How to Sell Your Home
Without a Broker

How to Sell Your Home
Without a Broker

Bill Carey
Suzanne Kiffmann

John Wiley & Sons
New York • Chichester • Brisbane • Toronto • Singapore

Library of Congress Cataloging-in-Publications Data

Carey, Bill. 1951–   : How to sell your home without a broker / by
  Bill Carey and Suzanne Kiffmann.
      p.   cm.
   Includes bibliographical references.
   ISBN 0-471-52562-6—ISBN 0-471-52561-8 (pbk.)
   1. House selling. I. Kiffmann, Suzanne, 1942–   . II. Title.
HD1379.C16   1990
33.33'83--dc20   90-31161
                                                                      CIP

Printed in the United States of America
90 91 10 9 8 7 6 5 4 3 2 1

CONTENTS

INTRODUCTION

Congratulations for choosing to become one of the smart homeowners that save thousands of dollars in commission by selling their own home! Results from a national study—recently published in *Consumers Report*—reveal that 1) in the last five years, nearly one out of five homesellers tried to sell their homes without a broker, and 2) 20% of homesellers overall are dissatisfied with the efforts of their brokers. Now, here's the first book to support the results of these growing trends. *How to Sell Your Home Without a Broker* is a step-by-step system designed to save thousands of dollars for you if you have
- Never sold a home before and know nothing about the process.
- Sold a home previously and need information in one or several areas.
- Sold a home fairly recently and want to be updated regarding specific aspects of a successful sale.

The book is designed to take you step-by-step through the entire real estate transaction from a planned beginning to a profitable end.

As property values increase, so does the amount of money you pay in real estate commission. The commission represents a substantial amount of your equity. For example, saving the typical 6 percent commission on the sale of your home is not just the simple percentage that it appears to be. The smaller your equity, the greater the percentage of your equity you save by paying yourself the commission.

Comparing two homes selling for $150,000, a 6 percent commission ($9,000), starts out the same in both cases. If one owner has a gross equity of $50,000 and the other a gross equity of $30,000, the commission as a *percent of equity* is decidedly different. (Gross equity is equal to the sales price minus the existing mortgage.)

Price of home	$ 150,000	$ 150,000
× Percent commission	6%	6%
= Commission	$ 9,000	$ 9,000
Commission	$ 9,000	$ 9,000
Gross equity	$ 50,000	$ 30,000
= Commission as a percent of owner's equity	18%	30%

Paying yourself the commission may provide you other benefits; you
- Have more flexibility in financing the sale of your present home to get the price and terms you desire.
- Receive more money with which to purchase options when choosing another home: another bedroom, another bath, a dining room, a family room, or a pool, to name a few.
- Gain more money to make upgrades in the home you buy: carpets, drapes, landscaping, pool, spa, and so on.
- Have more choices in financing your new real estate purchase.
- Net more money to make other investments.
- Start with more money to pay off other debts.

Using *How to Sell Your Home Without a Broker*, you can save money on real estate commissions and can successfully prepare, market, negotiate, close, and wrap up the sale of your home.

How to Use This Book

How to Sell Your Home Without a Broker is designed to work equally well for the novice, the experienced seller, and the "professional." The following list indicates which method you would probably find most useful based upon your prior experience.

- Novice, if this is your first or second sale of property or you have not sold property in the last three years.
- Experienced, if you sold at least two properties previously.
- Professional, if you sold a number of properties previously.

The checklists and worksheets are keys to the successful use of this book, whatever your level of expertise. Make notes as you read of which of the techniques and forms we provide will be most helpful to you.

Novice Seller

If this is your first or second home sale or you have not sold a home in the last three years,

1. Examine the contents before you read each chapter to get an overview.
2. Skim the chapter checklists.
3. Begin the preparations to sell your home yourself by
   a. Reading the entire Prepare section, Chapters 1 to 5.
   b. Checking off any method you feel you may want to use in the Use column of the checklist.
   c. Skimming the checklists of the Market, Negotiate, Close, and Wrap Up sections, to see the information they provide.
   d. Getting your property ready to market, as described in the Prepare section.
4. When you have *nearly completed* your preparations, continue with this book by
   a. Reading the entire Market section, Chapters 6 to 8.
   b. Checking off any method you want to use in the Use column of the checklist.
   c. Skimming the Negotiate, Close, and Wrap Up sections' checklists to review what techniques these sections contain.
   d. Proceeding to market your property as described in the Market section.
5. If buyers appear while you are marketing your property, prepare by
   a. Reading the entire Negotiate section, Chapters 9 to 13.
   b. Checking off any method you want to use in the Use column of the checklist.
   c. Skimming the contents for the Close and Wrap Up sections' checklists to refresh your memory about what they include.
   d. Negotiating the sale of your property following the guidelines suggested in the Negotiate section.
6. To complete the sale of your home, continue by
   a. Reading the entire Close section, Chapters 14 to 16.
   b. Checking off any methods you want to use in the Use column of the checklist.
   c. Skimming the contents of the Wrap Up section's checklist to devise your plan for the remaining tasks.
   d. Closing the sale of your property.

7. Wrap up the sale of your home by
    a. Reading the entire Wrap Up section, Chapters 17 and 18.
    b. Check off any method you want to use.
    c. Wrapping up the sale of your property.

Experienced Seller

If you have sold two or more properties before but feel you need more information about handling various aspects of the sale,

1. Skim the Table of Contents to get an overview of the entire sales process.
2. Use the chapter checklists in the following manner:
    a. Make a check in the Read column for areas that you need more in-depth information about.
    b. Skim the checklists for the sections of the book that deal with areas in which you feel competent.
    c. Read thoroughly the sections you checked off in the chapter checklists.
    d. Make a check in the Use column for material and forms you want to use in selling your home. Complete the forms you want to use; photocopy them if you feel you'll need more than one draft.
3. Read one section ahead of the section on which you are currently working.

Professional Seller

If you have sold a number of properties,

1. Skim the chapter checklists to get an overview of the entire sales process.
2. Use the chapter checklists in the following way:
    a. Make a check in the Read column for areas that you need more in-depth information about.
    b. Skim checklists for the sections of the book that deal with areas in which you feel competent to ensure there are no other areas for which you may need additional information.
    c. Read thoroughly the sections you checked off in the chapter checklists.
    d. Note form titles and headings for material and forms you want to use in selling your home. Complete the forms you want to use; photocopy them if you feel you'll need more than one draft.

Whatever your level of experience, we are confident that this book can help you sell your home without a broker.

CHAPTER CHECKLISTS

SECTION I   Prepare

CHAPTER 1   Decide on Your Goals

CHAPTER 5   Disclose!

CHAPTER 11 Understand Implications of Contract

CHAPTER 18 Move!

CHAPTER 1
Decide on Your Goals

Your preparation to effectively sell your home yourself includes determining the goals you wish to achieve.

Step 1: Decide on Your Goals

Decide what your primary goals are before you sell your property. Knowing your goals helps you determine many of the aspects of the sale. Your goals might include
- Deciding where and when to move.
- Selling your property quickly.
- Receiving as much cash as possible from the transaction in order to buy another home or make investments.
- Determining the lowest price you are willing to accept.
- Having a monthly income by financing part or all of the sale yourself.
- Minimizing the tax consequences of the sale.

The Goals Worksheet helps to make your priorities in selling your home clear to you. Fill out the Goals Worksheet as follows:
1. Write out goals you wish to achieve in selling your home under Preliminary Goals.
2. Prioritize your listed goals by placing a number to the left of each goal. Make the most important goal 1, the second most important goal 2, and so on.
3. Rewrite your goals in their order of importance on the Prioritized Goals Worksheet to provide a reference as you sell your home.

Step 2: Understand the Property Sale Variables

When you sell can affect how fast you sell your property and even how much you receive for it. Consider the time of year, economic climate in your area, interest rates, and tax regulations as you decide when to sell.

Timing of the Sale
Some months of the year are usually deemed better for the sales of homes, as the chart called Timing Your Property Sale indicates.

GOALS WORKSHEET

Name:_____ Date:_____
Property Address:_____

PRELIMINARY GOALS

Number   Goal

_____   _____
_____   _____
_____   _____
_____   _____
_____   _____
_____   _____
_____   _____
_____   _____
_____   _____
_____   _____
_____   _____
_____   _____
_____   _____
_____   _____
_____   _____
_____   _____

PRIORITIZED GOALS

Rank   Goal

_____   _____
_____   _____
_____   _____
_____   _____
_____   _____
_____   _____
_____   _____
_____   _____
_____   _____
_____   _____
_____   _____
_____   _____
_____   _____
_____   _____
_____   _____
_____   _____

TIMING YOUR PROPERTY SALE

Month	Condition	Possible Reasons
January	Few buyers available.	People recovering from the holidays.
February	More buyers in marketplace.	People in areas with cold winters find things wrong with present homes and begin to look.
March	More buyers in marketplace.	Compiling tax returns, potential first time home buyers may decide to take advantage of tax deductions for mortgage interest.
April	Demand often highest. Prices may increase if economy is good.	People begin to be interested in homes with outdoor amenities. Families with children begin thinking of finding a home to move into during summer.
May	Similar to April.	Similar to April.
June	Similar to April.	Similar to April.
July	Demand begins to diminish.	Many people take vacations. People with children want to be moved in before new school year starts.
August	Similar to July.	Similar to July.
September	Investor activity increases.	Family demand decreases. The percentage of investors increases.
October	Similar to September.	Similar to September.
November	Demand often low.	Weather is cold and people are preparing for the holidays.
December	Similar to November.	Similar to November.

Interest Rates

Interest rates obtainable by buyers at the time you sell your home may greatly influence the number of potential buyers available. When interest rates are low, the number of buyers generally increases. The number of potential buyers increases greatly if this period of low interest rates just follows a period of relatively high interest rates.

Regional Economy

A healthy economy in your region can be important in determining the best time to sell your home. When the area economy is good, the number of potential home buyers who feel confident enough about the future to invest in a home usually increases, and the price of homes often increases, too.

Because the number of potential home buyers generally decreases in areas experiencing an economic slump, it may be better to retain your property during these times if possible. An axiom in the real estate industry is to buy low (at a low price) and sell high (at a high price). If you must sell, you have an advantage because you can sell a comparable property for less than the seller who must pay a broker a real estate commission.

Tax Regulations

Two tax regulations relating to capital gains are particularly important because they may affect your timing in selling your home. More detailed information regarding both is discussed in Chapter 17, "Taxes." Because of rapidly changing tax laws, also contact your accountant or tax preparer for more current information.

24-Month Rule

When you sell your principal residence, you must defer the tax on the gain if you buy or construct another principal residence within 24 months before or after your sale of the first residence. To qualify, the transaction must meet certain criteria. See Chapter 17 for more complete details.

Over-55 One-Time Exclusion

A taxpayer (or spouse) who is 55 years old or older before the date of the sale of his or her home can be granted a one-time exclusion of up to $125,000 of capital gain on the difference between the price originally paid for a property and the selling price. To qualify, the taxpayer and the transaction must meet certain criteria. See Chapter 17 for more complete details.

Condition of Property

A well-maintained home that needs no repairs or improvements is most likely to be valued for the highest price. The condition of your home when real estate professionals or appraisers view your property will influence their opinions of its values.

- If you maintain your home in *excellent* condition, so that your home appears immaculate and needs no repairs or improvements, proceed as indicated.
- If your home is in less-than-excellent condition, consider
  1. Reading Chapter 6, "Prepare Property," about the cost effectiveness of improvement, repair, and attractiveness items, then follow *either* number 2 or number 3.
  2. Handling whichever improvement, repair, and/or attractiveness items you decide to take care of to increase the value of your home *before* requesting opinions about its condition.
  3. Requesting opinions of the value of your home in its *current* condition.
     a. Ask each consultant how much he or she thinks your home is now worth. Also ask how much he or she thinks the value of your home would change for each improvement or repair you are considering making.
     b. Decide what to do after you hear what your consultants consider most cost effective.

Step 3: Gather Pricing Information

The price you decide to ask for your property may be influenced by input from any number of sources. Methods may include finding out information yourself as well as asking local real estate professionals for free market evaluations. Other methods may include hiring an appraiser and asking a title company for values of comparable homes.

Consider choosing the method or methods you feel to be the most advantageous. Consider using at least six different values from at least two sources. For example, obtain three values from a title insurance company and three different values from a real estate professional.

Use the Asking Price Determination Worksheet to record your findings.
1. List the address of each property.
2. Enter the number of bedrooms and baths each home contains.
3. Write the number of square feet in the living area. (Do not include the garage or basement unless it has been converted into a permanent part of the living area.)

ASKING PRICE DETERMINATION WORKSHEET

Address:_____

<u>Property Information</u>   <u>Price</u>

Property Address	Bed-rooms	Bath-rooms	Square feet	Remarks	For Sale	Sold

Source: My home

_____	____	____	____	_____		

Source: Neighbors

_____	____	____	____	_____	____	____
_____	____	____	____	_____	____	____
_____	____	____	____	_____	____	____
_____	____	____	____	_____	____	____
_____	____	____	____	_____	____	____

Source: Real estate professionals

_____	____	____	____	_____	____	____
_____	____	____	____	_____	____	____
_____	____	____	____	_____	____	____
_____	____	____	____	_____	____	____
_____	____	____	____	_____	____	____
_____	____	____	____	_____	____	____

Source: Appraiser

_____	____	____	____	_____	____	____
_____	____	____	____	_____	____	____

Source: Title companies

_____	____	____	____	_____	____	____
_____	____	____	____	_____	____	____
_____	____	____	____	_____	____	____
_____	____	____	____	_____	____	____
_____	____	____	____	_____	____	____
_____	____	____	____	_____	____	____

Most comparable
   For sale _____   ____
   Sold _____   ____

ASKING PRICE $_____

4. Record remarks about other amenities or property condition.
5. Enter the price in the
   - For Sale column if the property has not closed.
   - Sold column if the property has closed.

Find Information Yourself

To find information yourself, locate several houses in your immediate neighborhood that are comparable to yours that are for sale or have recently sold. Do not comparison shop property based on square footage alone. Consider the following items when you are deciding which properties are comparable to your own:
- Physical characteristics of the property—the number of bedrooms and bathrooms; room types and layouts; size in area (square feet); special features; age; condition; architectural style; lot size, lot shape, and topography.
- Location—view, nearness to desirable community features, and distance from undesirable features.
- Financing terms—amount of down payment, type of loans (FHA, VA, conventional, all-inclusive trust deed), number of loans, rate of loans, terms of loans (assumable, due-on-sale, prepayment penalties, seller buy-down).

To find out the information you want, you can ask neighbors who are selling or have recently sold as well as those who have recently bought. You can also attend area open houses.

ADVANTAGES
- This is an inexpensive method in terms of dollars spent.

DISADVANTAGES
- Often the method is not too accurate, because sellers may exaggerate what they received, buyers may understate what they paid, and sellers of houses currently on the market often do not receive the price they are asking.
- Some people may be offended by your questions.
- This method uses a lot of your time for questionable results.

Ask Real Estate Professionals

Many real estate professionals will provide you with a market evaluation of your home, usually at no cost or obligation.
1. Contact several real estate professionals about providing you with a market evaluation at no cost or obligation to you.
2. Inform them that you are selling your home yourself but you may call them later if you decide differently.
3. Be aware that each professional will probably try to sell you on the advantages of listing your home with his or her firm.

ADVANTAGES
- Usually there is no charge for this type of information from a real estate professional.
- Obtaining the information is easy, because the real estate professional does the work.

DISADVANTAGES
- Some real estate professionals inflate their estimate of the value of your house to try to obtain a listing.

- Some real estate professionals may contact you repeatedly in an effort to list your property.

Hire an Appraiser

An *appraisal* is a supportable opinion or estimate of value as of a specific date. There are many types of appraisals for different purposes, and they may yield very different values on the same property. You need a *realistic* opinion of market value.

To get the most for your money in hiring an appraiser,

- Hire a qualified appraiser. Good sources of referrals include mortgage loan brokers, officers of a bank or savings and loan where you have accounts, real estate professionals, and real estate attorneys.
- Establish in advance the fee to be charged by the appraiser.
- Emphasize that you want a realistic opinion of market value of your residence in its present condition.

ADVANTAGES

- This process can be a useful aid in determining your asking price, especially if your house is unusual.
- The method is easy, because the appraiser does the work.

DISADVANTAGES

- It may cost several hundred dollars.
- The method may not be cost effective for properties that are similar to others in the area.

Ask Your Title Insurance Company

Your title insurance company is the organization that insured the title to your home when you purchased the property. To discover the identity of the company, see the certificate of title insurance you received when you purchased the property.

Title insurance companies usually are happy to provide at no charge information regarding similar properties that have sold recently in your neighborhood.

- Tell the title insurance company that you are selling your home yourself.
- Inform the company that you plan to use its services.

ADVANTAGES

- This method is accurate, because title companies have access to reliable, up-to-date information.
- It is easy, because the title company does the work.
- Usually the service is free.

DISADVANTAGES

- It provides data on actual sales prices of homes on which the sale is complete. You do not discover, however, what prices people asked or how long the home was on the market.
- You may feel you should use the title company's services when you sell your home.

Step 4: Determine Your Asking Price

After investigating the market value of properties similar to your own and filling in the Asking Price Determination Worksheet, you are ready to determine what price to ask for your home.

1. Decide which house *for sale* is most comparable to your own.
2. Enter this value in the Most comparable section under For Sale on the work-sheet.
3. Decide which house that *sold* is most comparable to yours.
4. Fill in the Most comparable section under Sold with this value.
5. Consider using the most comparable
   - For sale price as your ceiling or high price.
   - Sold price as your floor or low price.
6. Decide your asking price after judging the housing market.
   - If the price of houses for sale in your area is rising, set your asking price just below the most comparable property's for sale price from the worksheet.
   - If the price of houses for sale in your area is stagnant or declining, set your asking price just above the price of the most comparable Sold property.

After finding out asking and selling prices of other homes, you may still feel that your property is worth more than comparable properties. You may feel strongly that your home is worth more if you made significant upgrades. Avoid letting your subjective feelings about your taste and decorating influence your evaluation of your home.

After you have decided upon your goals and determined an asking price for your property, you are ready to assemble your property records, as described in Chapter 2.

CHAPTER 2
Assemble Property Records

Having your property records readily available greatly help you to complete the steps required to sell your home yourself.

Step 1: Prepare Property Records Worksheet

Understand the Reasons for Gathering Property Records
The Property Records Worksheet and property records file help you collect and organize much of the information you need to sell your home yourself as well as to calculate your income taxes.

Prepare the Property Records Worksheet
Prepare the Property Records Worksheet by checking the documents you need to find for your property records file.

Prepare the Property Records File
Create a large file in which you can store most documents, records, and information about your property. You may keep this file in your home. For documents that are of great importance and not easily replaced or irreplaceable,
1. Make a copy of the document for your property records file.
2. Place the original document in a safe deposit box.
3. Write on the copy where the original is located.
4. File the copy in your property records file.

Step 2: Collect Documents

Gather the documents you need regarding ownership, loans, insurance, capital improvements, maintenance, and fees. Consider copying items marked in this chapter with an asterisk (*) for your file and placing (or replacing) the originals in a safe deposit box.

Ownership Documents
These documents have to do with your property ownership. Place the documents or clear copies of them in your property records file.

PROPERTY RECORDS WORKSHEET

Name: _____

Address: _____

Found Filed Description

Ownership documentation

[ ]	[ ]	Purchase contract
[ ]	[ ]	Legal description
[ ]	[ ]	Conditions, covenants, and restrictions
[ ]	[ ]	Preliminary title report
		Inspection reports
[ ]	[ ]	Physical
[ ]	[ ]	Geological
[ ]	[ ]	Pest control
[ ]	[ ]	Warranties
[ ]	[ ]	Title insurance
[ ]	[ ]	Closing statement
[ ]	[ ]	Other _____

Mortgage documentation

[ ]	[ ]	Mortgage
[ ]	[ ]	Deed of trust
[ ]	[ ]	Promissory note
[ ]	[ ]	Loan disclosure statement
[ ]	[ ]	Payment statements
[ ]	[ ]	Property tax statements
[ ]	[ ]	Assessor's map of area
[ ]	[ ]	Assessment notices
[ ]	[ ]	Improvement notices
[ ]	[ ]	Satisfactions of mortgages
[ ]	[ ]	Reconveyance deeds
[ ]	[ ]	Other _____

Insurance documentation

[ ]	[ ]	Fire
[ ]	[ ]	Hazard
[ ]	[ ]	Homeowner's
[ ]	[ ]	Mortgage
[ ]	[ ]	Other _____

PROPERTY RECORDS WORKSHEET

Found Filed Description

Capital improvement documentation
Improvement: _____
[ ]	[ ]	Plans and specifications
[ ]	[ ]	Estimates
[ ]	[ ]	Contracts
[ ]	[ ]	Building permits
[ ]	[ ]	Inspection records
[ ]	[ ]	Payment records
[ ]	[ ]	Invoices
[ ]	[ ]	Notices of completion
[ ]	[ ]	Preliminary lien notices
[ ]	[ ]	Lien releases

Improvement: _____
[ ]	[ ]	Plans and specifications
[ ]	[ ]	Estimates
[ ]	[ ]	Contracts
[ ]	[ ]	Building permits
[ ]	[ ]	Inspection records
[ ]	[ ]	Payment records
[ ]	[ ]	Invoices
[ ]	[ ]	Notices of completion
[ ]	[ ]	Preliminary lien notices
[ ]	[ ]	Lien releases

Improvement: _____
[ ]	[ ]	Plans and specifications
[ ]	[ ]	Estimates
[ ]	[ ]	Contracts
[ ]	[ ]	Building permits
[ ]	[ ]	Inspection records
[ ]	[ ]	Payment records
[ ]	[ ]	Invoices
[ ]	[ ]	Notices of completion
[ ]	[ ]	Preliminary lien notices
[ ]	[ ]	Lien releases

PROPERTY RECORDS WORKSHEET

Found Filed Description

Maintenance records

Item: _____

[ ]	[ ]	Payment records
[ ]	[ ]	Invoices
[ ]	[ ]	Guarantees and warranties

Item: _____

[ ]	[ ]	Payment records
[ ]	[ ]	Invoices
[ ]	[ ]	Guarantees and warranties

Item: _____

[ ]	[ ]	Payment records
[ ]	[ ]	Invoices
[ ]	[ ]	Guarantees and warranties

Item: _____

[ ]	[ ]	Payment records
[ ]	[ ]	Invoices
[ ]	[ ]	Guarantees and warranties

Item: _____

[ ]	[ ]	Payment records
[ ]	[ ]	Invoices
[ ]	[ ]	Guarantees and warranties

Fees information

[ ]	[ ]	Electric
[ ]	[ ]	Gas
[ ]	[ ]	Water
[ ]	[ ]	Sewer
[ ]	[ ]	Trash
[ ]	[ ]	Taxes
[ ]	[ ]	Insurance
[ ]	[ ]	Homeowner's
[ ]	[ ]	Other_____
[ ]	[ ]	Other_____

Purchase Contract

This document includes all the terms and conditions to which you and the sellers agreed when the sellers accepted your offer to buy the property.

Legal Description

The legal description is a formal description detailing your property's exact location, dimensions, and boundaries. It may be in the form of a written description in addition to a map or maps.

Covenants, Conditions, and Restrictions (CC&Rs)

The CC&Rs is a document that lists private restrictions on property. *Covenants* are the promises and agreements to take or not take certain actions. *Conditions* are requirements before the performance or effectiveness of something else. *Restrictions* are encumbrances that limit the use of real estate in some manner.

Subdivisions in which the buyer has some interest in common areas—such as single family homes sharing common areas, condominiums, and time-share projects—generally have CC&Rs.

Preliminary Title Report

A preliminary title report summarizes the title search performed for your property.

Inspection Reports

Reports by inspectors about the condition of various aspects of your property, including defects and repairs considered necessary; they might document the results of the following types of examinations.

Physical Inspection. A physical inspection includes but is not limited to structure, plumbing, heating, electrical, built-in appliances, roof, soils, foundation, mechanical systems, pool, pool heater, pool filter, air conditioner, and possible hazards.

Geological Inspection. A geological inspection is an examination by a soils engineer for potential or actual geological problems, as well as examination of records to determine whether property falls within special zones.

Pest Control Inspection. A pest control inspection checks for infestation or infection or conditions that might lead to infestation or infection by wood-destroying pests or organisms.

Warranties

Warranties are documents, either printed or written, guaranteeing the condition of your property or its components.

Title Insurance Policy*

A title insurance policy is the coverage issued to you by the title company on completion of the final title search. The insurance provided by this document protects you against claims in the future based on circumstances in the past. This policy insures you or the lender (depending upon who is insured) against certain types of losses (depending on the type of coverage) if the title is defective.

Closing Statement

The closing statement is an itemized accounting given to you and the sellers at closing by the closing agent or escrow holder. This statement details receipts, disbursements, charges, credits, and prorations.

Deed to the Property

The deed you received when you bought the home may be any of the following types.

Grant Deed.* A grant deed is a document that uses the word *grant* to transfer ownership.

Quitclaim Deed.* A quitclaim deed is a document that uses the word *quitclaim* to transfer ownership and release the grantor from any interest in that property.

Warranty Deed.* A warranty deed is a property deed in which the grantor guarantees the title to be as indicated.

Gift Deed.* A gift deed is a property deed given for love and affection.

Trustee's Deed.* A trustee's deed is a document used by a trustee in a property foreclosure handled outside the court system to transfer the debtor's title to the buyer.

Sheriff's or Marshal's Deed.* A sheriff's or marshal's deed is a document used by courts in foreclosure or in carrying out a judgment. This deed transfers a debtor's title to a buyer.

Tax or Controller's Deed.* A tax or controller's deed is a document used by a state to transfer title to a grantee.

Insurance Documents

These documents are evidence of coverage on your property.

Fire Insurance

A fire insurance policy is a document from an insurance company showing to what amount a property is insured in the event of a fire.

Homeowner's Insurance

A homeowner's policy protects a homeowner from liability (damages to other people or property) and from casualty (loss of or damage to the structures or personal property). This insurance covers you for the hazards listed in the policy (such as fire, flood, and landslide). Fire and hazard insurance are types of homeowner's insurance with more limited coverage.

Mortgage Insurance

Mortgage insurance provides documents revealing that your loan is insured so that whomever you designate will be able to pay any of the following:

- The loan balance if you die and have purchased mortgage life insurance.
- The monthly mortgage charges if you are totally and permanently disabled and have purchased a mortgage disability policy.
- The lender's part of the outstanding balance in the event you default, if you purchase mortgage default insurance.

Loan Documents

Loan documents are evidence of a loan. They can include any or all of the following:

Mortgage*

A contract in which you promise your property to secure a loan. You retain title to and possession of the property.

Trust Deed*

A trust deed is a document, used as a security device for the loan on your property, by which you transfer bare (naked) legal title with the power of sale to a trustee. This transfer is in effect until you have totally paid off the loan.

Home Equity Line of Credit*

A loan you can obtain using your equity in your home as collateral for the loan is a home equity line of credit. A line of credit is a potential loan until you use some or all of it, at which time it becomes an actual loan.

Promissory Note*

A promissory note is a written contract you sign promising to pay a definite amount of money by a definite future date.

Payment Statements

Payment statements can be either monthly stubs or annual summary statements. Both should show your payment date, amounts applied to principal and interest, and remaining balance due.

Property Tax Statements

Property tax statements are documents that the county assessor's office mails to you as a homeowner. These statements itemize the semiannual or annual tax bill on your home and indicate the payment due dates.

Assessment Notices

Notice of assessment (or reassessment) is a document sent to you by the county assessor's office to give you notice of changes in the assessed value of your property.

Improvement Notices

Improvement notices are documents sent by governmental authorities giving you notice of planned improvements such as sidewalks, curbs, and sewers. These are one-time charges.

Satisfaction of Mortgage*

A satisfaction of mortgage is a document that indicates you paid your mortgage in full.

Reconveyance Deed*

A reconveyance deed is a document filed at the county recorder's office recording full satisfaction of a debt on your home and transferring legal title from the trustee to you.

Capital Improvement Documents

Capital improvements are additions to your property that
- Are permanent; they cannot be removed.
- Increase the value of the property.
- Have a useful life of more than one year.

Capital Improvements Worksheet

The total cost of all capital improvements is used to calculate your basis in your home for tax purposes. The Capital Improvements Worksheet makes it easy to collect this data. In the past, the items listed on the worksheet were considered capital improvements. Check with your accountant or tax preparer for the current status of these items.

Plans and Specifications

Plans and specifications are descriptions and drawings of the improvement, including but not limited to blueprints, prepared by you or a professional.

Estimates

Estimates include all written and signed approximations of the cost of the work required that are submitted by contractors for each property improvement.

Contracts

Contracts are the agreements spelling out all terms and conditions for each property improvement signed by both you and the contractors.

CAPITAL IMPROVEMENTS WORKSHEET

Name:_____

Address:_____

Did	Improvement	Date	Cost

Yard

[ ] Lawn area enlargement . . . . ____ ____

[ ] Shrub addition . . . . ____ ____

[ ] Tree addition . . . . ____ ____

[ ] Sprinkler system addition . . . . ____ ____

[ ] Decorative component addition . . . . ____ ____

[ ] Decorative component redesign . . . . ____ ____

[ ] Resurfacing for drainage . . . . ____ ____

[ ] Drains installation for drainage . . . . ____ ____

[ ] Equipment installation for drainage . . . . ____ ____

[ ] Other:_____ ____ ____

Driveway and Walks

[ ] Driveway added or extended . . . . ____ ____

[ ] Walk added or extended . . . . ____ ____

[ ] Curb addition or extension . . . . ____ ____

[ ] Other:_____ ____ ____

Walls and Fences

[ ] Wall or fence addition . . . . ____ ____

[ ] Other:_____ ____ ____

Patios, Decks, and Courts

[ ] Patio addition or enlargement . . . . ____ ____

[ ] Deck addition or enlargement . . . . ____ ____

[ ] Game court (such as tennis) addition . . . . ____ ____

[ ] Other:_____ ____ ____

Pools and Spas

[ ] Pool installation . . . . ____ ____

[ ] Spa installation . . . . ____ ____

[ ] Sauna installation . . . . ____ ____

[ ] Changing facilities installation . . . . ____ ____

[ ] Other:_____ ____ ____

Subtotal Page #1 $_____

CAPITAL IMPROVEMENTS WORKSHEET

Did	Improvements	Date	Cost
	Outdoor Equipment		
[ ]	Lighting equipment installation	_____	_____
[ ]	Sound system installation	_____	_____
[ ]	Barbecue installation	_____	_____
[ ]	Playground equipment installation	_____	_____
[ ]	Well installation	_____	_____
[ ]	Pump installation	_____	_____
[ ]	Incinerator installation	_____	_____
[ ]	Other:_____	_____	_____
	Structures		
[ ]	Tool shed addition or improvement	_____	_____
[ ]	Greenhouse addition or improvement	_____	_____
[ ]	Outbuilding addition or improvement	_____	_____
[ ]	Barn addition or improvement	_____	_____
[ ]	Stable addition or improvement	_____	_____
[ ]	Other:_____	_____	_____
	Roof and Gutters		
[ ]	Roof upgrades	_____	_____
[ ]	Gutter upgrades	_____	_____
[ ]	Other:_____	_____	_____
	Siding, Walls, and Foundation		
[ ]	Siding upgrades	_____	_____
[ ]	Wall upgrades	_____	_____
[ ]	Structural strengthening	_____	_____
[ ]	Foundation work for settling and seepage	_____	_____
[ ]	Floor jack installed	_____	_____
[ ]	Other:_____	_____	_____
	Windows and Doors		
[ ]	Windows or screens installed	_____	_____
[ ]	Shutter installed	_____	_____
[ ]	Awning installed	_____	_____
[ ]	Door installed	_____	_____
[ ]	Storm door installed	_____	_____
[ ]	Other:_____	_____	_____

Subtotal Page #2 $_____

CAPITAL IMPROVEMENTS WORKSHEET

Did	Improvement	Date	Cost

Entrance
[ ] Intercom installed . . . . _____ _____
[ ] Security system installed . . . . _____ _____
[ ] Ceiling upgraded . . . . _____ _____
[ ] Lighting fixtures installed . . . . _____ _____
[ ] Floor covering permanently installed . . . . _____ _____
[ ] Other:_____ _____ _____

Living Room
[ ] Ceiling upgraded . . . . _____ _____
[ ] Lighting fixtures installed . . . . _____ _____
[ ] Fireplace installed or upgraded . . . . _____ _____
[ ] Floor covering permanently installed . . . . _____ _____
[ ] Furnishings built-in . . . . _____ _____
[ ] Entertainment equipment built-in . . . . _____ _____
[ ] Other:_____ _____ _____

Dining Room
[ ] Ceiling upgraded . . . . _____ _____
[ ] Light fixture installed . . . . _____ _____
[ ] Floor covering permanently installed . . . . _____ _____
[ ] Furnishings permanently installed . . . . _____ _____
[ ] Closets, cabinets, or shelves added . . . . _____ _____
[ ] Other:_____ _____ _____

Family Room
[ ] Ceiling upgraded . . . . _____ _____
[ ] Lighting fixture installed . . . . _____ _____
[ ] Fireplace installation or upgraded . . . . _____ _____
[ ] Floor covering permanently installed . . . . _____ _____
[ ] Furnishings built-in . . . . _____ _____
[ ] Closets, cabinets, or shelves added . . . . _____ _____
[ ] Entertainment equipment built-in . . . . _____ _____
[ ] Other:_____ _____ _____

Kitchen
[ ] Ceiling upgraded . . . . _____ _____
[ ] Lighting fixture installed . . . . _____ _____
[ ] Floor covering permanently installed . . . . _____ _____
[ ] Furnishings built-in . . . . _____ _____
[ ] Closets, cabinets, or shelves added . . . . _____ _____

Subtotal Page #3 $_____

CAPITAL IMPROVEMENTS WORKSHEET

Did Improvement   **Date   Cost**

Kitchen (Continued)

[ ] Ovens or stoves built-in . . . .   _____ _____
[ ] Sink addition installed . . . .   _____ _____
[ ] Garbage disposal addition installed . . . .   _____ _____
[ ] Dishwasher addition installed . . . .   _____ _____
[ ] Refrigerator or freezer built-in . . . .   _____ _____
[ ] Counter added . . . .   _____ _____
[ ] Other:_____   _____ _____

Utilities

[ ] Electric switches and/or outlets added . . . .   _____ _____
[ ] Power lines added or upgraded . . . .   _____ _____
[ ] Plumbing pipes added or upgraded . . . .   _____ _____
[ ] Heating system upgraded . . . .   _____ _____
[ ] Air conditioning system installed or upgraded . . . .   _____ _____
[ ] Humidifier system installed or upgraded . . . .   _____ _____
[ ] Dehumidifier system installed or upgraded . . . . . .   _____ _____
[ ] Air-filtration system installed or upgraded . . . . .   _____ _____
[ ] Smoke detectors installed or upgraded . . . .   _____ _____
[ ] Water softener installed or upgraded . . . .   _____ _____
[ ] Burglar alarm installed or upgraded . . . .   _____ _____
[ ] Septic tank installed or upgraded . . . .   _____ _____
[ ] Leach line installed or upgraded . . . .   _____ _____
[ ] Other:_____   _____ _____

Den

[ ] Ceiling upgraded . . . .   _____ _____
[ ] Light fixture installed . . . .   _____ _____
[ ] Floor covering permanently installed . . . .   _____ _____
[ ] Furnishings built-in . . . .   _____ _____
[ ] Entertainment equipment built-in . . . .   _____ _____
[ ] Closets, cabinets, or shelves added . . . .   _____ _____
[ ] Other:_____   _____ _____

Bedroom 1 (Master Bedroom)

[ ] Ceiling upgraded . . . .   _____ _____
[ ] Light fixture installed . . . .   _____ _____
[ ] Floor covering permanently installed . . . .   _____ _____
[ ] Furnishings built-in . . . .   _____ _____
[ ] Closets, cabinets, or shelves added . . . .   _____ _____
[ ] Other:_____   _____ _____

Subtotal Page #4 $_____

CAPITAL IMPROVEMENTS WORKSHEET

Did	Improvement	Date	Cost

Bedroom 2
[ ] Ceiling upgraded . . . . _____ _____
[ ] Light fixture installed . . . . _____ _____
[ ] Floor covering permanently installed . . . . : _____ _____
[ ] Furnishings built-in . . . . _____ _____
[ ] Closets, cabinets, or shelves added . . . . _____ _____
[ ] Other:_____ _____ _____

Bedroom 3
[ ] Ceiling upgraded . . . . _____ _____
[ ] Light fixture installed . . . . _____ _____
[ ] Floor covering permanently installed . . . . _____ _____
[ ] Furnishings built-in . . . . _____ _____
[ ] Closets, cabinets, or shelves added . . . . _____ _____
[ ] Other:_____ _____ _____

Bedroom 4
[ ] Ceiling upgraded . . . . _____ _____
[ ] Light fixture installed . . . . _____ _____
[ ] Floor covering permanently installed . . . . _____ _____
[ ] Furnishings built-in . . . . _____ _____
[ ] Closets, cabinets, or shelves added . . . . _____ _____
[ ] Other:_____ _____ _____

Bedroom 5
[ ] Ceiling upgraded . . . . _____ _____
[ ] Light fixture installed . . . . _____ _____
[ ] Floor covering permanently installed . . . . _____ _____
[ ] Furnishings built-in . . . . _____ _____
[ ] Closets, cabinets, or shelves added . . . . _____ _____
[ ] Other:_____ _____ _____

Hall and Stairs
[ ] Ceiling upgraded . . . . _____ _____
[ ] Light fixture installed . . . . _____ _____
[ ] Floor covering permanently installed . . . . _____ _____
[ ] Furnishings built-in . . . . _____ _____
[ ] Closets, cabinets, or shelves added . . . . _____ _____
[ ] Laundry chute added . . . . _____ _____
[ ] Elevator added or upgraded . . . . _____ _____
[ ] Other:_____ _____ _____

Subtotal Page #5 $_____

CAPITAL IMPROVEMENTS WORKSHEET

Did	Improvement	Date	Cost

Bathroom 1 (Master Bath)
[ ] Ceiling upgraded . . . . _____ _____
[ ] Light fixture installed . . . . _____ _____
[ ] Floor covering permanently installed . . . . _____ _____
[ ] Furnishings built-in . . . . _____ _____
[ ] Closets, cabinets, or shelves added . . . . _____ _____
[ ] Plumbing fixtures added . . . . _____ _____
[ ] Other:_____ _____ _____

Bathroom 2
[ ] Ceiling upgraded . . . . _____ _____
[ ] Light fixture installed . . . . _____ _____
[ ] Floor covering permanently installed . . . . _____ _____
[ ] Furnishings built-in . . . . _____ _____
[ ] Closets, cabinets, or shelves added . . . . _____ _____
[ ] Plumbing fixtures added . . . . _____ _____
[ ] Other:_____ _____ _____

Bathroom 3
[ ] Ceiling upgraded . . . . _____ _____
[ ] Light fixture installed . . . . _____ _____
[ ] Floor covering permanently installed . . . . _____ _____
[ ] Furnishings built-in . . . . _____ _____
[ ] Closets, cabinets, or shelves added . . . . _____ _____
[ ] Plumbing fixtures added . . . . _____ _____
[ ] Other:_____ _____ _____

Utility Room
[ ] Ceiling upgraded . . . . _____ _____
[ ] Light fixture installed . . . . _____ _____
[ ] Floor covering permanently installed . . . . _____ _____
[ ] Furnishings built-in . . . . _____ _____
[ ] Closets, cabinets, or shelves added . . . . _____ _____
[ ] Plumbing fixtures added . . . . _____ _____
[ ] Other:_____ _____ _____

Garage or Carport
[ ] Ceiling upgraded . . . . _____ _____
[ ] Light fixture installed . . . . _____ _____
[ ] Floor covering permanently installed . . . . _____ _____
[ ] Furnishings built-in . . . . _____ _____

Subtotal Page #6 $_____

CAPITAL IMPROVEMENTS WORKSHEET

Did	Improvement	Date	Cost

Garage or Carport (Continued)

[ ] Closets, cabinets, or shelves added . . . . ____ ____

[ ] Plumbing fixtures added . . . . ____ ____

[ ] Other:_____ ____ ____

Attic

[ ] Ventilation improved . . . . ____ ____

[ ] Ceiling upgraded . . . . ____ ____

[ ] Light fixture installed . . . . ____ ____

[ ] Floor covering permanently installed . . . . ____ ____

[ ] Furnishings built-in . . . . ____ ____

[ ] Closets, cabinets, or shelves added . . . . ____ ____

[ ] Other:_____ ____ ____

Basement

[ ] Ceiling upgraded . . . . ____ ____

[ ] Light fixture installed . . . . ____ ____

[ ] Floor covering permanently installed . . . . ____ ____

[ ] Furnishings built-in . . . . ____ ____

[ ] Closets, cabinets, or shelves added . . . . ____ ____

[ ] Plumbing fixtures added . . . . ____ ____

[ ] Other:_____ ____ ____

Porch

[ ] Ceiling upgraded . . . . ____ ____

[ ] Light fixture installed . . . . ____ ____

[ ] Floor covering permanently installed . . . . ____ ____

[ ] Furnishings built-in . . . . ____ ____

[ ] Closets, cabinets, or shelves added . . . . ____ ____

[ ] Other:_____ ____ ____

Subtotal Page #7 $_____

Subtotal Page #1 $_____

#2 $_____

#3 $_____

#4 $_____

#5 $_____

#6 $_____

#7 $_____

TOTAL $_____

Building Permits
Building permits are documents that permit building after your plans are approved by the necessary city and/or county agencies.

Inspection Records
Inspection records are notices indicating inspections were conducted by the proper local authorities at the required points in the building process.

Payment Records
Payment records include all checks and receipts as well as written ledgers indicating date, amount paid, and type of work.

Invoices
Invoices are documents that provide proof of payment for any expenses you incur related to your property improvements. Invoices could cover material costs, labor costs, and/or subcontractor fees.

Preliminary Lien Notices
Preliminary lien notices are documents notifying you of liens (charges on property for the payment of a debt) presented to you.

Completion Notices
Completion notices are documents you file and record with your county when your home improvement is completed. These notices place time limits for filing mechanics' liens. Store a copy of the completion notice in your file.

Lien Releases*
Lien releases (also called waivers of lien) are documents that release you from monetary liability to the person listed on the release whom you paid in full. Obtain lien releases from suppliers, subcontractors, and general contractors.

Maintenance Records
Maintenance records encompass all documents relating to general upkeep for your property, including such items as repairs to plumbing and electrical systems, garden maintenance, and painting, as well as the purchase of carpet, drapes, furniture, and appliances.

Invoices
Invoices are documents that are proof of payment for any expense you incur in maintaining your home.

Guarantees and Warranties
Guarantees and warranties are documents providing assurances of the quality of or length of usage to be expected of a product. These assurances can be of aid in obtaining satisfaction if an object or service is not as promised or if it malfunctions within given time or usage limits.

Ownership Costs
Gather information for the preceding year about costs that would be of interest to potential buyers of your property. Costs include utilities, taxes, insurance, and homeowner's association dues.

Calculate Ownership Costs
Use the Ownership Costs Worksheet to gather and process the data as explained here:

OWNERSHIP COSTS WORKSHEET

Name:_____

Address:_____

Year Month	Electric	Gas/Oil	Water	Sewer	Trash
____ January	_____	_____	_____	_____	_____
____ February	_____	_____	_____	_____	_____
____ March	_____	_____	_____	_____	_____
____ April	_____	_____	_____	_____	_____
____ May	_____	_____	_____	_____	_____
____ June	_____	_____	_____	_____	_____
____ July	_____	_____	_____	_____	_____
____ August	_____	_____	_____	_____	_____
____ September	_____	_____	_____	_____	_____
____ October	_____	_____	_____	_____	_____
____ November	_____	_____	_____	_____	_____
____ December	_____	_____	_____	_____	_____
Total	_____	_____	_____	_____	_____
+ Number of months ____	____	____	____	____
=Average/month	_____	_____	_____	_____	_____

Year Month	Taxes	Insurance	Home-owner's Fees		
____ January	_____	_____	_____	_____	_____
____ February	_____	_____	_____	_____	_____
____ March	_____	_____	_____	_____	_____
____ April	_____	_____	_____	_____	_____
____ May	_____	_____	_____	_____	_____
____ June	_____	_____	_____	_____	_____
____ July	_____	_____	_____	_____	_____
____ August	_____	_____	_____	_____	_____
____ September	_____	_____	_____	_____	_____
____ October	_____	_____	_____	_____	_____
____ November	_____	_____	_____	_____	_____
____ December	_____	_____	_____	_____	_____
Total	_____	_____	_____	_____	_____
+ Number of months ____	____	____	____	____
=Average/month	_____	_____	_____	_____	_____

1. Write the property address.
2. Enter the year for which you gathered the information on the line preceding the name of each month.
3. Record the cost for each item for which you were charged that month.
4. Add the numbers in each column to obtain a total for that column.
5. Enter the total amount for each column on the appropriate line marked Total.
6. Record the number of months represented by the figures in each column on the appropriate line beside Number of months.
7. Divide the Total by the Number of months for each column.
8. Enter the answer for each column on the line marked Average/month.

Step 3: Organize Your Property Records File

If you have not done so already, organize the documents in your property records file in the order indicated on the Property Records Worksheet. With your documents organized this way, you can find them easily when you need to refer to them.

After you have gathered, processed, and organized all the available documents concerning your property, you are ready to estimate the financial impact of the sale of your property. This activity is the subject of Chapter 3.

CHAPTER 3
Determine Your Financial Requirements

Once you have collected the records that document the history of your property's purchase, mortgage, insurance, improvements, and maintenance, you are ready to determine your financial requirements.

Step 1: Estimate Costs

To best understand and plan for your financial requirements, you must understand and estimate your costs.

Prepare Net Proceeds Worksheet

Use the Net Proceeds Worksheet to calculate approximately how much money you will have remaining after deductions for your loans, marketing costs, and closing costs. This remaining amount is your *net proceeds*. Prepare this worksheet by
1. Entering the address of your property.
2. Recording your asking price.
3. Calling the lenders from whom you have your loans (mortgages, trust deeds, and/or home equity lines of credit) and asking
   • How much do I owe on this loan?
   • Is there a prepayment penalty if I pay off this loan?
   • If so, what is the prepayment penalty?
4. Writing information obtained from lenders on the worksheet.
5. Entering the expenses you estimate for the following costs on the cost section of the worksheet.

Mortgage Costs

Enter information about any mortgages or trust deeds that you have on the property.

Estimate Marketing Costs

Marketing costs to consider are fix-up and advertising expenses. We discuss each of these expenses briefly at this time so that you can estimate the costs involved. A more in-depth discussion of each of the items can be found in Chapter 7, "Advertise."

Improvement Costs. Improvement costs are expenses for permanent additions. These additions generally add to the value of your home if they are done well and are

NET PROCEEDS WORKSHEET

Name:_____Date:_____
Address:_____

Asking price $_____

Charges against asking price

Mortgage costs

1st Mortgage/Trust deed (TD)	+ $_____
1st Mortgage/TD prepayment penalty	+ $_____
2nd Mortgage/Trust deed (TD)	+ $_____
2nd Mortgage/TD prepayment penalty	+ $_____

Marketing costs

Improvement costs	+ $_____
Repair costs	+ $_____
Attractiveness costs	+ $_____
Advertising costs	+ $_____

Closing costs   + $_____
(Use 1.5% to 3.0% of asking price)

Total of charges against asking price   – $_____

Net Proceeds   = $_____

not over-improvements. Over-improving is adding to the worth of your home beyond the reasonable market value of comparable homes in your area. If you over-improve, you may not be able to recover the cost of the work. Consider making no improvements after you decide to sell your home.

Repair Costs. Repair costs are expenditures for work that maintains your home's condition. Repairs include replacement of items as well as restoring function to items. Repairing obvious problems generally makes your home more salable to a greater number of buyers. In their minds, buyers may exaggerate a repair that seems minor to you into a major reason for not purchasing your home. Repairs of obvious problems you are able to fix for a reasonable price are usually very cost effective.

Outside repairs might include such things as removing or replacing plantings; or removing, repairing, or replacing outdoor structures or exterior items on your home. Inside repairs could involve repairing or replacing interior items in your home.

Do not attempt to conceal problems by making poor or cosmetic repairs. Whether or not your state has disclosure laws, you may make yourself liable to lawsuits if you make this type of repair and do not disclose significant problems.

Attractiveness Costs. Attractiveness costs are charges for items that are not repairs or improvements, but make your home more appealing to buyers. Attractiveness is in the eye, ear, and nose of the beholder. If your home makes a good first impression, viewers are more likely to want to purchase it and pay top dollar.

Attractiveness costs are usually minimal to negligible. They include work you can usually hire someone to do for a minimal charge or do yourself. The costs are generally for such items as house cleaning as well as yard and perhaps pool maintenance.

Advertising Costs. Advertising costs include the expenses you incur in letting people know that your home is for sale. These charges include such items as signs and flags, classified or display newspaper advertisements, newsletter and magazine advertisements, flyers, and open houses.

Costs can vary widely, depending on the advertising you plan to do and the charges for this advertising in your area. For the purposes of this estimate, consider allocating about $300 to $500 for the first week you plan to have your home on the market and approximately $100 per week for each week thereafter.

Estimate Closing Costs

Closing costs (costs of sale) are expenses over and above the purchase price in buying and selling real estate.

The closing costs typically run between 1.5 percent to 3 percent of the sales price, excluding any real estate commission. This percentage estimates that you will pay the usual costs that sellers in your area generally pay.

Negotiability of Costs. Your net proceeds depend also on who actually pays which costs. Costs are negotiable except for fees on Veterans Administration (VA) loans. Study the Market Effect on Payment of Closing Costs chart. It explains how your closing costs may vary depending upon the type of market at the time you sell your home and whether there is an excess of sellers or buyers.

MARKET EFFECT ON PAYMENT OF CLOSING COSTS

Market	Excess	You Might Consider
Normal	Neither	Paying the usual closing costs.
Buyers'	Sellers	Paying more closing costs than usual yourself.
Sellers'	Buyers	Asking buyers to pay more costs than usual.

Costs Included. The list of costs to consider as closing costs is too long and detailed to include here or to fully factor as you calculate your estimated net proceeds. If you want to know more about closing costs, see Chapter 9.

Estimate Moving Expenses

Estimate your moving costs if you plan to move from the home you are selling. Moving costs, while not strictly regarded as expenses of selling your home, may definitely be substantial enough to be budgeted for when you sell. Moving costs depend upon many factors, such as how many pounds of goods you move, how far you move, and what method(s) you choose to move the items. If you are concerned about these costs, read Chapter 18, "Move!"

Estimate Tax Consequences

The immediate tax consequences of your sale of your home may be negligible to substantial, depending on many factors, such as your timing, your use of an exemption, and your costs. If you are concerned about estimating your tax consequences, see Chapter 17, "Handle Taxes," and contact your accountant or tax preparer.

Step 2: Calculate Estimated Net Proceeds

To calculate your estimated net proceeds from your home sale on your Net Proceeds Worksheet,
1. Total all the items you listed as Charges against the asking price.
2. Enter this value on the line labeled Total of charges against asking price.
3. Subtract this Total of charges against asking price from the Asking price above to obtain the Net Proceeds.

Step 3: Understand Financial Arrangements

Numerous methods for financing the sale of your home exist. Understanding the most commonly used methods and choosing the one(s) that best fits your needs can be an important part of putting money in your pocket.

Understand All Cash Offers

With all cash offers, you can receive all cash (less the costs of the sale) from selling your house. This occurs in two ways. Usually buyers put some cash down and obtain financing for the balance from a lender other than yourself. Sometimes buyers may have enough money to buy your home outright. This happens in only about 4 percent of home purchases.

ADVANTAGES
- You have received all your money from the house.
- You have no further interest in the property.

DISADVANTAGES
- You may have a large tax bill to pay, depending on your financial situation.
- You may need to find a way to invest your money.

Understand Buyers Taking Over Your Loan

Your participation in financing the sale of your home may make your home easier to sell. This is particularly true when mortgage money is expensive or difficult for buyers to obtain from the usual sources.

Assumable Loan

An assumable loan is an existing trust deed or mortgage that is kept at the same interest rate and terms as you agreed to when you financed the property and for which buyers become primarily liable. You become secondarily liable for the loan and for any deficiency judgment arising from it. A *deficiency judgment* is a court decision making an individual personally liable for the payoff for a remaining amount due because less than the full amount was obtained by foreclosure on the property.

Buyers may want to assume a loan on the property if the terms and conditions of the existing loan are more attractive than those on a new loan. Most VA and Federal Housing Administration (FHA) loans are currently assumable loans.

If you wish to allow buyers to assume your loan, consider these steps:

1. Reading your existing loan to be sure the loan is assumable.
2. Consulting a loan officer in your local bank or your attorney if you are unsure whether your loan is assumable.
3. Asking the lender of an assumable loan if the lender requires
   - Qualification of the buyers. Buyers must prove to a lender that they can make the payments and are good credit risks.
   - Assumption fee. Lenders charge to let buyers assume primary liability for payment of the loan.
   - Renegotiation of the loan. Lenders requiring buyers to renegotiate the loan, so the terms and conditions differ—sometimes substantially—from the original loan.
4. Request that you be released from all liability if buyers assume the loan. For most assumable loans, buyers become primarily liable but you remain *secondarily liable* for the loan and any deficiency judgment arising from it.

ADVANTAGES
- Property may be easier to sell with this loan.
- Buyers may become primarily liable for the loan.

DISADVANTAGES
- You may remain secondarily liable for the loan.
- Buyers may not want an assumable loan if the lender requires them to qualify for the loan, pay an assumption fee, and/or renegotiate the loan.

Subject to Loan

A subject to loan is an existing loan for which buyers agree to take over responsibility for payments under the same terms and conditions as existed when you agreed to the loan. You remain primarily liable for any deficiency judgment. The loan's name comes from the fact that buyers taking over the loan are subject to your approval. These loans are typically pre-1988 VA and FHA loans.

ADVANTAGES
- Property may be easier to sell with this type of loan.
- Buyers do not have to qualify for the loan.
- Escrow may be shorter because no new loan is required.

DISADVANTAGES
- You remain primarily liable for the loan if the buyers do not pay.
- You could lose a portion or all of your VA eligibility to purchase your next home.

Due-on-Sale Clause

A due-on-sale clause is a type of acceleration clause in a mortgage, trust deed, and/or promissory note that gives a lender the right to demand all sums owed be paid immediately if the owner of the property transfers title.

ADVANTAGES
- If you make a loan to the buyer to purchase your home, when buyer transfers title, you get your money back sooner than you expected.

DISADVANTAGES
- You must pay off the loan during the closing.
- If you make a loan to buyers to purchase your home, when buyers transfer title, you get your money back. You cannot choose when that time will be.

Prepayment Penalty

A prepayment penalty is a fine imposed on a borrower by a lender for the early payoff of a loan or any substantial part of a loan. To find out if you have a prepayment penalty on your loan, check your loan documents. If the documents contain such a clause, you can determine what its cost is using this procedure:
1. To calculate the amount of your prepayment penalty, check your loan documents. The amount of the prepayment penalty is usually stated as a certain number of months interest in addition to the amount you owe as of that date.
2. To determine the tax implications of this punitive interest, consult your accountant or tax preparer.

ADVANTAGES
- If you make a loan to buyers to purchase your property that includes a prepayment penalty, they must pay you the fine you agreed on if they pay the loan off early.

DISADVANTAGES
- If you must pay a prepayment penalty when you sell, you must come up with an agreed upon amount of extra money when you may have little extra available.

Understand Buyers Obtaining New Financing

When buyers obtain new financing, they pay you the full amount of the proceeds in cash. Whether buyers obtain a conventional loan or a government guaranteed or insured loan has an effect on your sale. The details of the loan (fixed rate, adjustable rate, and so on) do not affect your cash proceeds.

Conventional Loans

Conventional loans—those obtained from commercial banking institutions such as banks, S&Ls, or mortgage companies—are not guaranteed or insured by government agencies.

ADVANTAGES
- These loans require a shorter time and less paperwork.
- There are no rules requiring you to pay some of buyers' points.

DISADVANTAGES
- A larger down payment is usually required, so not as many buyers qualify for the loan.
- Interest rates are usually higher.

VA and FHA Loans

VA and FHA loans are ones guaranteed by the Veterans Administration and ones insured by the Federal Housing Administration, respectively. Existing VA and FHA loans are described under assumable loans earlier in the chapter. New VA and FHA loans have certain advantages and disadvantages.

ADVANTAGES
- Buyers who do not qualify for a conventional loan may be able to buy your home because of the low down payment and/or low interest rates.

DISADVANTAGES
- A new VA or FHA loan typically requires 30 to 45 days longer and much more paperwork to process than does a conventional loan.
- You must pay certain buyer's closing costs on both VA and FHA loans.
- You must pay points on a VA loan.

Understand Your Participation in Buyers' Financing

Your participation in financing the sale of your home may make your home easier to sell. This is particularly true when mortgage money is expensive or difficult for a buyer to obtain from the usual sources.

The *down payment* is the amount of money that you and buyers agree should be paid or that the lender requires that buyers pay toward the property purchase before the closing. A *deposit* or *earnest money* is money the buyers present with a purchase offer as a sign of their good faith and ability to purchase your home. A deposit generally represents part of the down payment.

Weigh the advantages and disadvantages of different amounts of down payment. Decide a range of down payments within which you are comfortable selling your home.

Large Down Payments

Down payments of 20 percent or more are usually considered large. For most sellers, the advantages of requiring buyers to make a large down payment outweigh the disadvantages.

ADVANTAGES
- Large down payments enable buyers to qualify for a loan, for which they might not otherwise be able to qualify.
- It encourages buyers to take better care of the property than if buyers have less invested.
- A large financial stake makes buyers less likely to default on the loan because of the large loss should they default.
- Such a down payment makes more money available for you to put into investments that have a higher rate of return.

DISADVANTAGES
- Large down payments give you a smaller monthly income from the sale of your property if you make the loan to the buyers yourself.
- Buyers with a large monthly income but a small down payment may not qualify to buy your home.

Small Down Payments

Down payments of 10 percent or less are generally considered small. The benefits of permitting buyers to make a small down payment may outweigh the drawbacks in some situations.

ADVANTAGES
- A smaller down payment makes it easier to sell your property, because more buyers can qualify.
- It allows buyers who have a large monthly income but a small down payment to buy the property.
- A small down payment may provide you with a high return if what you are making on the loan is the highest rate of return you can get on your money at equal risk.
- This type of financing provides you with a larger monthly income if you decide to make the loan to the buyer yourself.

DISADVANTAGES
- Buyers may be more likely to default on the loan. They have less to lose.
- You could lose the whole loan amount if the buyers default and the underlying lender forecloses.

Seller Buy-down Loan

A seller buy-down loan is financing in which the effective interest rate is bought down (reduced) during the beginning years of the loan by your contributions. You are really paying for the buyers' interest in advance. This lower interest rate usually lasts two to three years. You may increase the price to cover this additional cost. The following is an example of a seller buy-down loan:

A loan for $100,000 at 12 percent interest has payments totaling $12,000 per year.
Seller pays $3,000 for a two-year buy-down, of which
    $2000 is applied to buyer's first year's payments
    $1000 is applied to buyer's second year's payments
Buyer pays on $100,000 loan
    $10,000 during first year for an effective rate of 10 percent
    $11,000 during second year for an effective rate of 11 percent

ADVANTAGES
- More buyers may be interested in buying your house if you offer the buy-down loan.
- It enables buyers to purchase the property who might not otherwise qualify.
- You may be able to sell your property sooner.

DISADVANTAGES
- Buyers may be more likely to default because they don't have as much invested.
- If you pay buyers' interest in advance and do not increase the price, you will obtain less money from the sale.

Seller Carry Back Loan

Under a seller carry back loan agreement, you act as a lender to "carry back," or hold, loan notes from the buyers. These notes may be first, second, or even third loans.

ADVANTAGES
- Terms and conditions of the loan are negotiable.
- You may receive monthly income from the loan.

- You may be eligible for capital gains tax deferment.
- Buyers do not need to qualify for an institutional loan.
- Buyers do not pay loan origination fees or points, which may make them more likely to purchase your home.

DISADVANTAGES

- You may spend time and effort to qualify the buyers to ensure that they have the ability to pay.
- More time and effort is necessary to find out about any regulations that may apply, in order to avoid breaking any laws.
- You may spend time, effort, and possibly money to make sure the agreement is written properly.

Consider consulting a professional such as your attorney before signing a seller carry back loan agreement in order to
- Qualify buyers to be sure that they have the ability to pay.
- Write the agreement properly.
- Inform you of any rules that may apply, such as federally required and imputed (assigned) interest rates.

All Inclusive Trust Deed (AITD, Wraparound Mortgage)

The all inclusive trust deed (AITD), also known as a wraparound mortgage, is a junior (second, third, and so on) loan at one overall interest rate used to wrap the existing loans into a package. The amount of this loan you make to the buyers is sufficient to cover the existing loan and provide additional funds for you. You make payments on the existing loans from buyers' payments. You remain primarily responsible for the loans that are wrapped. These loans are also referred to as overriding deeds of trust. The following is an example of an AITD:

Purchase price	$ 125,000
Down payment	− 25,000
Buyer's AITD at 11%	100,000
Buyer's AITD at 11%	100,000
Seller's 1st trust deed (TD) at 8 percent	− 70,000
Seller's equity	30,000
Buyer's 12 month interest on AITD to seller ($100,000 times 11 percent)	11,000
Seller's 12 month interest on 1st TD to lender ($70,000 times 8 percent)	− 5,600
Seller's return on equity ($11,000 − $5,600)	5,400
Seller's return on equity ($5,400/$30,000)	18 percent

ADVANTAGES

- The wraparound mortgage allows you more price and sales flexibility, because you do the financing.
- This may be the only practical way to sell a home where the existing loan contains a lock-in clause. A lock-in clause prohibits the prepayment of a note.
- The wraparound mortgage retains favorable terms on existing loans.

DISADVANTAGES

- You are responsible for the loans in the case of foreclosure.
- To be safe you may want to go to the effort and/or expense of qualifying buyers to be sure that they have the ability to pay.
- You must find out about any regulations that apply.

- You may have to pay a professional to make sure the agreement is written properly.

Consult persons knowledgeable in real estate finance to design the loan. Establishing this loan may include these tasks:
- Paying off or renegotiating an existing loan that restricts the sale or other transfer of title (alienation).
- Participating in the Federal National Mortgage Association (FNMA) Refinance and Resale Program.
- Determining what conditions constitute default.
- Preparing a realistic payment schedule to cover existing loans.
- Deciding who will set up, pay for, and administer collection procedures. (Both seller and buyers may be most protected from default if the AITD is set up so that a trustee handles all the payments and holds the AITD.)
- Writing a legally binding AITD contract.

Land Sale Contract (Conditional Sales Contract, Contract for Deed)

A land sale contract is a type of installment sale agreement that stipulates that the seller retain title to the property until the buyers perform all the conditions of the contract. Because this contract is less frequently used than other loan forms and can be quite complex, consider consulting your real estate attorney if you desire to use this form of financing.

Now that you have determined your financial requirements, you are ready to select consultants to aid you with various aspects of the sales process.

CHAPTER 4
Select Consultants

Having consultants provide you with professional advice and/or services can be very useful when you sell your home yourself. The consultants you might want to consider include accountants or tax preparers, attorneys, closing agents/escrow holders, home inspectors, lenders, title insurance companies—and sometimes even real estate professionals.

Step 1: Select Consultants

Consider selecting consultants to provide services at this point, if you have not already done so, to
- Obtain maximum benefit from the services that they offer.
- Avoid choosing a consultant or company that does not like to deal with people who sell their own homes.

As you interview these professionals, complete the worksheet for that profession that accompanies the descriptions here.

Accountants or Tax Preparers

An accountant is a person who keeps, audits, and inspects financial records, prepares financial reports, gives tax advice, and prepares tax returns. The more complicated your financial affairs, the more you may be able to profit from consulting an accountant before you sell your home.

Tax preparers prepare tax returns. They can tell you about the laws regarding taxes.

Consider using an accountant or tax preparer to
- Aid you in determining financial implications of your sale.
- Help you to determine possible tax implications before you sell your home.
- Prepare tax returns after you have sold your home.

Attorneys

Attorneys are people licensed to practice law. An attorney's business is to give legal advice and/or assistance as well as to prosecute and defend causes in courts. Choose an attorney who specializes in real estate and who can guide your sale through the entire process, as needed. Hire a local attorney, because laws as well as local customs affecting real estate sales vary. Depending on where you live, you might consider using an attorney to
- Write or review the purchase contract before you sign it.

ACCOUNTANT QUESTIONS WORKSHEET

Name:_____Telephone:_____

Address:_____

<u>Ask</u> <u>Ans.</u> <u>Questions</u>

Prepare

[ ] [ ] What are your credentials?_____

_____

[ ] [ ] What do you charge per hour? $_____

[ ] [ ] How does 24-month tax rule affect my timing selling my home?__

_____

[ ] [ ] Am I eligible for the over-55 one-time exclusion? [ ] Yes [ ] No

[ ] [ ] How does use of the over-55 one-time exclusion affect the timing of
my sale? _____

[ ] [ ] Will you provide me with list of items currently considered capital
improvements?   [ ] Yes [ ] No

[ ] [ ] How much of a deposit do you suggest I ask for? $_____

[ ] [ ] Does my loan have a prepayment penalty?   [ ] Yes [ ] No

[ ] [ ] If so, how much? $ _____

[ ] [ ] Is my loan assumable?   [ ] Yes [ ] No

[ ] [ ] Lender charge an assumption fee?   [ ] Yes [ ] No

[ ] [ ] If so, how much? $_____

[ ] [ ] Lender requiring qualification of buyers to assume my loan?
                                                        [ ] Yes [ ] No

[ ] [ ] Lender requiring renegotiation of loan with buyers who want to
assume my loan?   [ ] Yes [ ] No

[ ] [ ] Is my loan a subject to loan?   [ ] Yes [ ] No

[ ] [ ] Is my loan due-on-sale?   [ ] Yes [ ] No

[ ] [ ] My tax result leasing to buyers before closing? $_____

[ ] [ ] My tax result leasing from buyers after closing? $_____

[ ] [ ] My tax result using a lease option? $_____

[ ] [ ] What are the names and phone numbers of attorneys you
recommend?_____

_____

[ ] [ ] What are the names and phone numbers of closing agents you
recommend?_____

_____

[ ] [ ] What are the names and phone numbers of escrow holders you
recommend?_____

_____

ACCOUNTANT QUESTIONS WORKSHEET

Ask Ans. Questions

Prepare (*continued*)

[ ] [ ] What are the names and phone numbers of title companies you recommend?_____

_____

[ ] [ ] What are the names and phone numbers of real estate professionals you recommend?_____

[ ] [ ] _____

[ ] [ ] _____

[ ] [ ] _____

[ ] [ ] _____

[ ] [ ] _____

Market

[ ] [ ] _____

[ ] [ ] _____

[ ] [ ] _____

Negotiate

Ask	Ans.	Question		
[ ]	[ ]	How much initial deposit do you suggest?	$_____	
[ ]	[ ]	By how much do you suggest buyers increase the deposit?	$_____	
[ ]	[ ]	How much down payment do you recommend?	$_____	
[ ]	[ ]	Do you suggest buyers get a new loan?	[ ] Yes	[ ] No
[ ]	[ ]	Do you suggest buyers assume my loan?	[ ] Yes	[ ] No
[ ]	[ ]	Do you suggest buyers take title subject to?	[ ] Yes	[ ] No
[ ]	[ ]	Do you suggest I make a seller carry back loan?	[ ] Yes	[ ] No
[ ]	[ ]	If so, for how much?	$_____	
[ ]	[ ]	If so, for how long?	_____	
[ ]	[ ]	If so, what are my tax consequences?	$_____	
[ ]	[ ]	Do you suggest I use an AITD or wraparound?	[ ] Yes	[ ] No

ACCOUNTANT QUESTIONS WORKSHEET

<u>Ask</u> <u>Ans.</u> <u>Questions</u>
Negotiate (*continued*)

[ ]	[ ]	If so, for how much?	$_____
[ ]	[ ]	If so, for how long?	_____
[ ]	[ ]	If so, at what interest rate?	_____
[ ]	[ ]	If so, will you qualify the buyers?	[ ] Yes [ ] No
[ ]	[ ]	If so, will you write the contract?	[ ] Yes [ ] No
[ ]	[ ]	If so, what rules apply?_____	

[ ] [ ] Do you suggest I use a seller buy-down loan?   [ ] Yes [ ] No
[ ] [ ] If so, for how much? $_____
[ ] [ ] If so, for how long?   _____
[ ] [ ] Do you suggest leasing to buyers before closing?   [ ] Yes [ ] No
[ ] [ ] If so, for how much? $_____
[ ] [ ] If so, for how long?   _____
[ ] [ ] Do you suggest leasing from buyers escrow closing?[ ] Yes [ ] No
[ ] [ ] If so, for how much? $_____
[ ] [ ] If so, for how long?   _____
[ ] [ ] Do you suggest I use a lease option?   [ ] Yes [ ] No
[ ] [ ] What do you suggest for an option fee? $_____
[ ] [ ] How long do you suggest the option last?   _____
[ ] [ ] Do you suggest I use a purchase option?   [ ] Yes [ ] No
[ ] [ ] What amount do you suggest for an option fee? $_____
[ ] [ ] For how long do you suggest the option be good?   _____
[ ] [ ] Do you suggest I use an escrow?   [ ] Yes [ ] No
[ ] [ ] How long of an escrow do you suggest?   _____
[ ] [ ] By whom do you recommend the escrow fees be paid?
     _____

[ ] [ ] _____

[ ] [ ] _____

[ ] [ ] _____

[ ] [ ] _____

[ ] [ ] _____

ACCOUNTANT QUESTIONS WORKSHEET

<u>Ask</u> <u>Ans.</u> <u>Questions</u>

Close

[ ] [ ] Will you reconcile the closing statement for me?   [ ] Yes [ ] No

[ ] [ ] Will you explain the closing statement to me?   [ ] Yes [ ] No

[ ] [ ] _____

[ ] [ ] _____

[ ] [ ] _____

[ ] [ ] _____

Wrap Up

[ ] [ ] What moving costs are currently tax deductible?

[ ] [ ] What is effect of the 24-month rule on my transaction?

[ ] [ ] What is effect of the over-55 one-time exclusion on my sale?

[ ] [ ] What expenses are currently tax deductible?

[ ] [ ] What is effect of installment sale imputed interest rate on my sale?

[ ] [ ] What is effect of conversion of my residence to a rental property?

[ ] [ ] What is the effect of FIRPTA regulations on my transaction?

[ ] [ ] How much do I owe in taxes when I sell my home?$_____

[ ] [ ] _____

[ ] [ ] _____

[ ] [ ] _____

- Write or review other contracts, such as leases and options.
- Hold the earnest money in a trust account.
- Qualify buyers.
- Remedy any defects in your title.
- Handle any legal complications that could prevent closing.
- Manage the closing.
- Represent you in any actions against the buyer.

Closing Agents/Escrow Holders

The closing is the final stage of a real estate transaction. It involves signing loan documents, paying closing costs, and delivering the deed. A closing agent is a person you authorize to carry out the closing process for you.

Escrow is a type of closing. In this process you and buyers deposit documents and/or money with a neutral third party, the escrow holder. You and buyers give instructions to the escrow holder to hold and deliver documents and/or money upon the performance of certain conditions. The escrow officer is the person within an escrow company with whom you will be dealing.

Consider using an escrow, although you are not legally required to do so. Because the mechanics of property transfer are fairly complex, the advantages of having an escrow are numerous:

- An escrow officer can answer many of your questions.
- Safekeeping of documents and money is handled by a neutral third party.
- The escrow agent will carry out contract terms, including
  - Receiving and disbursing money.
  - Preparing, obtaining, and recording documents.
  - Calculating the proration of interest, taxes, insurance, and other funds.
- The system provides an assurance that all the conditions of the sale will be met before buyers receive documents and you receive funds.

Home Inspectors

Home inspectors can provide you and buyers with detailed information about the condition of your home. A home inspector first thoroughly examines the general physical condition of your property's site and structures. The inspector then submits a detailed written report on the quality and condition of its site and structures. This report usually lists what is in good repair as well as current and impending possible problems.

Providing a physical inspection report to buyers generally makes your home easier to sell. A physical inspection report may

- Convince buyers you are not trying to hide problems.
- Allow buyers to understand what problems they must deal with, if they buy your property.
- Convert most physical problems from contingencies to bargaining issues to be dealt with immediately.
- Aid you in filling out a real estate disclosure statement.

Lenders

Institutional real estate lenders are organizations that loan money for real estate loans. Such lenders include banks, savings and loans, thrifts, credit unions, and mortgage companies.

ATTORNEY QUESTIONS WORKSHEET

Name:_____Telephone:_____

Address:_____

<u>Ask</u> <u>Ans.</u> <u>Questions</u>

Prepare

[ ] [ ]   What are your credentials?_____

_____

[ ] [ ]   Do you specialize in real estate?   [ ] Yes [ ] No
[ ] [ ]   What do you charge per hour? $_____
[ ] [ ]   Will you represent me?   [ ] Yes [ ] No
[ ] [ ]   Names and phone numbers of appraisers you recommend?

_____

_____

[ ] [ ]   How much deposit do you suggest from buyers? $_____
[ ] [ ]   Does my loan have a prepayment penalty?   [ ] Yes [ ] No
[ ] [ ]   If so, how much? $_____
[ ] [ ]   Is my loan assumable?   [ ] Yes [ ] No
[ ] [ ]   Does the lender charge an assumption fee?   [ ] Yes [ ] No
[ ] [ ]   If so, how much is it? $_____
[ ] [ ]   Lender requiring to qualify buyers to assume my loan?
                                                       [ ] Yes [ ] No
[ ] [ ]   Lender requiring to renegotiate loan with buyers who want to assume
           my loan?   [ ] Yes [ ] No
[ ] [ ]   Is my loan a subject to loan?   [ ] Yes [ ] No
[ ] [ ]   Is my loan due-on-sale?   [ ] Yes [ ] No
[ ] [ ]   Do you recommend I use a seller buy-down loan? [ ] Yes [ ] No
[ ] [ ]   If so, for how much? $_____
[ ] [ ]   Do you recommend I use a seller carry back loan? [ ] Yes [ ] No
[ ] [ ]   If so, for how much? $_____
[ ] [ ]   If so, will you qualify buyers?   [ ] Yes [ ] No
[ ] [ ]   If so, will you write the loan agreement?   [ ] Yes [ ] No
[ ] [ ]   If so, what rules apply?

_____

[ ] [ ]   Do you suggest I use an AITD or wraparound mortgage?
                                                       [ ] Yes [ ] No
[ ] [ ]   If so, for how much? $_____
[ ] [ ]   If so, for how long?   _____
[ ] [ ]   If so, at what interest rate?   _____
[ ] [ ]   If so, will you qualify the buyers?   [ ] Yes [ ] No
[ ] [ ]   If so, will you write the contract?   [ ] Yes [ ] No

ATTORNEY QUESTIONS WORKSHEET

Ask Ans. Questions
Prepare (*continued*)

[ ] [ ] If so, what rules apply?

_____

_____

[ ] [ ] Do you suggest I use a lease?   [ ] Yes [ ] No
[ ] [ ] If so, will you write the lease?   [ ] Yes [ ] No
[ ] [ ] Do you suggest I use a lease option?   [ ] Yes [ ] No
[ ] [ ] If so, will you write the lease option?   [ ] Yes [ ] No
[ ] [ ] What are the names and phone numbers of accountants you recommend?_____

[ ] [ ] What are the names and phone numbers of appraisers you recommend?_____

[ ] [ ] What are the names and phone numbers of closing agents you recommend?_____

[ ] [ ] What are the names and phone numbers of escrow holders you recommend?_____

[ ] [ ] What are the names and phone numbers of home inspectors you recommend?_____

[ ] [ ] What are the names and phone numbers of title companies you recommend?_____

[ ] [ ] What are the names and phone numbers of real estate professionals you recommend?_____

[ ] [ ] What are the names and phone numbers of pest control operators you recommend?_____

[ ] [ ] Are you a closing agent/escrow holder?   [ ] Yes [ ] No
[ ] [ ] How many closings/escrows do you handle each year?

_____

[ ] [ ] Will you handle my closing/escrow?   [ ] Yes [ ] No
[ ] [ ] _____

[ ] [ ] _____

_____

[ ] [ ] _____

_____

ATTORNEY QUESTIONS WORKSHEET

Ask Ans. Questions
         Prepare (*continued*)

[ ] [ ] _____
         _____
[ ] [ ] _____
         _____
[ ] [ ] _____
         _____
[ ] [ ] _____
         _____
[ ] [ ] _____
         _____

         Market
[ ] [ ] Will you review my contract with a contractor for an improvement?
                                          [ ] Yes [ ] No
[ ] [ ] What are the mechanic's lien laws that apply to this contract?
         _____

[ ] [ ] What are the sign laws in this community?_____
         _____

[ ] [ ] What are the laws regarding discrimination that apply to this sale?
         _____

[ ] [ ] What laws regarding transfer disclosure apply to this sale?
         _____

[ ] [ ] Is a physical inspection necessary by law?   [ ] Yes [ ] No
[ ] [ ] If so, who must pay?   _____
[ ] [ ] Is a geological inspection necessary by law?   [ ] Yes [ ] No
[ ] [ ] If so, who must pay?   _____
[ ] [ ] Is a pest control inspection necessary by law? [ ] Yes [ ] No
[ ] [ ] If so, who must pay?   _____
[ ] [ ] _____
[ ] [ ] _____
         _____
[ ] [ ] _____
         _____
[ ] [ ] _____
         _____

ATTORNEY QUESTIONS WORKSHEET

<u>Ask</u> <u>Ans.</u> <u>Questions</u>

Negotiate

[ ] [ ] How much initial deposit do you suggest? $_____

[ ] [ ] How much do you suggest that buyers increase the deposit?

$_____

[ ] [ ] How much down payment do you recommend? $_____

[ ] [ ] Do you suggest buyers get a new loan? [ ] Yes [ ] No

[ ] [ ] Do you suggest buyers assume my loan? [ ] Yes [ ] No

[ ] [ ] Do you suggest buyers take title subject to? [ ] Yes [ ] No

[ ] [ ] Do you suggest I make a seller carry back loan? [ ] Yes [ ] No

[ ] [ ] If so, for how much? $_____

[ ] [ ] If so, for how long? _____

[ ] [ ] Do you suggest I use an AITD or wraparound mortgage?

[ ] Yes [ ] No

[ ] [ ] If so, for how much? $_____

[ ] [ ] If so, for how long? _____

[ ] [ ] If so, at what interest rate? _____

[ ] [ ] If so, will you qualify the buyers? [ ] Yes [ ] No

[ ] [ ] If so, will you write the contract? [ ] Yes [ ] No

[ ] [ ] If so, what rules apply?_____

_____

_____

[ ] [ ] Do you suggest I use a seller buy-down loan? [ ] Yes [ ] No

[ ] [ ] If so, for how much? $_____

[ ] [ ] If so, for how long? _____

[ ] [ ] Do you suggest leasing to buyers before closing? [ ] Yes [ ] No

[ ] [ ] If so, for how much? $_____

[ ] [ ] If so, for how long? _____

[ ] [ ] Do you suggest leasing from buyers after closing? [ ] Yes [ ] No

[ ] [ ] If so, for how much? $_____

[ ] [ ] If so, for how long? _____

[ ] [ ] Do you suggest I use a lease option? [ ] Yes [ ] No

[ ] [ ] If so, for how much? $_____

[ ] [ ] If so, for how long? _____

[ ] [ ] Do you suggest I use a purchase option? [ ] Yes [ ] No

[ ] [ ] If so, for how much? $_____

[ ] [ ] If so, for how long? _____

[ ] [ ] Do you suggest I use an escrow? [ ] Yes [ ] No

[ ] [ ] By whom do you recommend the escrow fees be paid?

_____

[ ] [ ] What type of title insurance do you recommend?

_____

_____

ATTORNEY QUESTIONS WORKSHEET

<u>Ask</u> <u>Ans.</u> <u>Questions</u>
Negotiate (*continued*)

[ ] [ ] Who do you recommend pay title insurance fees?

[ ] [ ] As of what date do you suggest prorations be calculated?

[ ] [ ] Who pays the transfer tax on this transaction?

[ ] [ ] What date do you suggest buyers take possession?

[ ] [ ] What are the regulations regarding smoke detectors?

[ ] [ ] What are the laws regarding transfer disclosure in this state?

[ ] [ ] Do you suggest I have a physical inspection?   [ ] Yes [ ] No
[ ] [ ] Do you suggest I have a geological inspection?   [ ] Yes [ ] No
[ ] [ ] Is Flood Hazard Area Disclosure required?   [ ] Yes [ ] No
[ ] [ ] Is disclosure for earthquake potential required?   [ ] Yes [ ] No
[ ] [ ]

[ ] [ ]

[ ] [ ]

[ ] [ ]

[ ] [ ]

[ ] [ ]

Close
[ ] [ ] Do you suggest I renegotiate with this buyer?   [ ] Yes [ ] No
[ ] [ ] Do you suggest I remarket my home?   [ ] Yes [ ] No
[ ] [ ]

[ ] [ ]

Wrap Up
[ ] [ ]

CLOSING AGENT/ESCROW HOLDER QUESTIONS WORKSHEET

Name:_____Telephone:_____
Address:_____

Ask Ans. Questions

Prepare
[ ] [ ]   What are your credentials?_____

[ ] [ ]   How many transactions do you handle each year? _____
[ ] [ ]   What do you charge? $_____
[ ] [ ]   Do you mind answering my questions?   [ ] Yes [ ] No
[ ] [ ]   What are the names and phone numbers of accountants you recommend?_____

[ ] [ ]   What are the names and phone numbers of appraisers you recommend?_____

[ ] [ ]   What are the names and phone numbers of home inspectors you recommend?_____

[ ] [ ]   What are the names and phone numbers of lenders you recommend?

[ ] [ ]   What are the names and phone numbers of title companies you recommend?_____

[ ] [ ]   What are the names and phone numbers of real estate professionals you recommend?_____

[ ] [ ]   What are the names and phone numbers of pest control operators you recommend?_____

[ ] [ ]   _____

[ ] [ ]   _____

[ ] [ ]   _____

[ ] [ ]   _____

[ ] [ ].   _____

CLOSING AGENT/ESCROW HOLDER QUESTIONS WORKSHEET

<u>Ask</u> <u>Ans.</u> <u>Questions</u>
Market

[ ]   [ ]   What laws regarding discrimination apply to this sale?

_____

[ ]   [ ]   What laws regarding transfer disclosure apply to this sale?

_____

[ ]   [ ]   Is a physical inspection necessary by law?   [ ] Yes [ ] No
[ ]   [ ]   If so, who must pay?   _____
[ ]   [ ]   Is a geological inspection necessary by law?   [ ] Yes [ ] No
[ ]   [ ]   If so, who must pay?   _____
[ ]   [ ]   Is a pest control inspection necessary by law?   [ ] Yes [ ] No
[ ]   [ ]   If so, who must pay?   _____
[ ]   [ ]   Your cost estimate for an appraisal fee? $_____
[ ]   [ ]   Your cost estimate for an assumption fee? $_____
[ ]   [ ]   Your cost estimate for a beneficiary statement? $_____
[ ]   [ ]   Your cost estimate for closing/escrow fees? $_____
[ ]   [ ]   _____

[ ]   [ ]   _____

[ ]   [ ]   _____

[ ]   [ ]   _____

[ ]   [ ]   _____

[ ]   [ ]   _____

Negotiate

[ ]   [ ]   Who usually pays closing/escrow fees?   _____
[ ]   [ ]   Your cost estimate for a credit report fee? $_____
[ ]   [ ]   Your cost estimate for delinquent payments on my account?
                                                              $_____
[ ]   [ ]   Your cost estimate for a demand fee? $_____
[ ]   [ ]   Your cost estimate for document preparation fees?
                                                              $_____
[ ]   [ ]   Your cost estimate for drawing deed fees? $_____
[ ]   [ ]   Your cost estimate for hazard insurance costs? $_____
[ ]   [ ]   Your cost estimate for home warranty costs? $_____
[ ]   [ ]   Your cost estimate for impounds? $_____

CLOSING AGENT/ESCROW HOLDER QUESTIONS WORKSHEET

Ask Ans. Questions
          Negotiate (*continued*)
[ ] [ ]   Your cost estimate for interest? $_____
[ ] [ ]   Your cost estimate for a loan tie-in fee? $_____
[ ] [ ]   Your cost estimate for a loan origination fee? $_____
[ ] [ ]   Your cost estimate for notary fees? $_____
[ ] [ ]   Your cost estimate for pest control inspection? $_____
[ ] [ ]   Who usually pays pest control inspection fees?   _____
[ ] [ ]   Your cost estimate for physical inspection fee? $_____
[ ] [ ]   Who usually pays physical inspection fees?   _____
[ ] [ ]   Your cost estimate for points? $_____
[ ] [ ]   Your cost estimate for a prepayment penalty? $_____
[ ] [ ]   Your cost estimate for a reconveyance deed? $_____
[ ] [ ]   Your cost estimate for recording fee? $_____
[ ] [ ]   Your cost estimate for satisfaction of mortgage? $_____
[ ] [ ]   Your cost estimate for the title insurance? $_____
[ ] [ ]   Your cost estimate for the transfer fee? $_____
[ ] [ ]   Your cost estimate for transfer tax? $_____
[ ] [ ]   How do I calculate the transfer tax?

_____

[ ] [ ]   As of what date do you suggest prorations be calculated?

_____

[ ] [ ]   What are the regulations regarding smoke detectors in this area?

_____

[ ] [ ]   What are the laws regarding transfer disclosure in this state?

_____

[ ] [ ]   Is Flood Hazard Area Disclosure required?   [ ] Yes [ ] No
[ ] [ ]   Is disclosure for earthquake potential required?   [ ] Yes [ ] No
[ ] [ ]   _____

[ ] [ ]   _____

[ ] [ ]   _____

[ ] [ ]   _____

[ ] [ ]   _____

[ ] [ ]   _____

CLOSING AGENT/ESCROW HOLDER QUESTIONS WORKSHEET

Ask Ans. Questions

Close

[ ] [ ] How do I set up a closing or escrow?

_____

[ ] [ ] What information do you need for closing or setting up an escrow?

_____

[ ] [ ] What responsibilities do I have for the escrow?

_____

[ ] [ ] What is the procedure you require for amending escrow instructions?

_____

[ ] [ ] Do you require a walk-through inspection before closing?

[ ] Yes [ ] No

[ ] [ ] What timing do you suggest on the walk-through?

_____

[ ] [ ] What else needs to be done so that closing can occur?

_____

[ ] [ ] When do you think closing will occur? _____

[ ] [ ] _____

[ ] [ ] _____

[ ] [ ] _____

[ ] [ ] _____

[ ] [ ] _____

[ ] [ ] _____

Wrap Up

[ ] [ ] _____

[ ] [ ] _____

[ ] [ ] _____

HOME INSPECTOR QUESTIONS WORKSHEET

Name:_____ Telephone:_____

Address:_____

Ask Ans. Questions

Prepare

[ ] [ ] What are your credentials?

_____

[ ] [ ] Are you a licensed home inspector? [ ] Yes [ ] No

[ ] [ ] For how long have you been doing home inspections?

_____

[ ] [ ] What do you charge for a home inspection? $_____

[ ] [ ] On what items do you report?

_____

[ ] [ ] Do you report on items in good condition? [ ] Yes [ ] No

[ ] [ ] Do you report on items that are not currently problems but that may need repair or replacement in the next few years? [ ] Yes [ ] No

[ ] [ ] Do you have a vested interest in my property? [ ] Yes [ ] No

[ ] [ ] Which repairs do you think would be most cost effective when I sell?_____

[ ] [ ] Who do you recommend to make the repairs?

_____

[ ] [ ] _____

[ ] [ ] _____

[ ] [ ] _____

Market

[ ] [ ] What are the names and phone numbers of closing agents you recommend?_____

[ ] [ ] What are the names and phone numbers of escrow holders you recommend?_____

[ ] [ ] What are the names and phone numbers of geological inspectors you recommend?_____

HOME INSPECTOR QUESTIONS WORKSHEET

Ask Ans. Questions

Market (*continued*)

[ ] [ ] What are the names and phone numbers of real estate professionals you recommend?_____

_____

[ ] [ ] What are the names and phone numbers of pest control operators you recommend?_____

_____

[ ] [ ] _____

[ ] [ ] _____

[ ] [ ] _____

[ ] [ ] _____

Negotiate

[ ] [ ] _____

[ ] [ ] _____

[ ] [ ] _____

Close

[ ] [ ] _____

[ ] [ ] _____

[ ] [ ] _____

Wrap Up

[ ] [ ] _____

[ ] [ ] _____

[ ] [ ] _____

If you do not have the knowledge and experience to prequalify buyers (decide what buyers are able to afford), consider

1. Finding a lender with whom you like to deal. This may be the lender who holds a loan on your present home.
2. Asking the lender to answer any questions you may have regarding financing the sale of your property.
3. Having that lender prequalify buyers for you.
4. Being sure that the prequalifying interview
   - Is free to the buyer who is being prequalified.
   - Does not obligate buyers to that particular lender.

Title Insurance Companies

Title insurance companies issue policies of title insurance. These policies ensure that the title is free of liens (a charge upon real property to pay some debt). The nature and extent of the liens depend on the type of policy purchased. In some states, a title insurance policy must be issued before you can close the sale of your property.

In some areas, title insurance companies act as escrow holders. Check with a real estate professional or title company if you are unsure about who handles the duties in your area.

Title companies often provide other services, most of which are available without charge. They usually answer questions and give explanations, provide information about properties comparable to yours that have been recently sold in your area, and deliver important documents to the offices of city, county, and lenders.

Real Estate Professionals

Because the real estate industry is rather complex and has a specific terminology, this chapter includes the descriptions of various real estate professionals, the ways in which they may be able to serve you, and questions you may want to ask them.

Step 2: Ask Needed Questions

The following worksheets contain some of the questions most frequently asked of professionals involved in real estate transactions. These worksheets enable you to keep track of questions to ask consultants as well as to record their answers. The consultants' time may be expensive. Even if you are not paying for that time directly, consultants will probably appreciate your thoroughness and thoughtfulness.

1. Write an X in the Ask column for all questions you want to ask a particular consultant.
2. Enter any other questions in the spaces provided.
3. When you receive an answer,
   A. Write an X in the Ans. column.
   B. Write or check off the response you receive in the space provided following the question.
4. Keep sheets handy so that you can refer to them easily.

A worksheet of questions you might want to ask real estate professionals appears later in this chapter. The Real Estate Professional Questions Worksheet appears at the end of the chapter. This is due to the number and complexity of the terms about and relationships with real estate professionals that you need to know before you can complete the worksheet easily.

LENDER QUESTIONS WORKSHEET

Name:_____Telephone:_____

Address:_____

<u>Ask</u> <u>Ans.</u> <u>Questions</u>

Prepare

[ ] [ ] How much do I owe on my loan? $_____

[ ] [ ] Does my loan have a prepayment penalty?   [ ] Yes [ ] No

[ ] [ ] If so, how much? $_____

[ ] [ ] Is my loan assumable?   [ ] Yes [ ] No

[ ] [ ] Do you charge an assumption fee?   [ ] Yes [ ] No

[ ] [ ] If so, how much? $_____

[ ] [ ] Do you require that you qualify buyers to assume my loan?
                                                            [ ] Yes [ ] No

[ ] [ ] Do you require that you renegotiate the loan with buyers who want
to assume my loan?   [ ] Yes [ ] No

[ ] [ ] Will you release me from liability if the buyers assume my loan?
                                                            [ ] Yes [ ] No

[ ] [ ] Is my loan a subject to loan?   [ ] Yes [ ] No

[ ] [ ] Is my loan due-on-sale?   [ ] Yes [ ] No

[ ] [ ] Would you approve a lease option?   [ ] Yes [ ] No

[ ] [ ] What are the names and phone numbers of appraisers you
recommend?_____

_____

[ ] [ ] What are the names and phone numbers of attorneys you
recommend?_____

_____

[ ] [ ] What are the names and phone numbers of closing agents or escrow
holders you recommend?_____

_____

[ ] [ ] What are the names and phone numbers of title companies you
recommend?_____

_____

[ ] [ ] What are the names and phone numbers of real estate professionals
you recommend?_____

_____

[ ] [ ] _____

_____

[ ] [ ] _____

_____

[ ] [ ] _____

_____

LENDER QUESTIONS WORKSHEET

Ask Ans. Questions

Market

[ ]	[ ]	Will you prequalify my buyers?	[ ] Yes [ ] No
[ ]	[ ]	Will you make a loan commitment in writing?	[ ] Yes [ ] No
[ ]	[ ]	Will you approve a bridge loan?	[ ] Yes [ ] No

[ ] [ ] _____
_____

[ ] [ ] _____
_____

[ ] [ ] _____
_____

Negotiate

[ ]	[ ]	Are you an escrow holder?	[ ] Yes [ ] No
[ ]	[ ]	Must buyers get new first loan?	[ ] Yes [ ] No
[ ]	[ ]	Your cost estimate for an appraisal fee?	$_____
[ ]	[ ]	Your cost estimate for an assumption fee?	$_____
[ ]	[ ]	Your cost estimate for beneficiary statement fee?	$_____
[ ]	[ ]	Your cost estimate for a credit report fee?	$_____
[ ]	[ ]	Your cost estimate for delinquent payments on my account?	$_____
[ ]	[ ]	Your cost estimate for a demand fee?	$_____
[ ]	[ ]	Your cost estimate for impounds?	$_____
[ ]	[ ]	Your cost estimate for interest?	$_____
[ ]	[ ]	Your cost estimate for a loan tie-in fee?	$_____
[ ]	[ ]	Your cost estimate for a loan origination fee?	$_____
[ ]	[ ]	Your cost estimate for points?	$_____
[ ]	[ ]	Your cost estimate for a prepayment penalty?	$_____
[ ]	[ ]	Do I have your permission for buyer to assume second loan?	[ ] Yes [ ] No
[ ]	[ ]	Do I have your permission for buyer to take title subject to?	[ ] Yes [ ] No
[ ]	[ ]	Do you require escrow to make a loan?	[ ] Yes [ ] No
[ ]	[ ]	Is standard coverage title insurance required?	[ ] Yes [ ] No
[ ]	[ ]	Is extended coverage title insurance required?	[ ] Yes [ ] No
[ ]	[ ]	Who usually pays title insurance fee?	_____
[ ]	[ ]	If repairs are needed, can amount price reduced be used to make repairs?	[ ] Yes [ ] No
[ ]	[ ]	Pest control inspection and report required?	[ ] Yes [ ] No
[ ]	[ ]	Does property need flood hazard disclosure?	[ ] Yes [ ] No
[ ]	[ ]	Does property need flood insurance?	[ ] Yes [ ] No
[ ]	[ ]	If so, how much?	$_____

LENDER QUESTIONS WORKSHEET

Ask Ans. Questions

Negotiate (*continued*)

[ ] [ ]   Does property need any other special disclosures? [ ] Yes [ ] No
[ ] [ ]   If so, which disclosure?_____
_____

[ ] [ ]   What are the names and phone numbers of sellers of home protection
plans?_____
_____

[ ] [ ]   Who pays notary fees?   _____
[ ] [ ]   _____
_____

[ ] [ ]   _____
_____

[ ] [ ]   _____
_____

Close

[ ] [ ]   Is escrow a condition of making a loan?   [ ] Yes [ ] No
[ ] [ ]   When will your appraiser come to evaluate my property?

[ ] [ ]   Can I have a written loan commitment?   [ ] Yes [ ] No
[ ] [ ]   Has closing agent contacted lender for demands?   [ ] Yes [ ] No
[ ] [ ]   Accounting of property taxes paid to tax office?

[ ] [ ]   Do you require a statement of impound account?   [ ] Yes [ ] No
[ ] [ ]   Do you require a copy of reconveyance deed?   [ ] Yes [ ] No
[ ] [ ]   _____
_____

[ ] [ ]   _____
_____

[ ] [ ]   _____
_____

Wrap Up

[ ] [ ]   _____
_____

[ ] [ ]   _____
_____

[ ] [ ]   _____
_____

TITLE COMPANY QUESTIONS WORKSHEET

Name:_____Telephone:_____

Address:_____

<u>Ask</u> <u>Ans.</u> <u>Questions</u>

Prepare

[ ] [ ] Why should I use your services?_____

_____

[ ] [ ] What is your charge for comparables? $_____

[ ] [ ] What are the sales prices of comparable properties in my
neighborhood?_____

_____

_____

[ ] [ ] What do you charge for a title survey? $_____

[ ] [ ] Will you work with me?   [ ] Yes [ ] No

[ ] [ ] What are the names and phone numbers of appraisers you
recommend?_____

[ ] [ ] What are the names and phone numbers of closing agents or escrow
holders you recommend?_____

[ ] [ ] What are the names and phone numbers of home inspectors you
recommend?_____

[ ] [ ] What are the names and phone numbers of lenders you recommend?

_____

[ ] [ ] What are the names and phone numbers of real estate professionals
you recommend?_____

[ ] [ ] _____

[ ] [ ] _____

[ ] [ ] _____

Market

[ ] [ ] _____

[ ] [ ] _____

TITLE COMPANY QUESTIONS WORKSHEET

Ask Ans. Questions

Negotiate

[ ] [ ] Your cost estimate for judgments against me? $_____

[ ] [ ] Your cost estimate for subescrow fee? $_____

[ ] [ ] Your cost estimate for title search fee? $_____

[ ] [ ] Your cost estimate for a title insurance? $_____

[ ] [ ] _____

[ ] [ ] _____

[ ] [ ] _____

Close

[ ] [ ] What are the results of the preliminary title report?

_____

[ ] [ ] Which of the items on the report might prevent closing?

_____

[ ] [ ] How do you recommend I handle these items?

_____

[ ] [ ] _____

[ ] [ ] _____

[ ] [ ] _____

Wrap Up

[ ] [ ] _____

[ ] [ ] _____

[ ] [ ] _____

Step 3: Understand Real Estate Terms

Due to the involved nature of real estate terminology, you need to understand the definitions of some terms before you read the listing of the most usual ways to interact with real estate professionals. Real estate professionals will contact you after you have placed your home on the market. They usually try to get you to sign a listing with the agency that they represent. You can deal most effectively with them if you understand terms that they use.

Agent

An agent is a person authorized by another—the principal—to act for the principal in dealings with third parties. An agent has certain duties to the principal resulting from the trust relationship, including always acting with the principal's consent, betraying no confidential information, making no secret profit, using reasonable skill and care in performing duties, obeying all lawful instructions, disclosing any material facts (facts that if known would influence a person's decision), and providing an accounting of all money received and disbursed.

You are responsible for the actions of any person you employ as an agent, just as real estate brokers are responsible for the sales associates they employ.

Real Estate Broker

A broker is a real estate agent who represents another person in dealing with third parties. To become a broker, a person must take required courses, pass a broker's exam, and be licensed by the state. The broker may employ sales associates, including real estate sales agents and other brokers. The broker is responsible for their actions.

Sales Associate

A sales associate is a real estate professional with either a broker's or salesperson's license, who acts as an agent for a broker.

Single Agent

A single agent is an agent representing only one party in a real estate transaction. Types of single agents include a listing agent or seller's agent who represents the seller in a transaction and the selling agent or buyer's agent who represents the buyer.

Dual Agent

A broker acting either directly or through a sales associate as the agent for both the seller and the buyer is known as a dual agent. With both parties represented by one agent, great potential exists for imagined or actual conflict of interest.

Divided Agency

The action of an agent in representing both parties in a transaction without the knowledge and consent of both parties creates a divided agency. A divided agency is illegal.

Termination of Agency

The representation by an agency may be ended (terminated) by various methods, including
- Expiration of the agency agreement, the most common method.

- Revocation (cancellation) of the agency by the principal, which may not relieve you of paying commission to a broker.
- Death or incapacity of either the principal or the broker, but not the sales associate.
- Destruction of the property.
- Mutual decision by you and the broker to revoke the agency.
- Renunciation of the agency agreement by the broker.

Commission

Commissions legally belong to and must be paid only to brokers, no matter which sales associate in their organization obtained the listing or made the sale.

Step 4: Use Real Estate Professionals Most Advantageously

The following are options for dealing with real estate professionals who approach you for a listing. The options are in order from what are generally considered to be the least expensive and restrictive options to those considered the most expensive and restrictive. Legally, commissions are negotiable.

Tell Professional You Are Selling Your Home Yourself

Thank the real estate professional politely for his or her interest but firmly decline any involvement with an agency.

ADVANTAGES
- It encourages real estate professionals to stop calling.
- It maintains good relationships.
- You owe no fees.

DISADVANTAGES
- Professional real estate help is not immediately available in case of questions or problems.

Allow Professional to Represent Buyers

Allow a real estate professional to represent the buyers only if the buyers pay the commission. Make it clear you will *not* sign a listing contract or pay a commission.

ADVANTAGES
- You sign no listing contract.
- You pay no real estate commission.
- You have a professional available for aid in some areas. However, remember the agent represents buyers.

DISADVANTAGES
- Because the professional is representing the buyer, this person is not the best source for answers.

Pay Professional by the Hour

If you decide to hire a professional to consult with you at an hourly rate, consider
1. Checking with independent brokers. They are often the best source of referrals to professional real estate consultants.

2. Asking at several real estate offices to get consultants' names.
3. Signing a contract with the consultant to protect you both.

ADVANTAGES
- You pay only for the services you use.
- Costs are commonly far less than the usual commission.
- You have the services of a real estate professional immediately available.

DISADVANTAGES
- You only get the services for which you pay.
- You pay some fees.

Negotiate Listing Contract for Less Than Usual Fee

The listing fee you negotiate with these brokers could be on a flat fee or commission basis. Some areas have discount brokers who charge less than the usual fee.

Understand *exactly* what you are getting for what price. Some real estate professionals limit the services they provide on reduced commission or flat fee contracts. Adding services you need to the basic charge might increase your cost of sale to more than the cost of a usual commission.

ADVANTAGES
- You generally pay less than the usual commission.
- You have the services of a professional immediately available to you.

DISADVANTAGES
- You pay some fees.
- You may have to negotiate to get the rate you want.
- You may receive less than the usual degree of service from the professional by choice or by default.

Sign a Permission to Show Listing

The permission to show listing contract allows a professional to show your property only to the person or persons named in that contract. It also provides that you will pay the commission you negotiate only if someone on the list purchases your home.

ADVANTAGES
- Your home may sell more quickly than it might otherwise.
- You must pay a commission only if you sell your home to a person listed on the contract.
- If you sell your home through the professional, you have his or her services immediately available.

DISADVANTAGES
- You must pay the commission if you sell your home to a person listed in the contract.
- You have the professional's services during only part of the process (negotiation and closing).

Have a Broker Submit Your Listing to MLS for a Fee

Find a broker to submit information about your house to your local multiple listing service (MLS) for a fee. Some brokers may do this without having you sign a listing agreement. You then pay a commission only to the broker who brings you buyers. You can set the commission at whatever level you desire. Remember, the lower you set the commission, the less likely real estate professionals will be to show your property.

ADVANTAGES
- Information regarding your home reaches more people who can actively help you sell your home.
- You determine the real estate commission.

DISADVANTAGES
- You pay a fee to list your property with an MLS.
- You pay a commission to sell your listing.
- Usually only real estate professionals have access to this information.

Sign an Open Listing

You can sign a nonexclusive open listing granting the right to sell agreement with one or more real estate professionals. It provides that if you sell your home yourself, you are not liable to the broker for a commission. If, however, a real estate professional obtains buyers for the property, you must pay the broker the commission you have negotiated.

ADVANTAGES
- You may sell your home yourself and pay no commission.
- You have the services of a real estate professional available during the whole process.
- Your property may be advertised by more than one real estate professional.

DISADVANTAGES
- Most real estate professionals will not concentrate their money, time, and effort on this type of listing.
- You must pay the commission if a professional procures the buyers.

Sign an Exclusive Agency Listing

Under an exclusive agency listing, which you may sign with only one broker, if that agency obtains the buyers you must pay the broker the commission negotiated. If you sell your home yourself, you are not liable to the broker for the commission.

ADVANTAGES
- You may sell your home yourself and pay no commission.
- You have the services of a real estate professional available during the entire period.

DISADVANTAGES
- Many real estate professionals will not concentrate their sales efforts on this type of listing.
- You must pay the commission you have negotiated if the professional finds the buyers.

Sign an Exclusive Right to Sell Listing

A restricted listing called an exclusive right to sell listing provides that, during the specified term, the broker has the sole and exclusive right to sell your home. It also provides that you must pay the real estate broker the negotiated commission, no matter who makes the sale.

ADVANTAGES
- A real estate professional is most likely to spend the most money, time, and effort on this listing.
- You have the services of the real estate professional during the entire period.

DISADVANTAGES
- You must pay the negotiated commission no matter who sells your home.

Sign a Net Listing

This type of listing provides that the broker retain as commission all money received in excess of the price you set.

ADVANTAGES
- A real estate professional is likely to spend much time, energy, and money on this type of listing.
- You have the services of a real estate professional during the entire period.

DISADVANTAGES
- You may receive far less for your property if you sign this type of listing than if you sign any other.
- Chances of fraud, misrepresentation, and other abuses are more common with this type of listing because of the inexact nature of the commission structure.

Ask Questions!

Now that you understand what real estate professionals are able to do for you, you can choose to interact with them in a manner that best satisfies your needs.

The questions on the Real Estate Professional Questions Worksheet encompass all levels of interaction with real estate professionals. Not all questions may be appropriate, depending upon the level of interaction you have chosen to pursue. As with most questions on all the lists, there are alternative sources of the information, depending on the nature of the question. Complete the worksheet just as you used the other worksheets in this chapter.

After you have selected your mix of consultants and have asked them some specific questions about your real estate concerns, you are ready to make a real estate disclosure statement concerning your property. This is the material covered in Chapter 5.

REAL ESTATE PROFESSIONAL QUESTIONS WORKSHEET

Name:_____Telephone:_____
Address:_____

<u>Ask</u> <u>Ans.</u> <u>Questions</u>

Prepare

[ ] [ ]   What are your credentials?_____

_____

[ ] [ ]   Provide a market evaluation at no cost or obligation?[ ] Yes [ ] No
[ ] [ ]   What are the prices of comparable properties in the neighborhood?

_____

[ ] [ ]   What are the names and phone numbers of appraisers you
           recommend?_____

_____

Ask	Ans.	Question		
[ ]	[ ]	Does my loan have a prepayment penalty?	[ ] Yes	[ ] No
[ ]	[ ]	If so, how much?	$_____	
[ ]	[ ]	Is my loan assumable?	[ ] Yes	[ ] No
[ ]	[ ]	Does the lender charge an assumption fee?	[ ] Yes	[ ] No
[ ]	[ ]	If so, how much?	$_____	
[ ]	[ ]	Is my loan a subject to loan?	[ ] Yes	[ ] No
[ ]	[ ]	Is my loan due-on-sale?	[ ] Yes	[ ] No

[ ] [ ]   What are the names and phone numbers of accountants you
           recommend?_____

_____

[ ] [ ]   What are the names and phone numbers of appraisers you
           recommend?_____

_____

[ ] [ ]   What are the names and phone numbers of closing agents you
           recommend?_____

_____

[ ] [ ]   What are the names and phone numbers of escrow holders you
           recommend?_____

_____

[ ] [ ]   What are the names and phone numbers of home inspectors you
           recommend?_____

_____

[ ] [ ]   What are the names and phone numbers of title companies you
           recommend?_____

_____

[ ] [ ]   What are the names and phone numbers of pest control operators you
           recommend?_____

_____

REAL ESTATE PROFESSIONAL QUESTIONS WORKSHEET

Ask Ans. Questions

Prepare (*continued*)

[ ] [ ] Do you consult?   [ ] Yes [ ] No
[ ] [ ] How much do you charge per hour for consulting?
                                                                    $_____

[ ] [ ] Will you review a contract for me?   [ ] Yes [ ] No
[ ] [ ] If I sign a one-time permission to show, will you show my property?
                                                                 [ ] Yes [ ] No
[ ] [ ] Will you submit my listing to the MLS for a fee? [ ] Yes [ ] No
[ ] [ ] If so, how much? $_____
[ ] [ ] What services do you provide for a discounted commission?
          _____
          _____

[ ] [ ] _____
          _____

[ ] [ ] _____
          _____

[ ] [ ] _____
          _____

[ ] [ ] _____
          _____

Market

[ ] [ ] Will you review my contract with a contractor?   [ ] Yes [ ] No
[ ] [ ] What mechanic's lien laws apply to this contract?
          _____

[ ] [ ] What are the sign laws in this community?
          _____

[ ] [ ] What laws regarding discrimination apply to this sale?
          _____

[ ] [ ] What laws regarding transfer disclosure apply to this sale?
          _____

[ ] [ ] Is a physical inspection necessary by law?   [ ] Yes [ ] No
[ ] [ ] If so, who must pay?   _____
[ ] [ ] Is a pest control inspection necessary by law?   [ ] Yes [ ] No
[ ] [ ] If so, who must pay?   _____
[ ] [ ] How much initial deposit do you suggest? $_____
[ ] [ ] How much might buyers increase the deposit? $_____

REAL ESTATE PROFESSIONAL QUESTIONS WORKSHEET

<u>Ask</u> <u>Ans.</u> <u>Questions</u>
Market (*continued*)

[ ] [ ] _____

[ ] [ ] _____

[ ] [ ] _____

Negotiate

Ask	Ans.	Questions		
[ ]	[ ]	Do you suggest buyers get a new loan?	[ ] Yes	[ ] No
[ ]	[ ]	Do you suggest buyers assume my loan?	[ ] Yes	[ ] No
[ ]	[ ]	Do you suggest buyers take title subject to?	[ ] Yes	[ ] No
[ ]	[ ]	Do you suggest I use a seller buy-down loan?	[ ] Yes	[ ] No
[ ]	[ ]	If so, for how much?	$_____	
[ ]	[ ]	If so, what rules apply?		

Ask	Ans.	Questions		
[ ]	[ ]	Do you recommend I use a seller carry back loan?	[ ] Yes	[ ] No
[ ]	[ ]	If so, for how much?	$_____	
[ ]	[ ]	If so, at what interest rate?	_____	
[ ]	[ ]	If so, will you qualify buyers?	[ ] Yes	[ ] No
[ ]	[ ]	If so, will you write the loan agreement?	[ ] Yes	[ ] No
[ ]	[ ]	If so, what rules apply?		

Ask	Ans.	Questions		
[ ]	[ ]	Do you suggest using an AITD or wraparound?	[ ] Yes	[ ] No
[ ]	[ ]	If so, for how much?	$_____	
[ ]	[ ]	If so, at what interest rate?	_____	
[ ]	[ ]	If so, will you qualify buyers?	[ ] Yes	[ ] No
[ ]	[ ]	If so, will you write the loan agreement?	[ ] Yes	[ ] No
[ ]	[ ]	If so, what rules apply?		

Ask	Ans.	Questions		
[ ]	[ ]	Do you suggest leasing to buyers before closing?	[ ] Yes	[ ] No
[ ]	[ ]	If so, for how much?	$_____	
[ ]	[ ]	If so, for how long?	_____	
[ ]	[ ]	If so, will you write the lease?	[ ] Yes	[ ] No
[ ]	[ ]	Do you suggest leasing from buyers after closing?	[ ] Yes	[ ] No
[ ]	[ ]	If so, for how much?	$_____	
[ ]	[ ]	If so, for how long?	_____	
[ ]	[ ]	If so, will you write the lease?	[ ] Yes	[ ] No
[ ]	[ ]	Do you suggest I use an option?	[ ] Yes	[ ] No

REAL ESTATE PROFESSIONAL QUESTIONS WORKSHEET

<u>Ask</u> <u>Ans.</u> <u>Questions</u>
Negotiate (*continued*)

Ask	Ans	Question	Answer
[ ]	[ ]	If so, for how much?	$_____
[ ]	[ ]	If so, for how long?	_____
[ ]	[ ]	If so, will you write the option?	[ ] Yes [ ] No
[ ]	[ ]	Do you suggest I use an escrow?	[ ] Yes [ ] No
[ ]	[ ]	Who do you recommend pay the escrow fees?	_____
[ ]	[ ]	Who do you recommend pay title insurance fees?	_____
[ ]	[ ]	As of what date should prorations be calculated?	_____
[ ]	[ ]	Who pays the transfer tax on this transaction?	_____
[ ]	[ ]	What date do you suggest buyers take possession?	_____
[ ]	[ ]	What are the laws regarding transfer disclosure in this state?	

_____

Ask	Ans	Question	Answer
[ ]	[ ]	Do you suggest I have a physical inspection done?	[ ] Yes [ ] No
[ ]	[ ]	Do you suggest I have a geological inspection done?	[ ] Yes [ ] No
[ ]	[ ]	Is Flood Hazard Area Disclosure required?	[ ] Yes [ ] No
[ ]	[ ]	Is disclosure for earthquake potential required?	[ ] Yes [ ] No
[ ]	[ ]	Your cost estimate for an appraisal fee?	$_____
[ ]	[ ]	Your cost estimate for an assumption fee?	$_____
[ ]	[ ]	Your cost estimate for a beneficiary statement?	$_____
[ ]	[ ]	Your cost estimate for closing/escrow fees?	$_____
[ ]	[ ]	Who usually pays closing/escrow fees?	_____
[ ]	[ ]	Your cost estimate for a credit report fee?	$_____
[ ]	[ ]	Your cost estimate for my delinquent payments?	$_____
[ ]	[ ]	Your cost estimate for a demand fee?	$_____
[ ]	[ ]	Your cost estimate for document preparation?	$_____
[ ]	[ ]	Your cost estimate for drawing deed fees?	$_____
[ ]	[ ]	Your cost estimate for hazard insurance costs?	$_____
[ ]	[ ]	Your cost estimate for home warranty costs?	$_____
[ ]	[ ]	Your cost estimate for interest?	$_____
[ ]	[ ]	Your cost estimate for a loan tie-in fee?	$_____
[ ]	[ ]	Your cost estimate for a loan origination fee?	$_____
[ ]	[ ]	Your cost estimate for notary fees?	$_____
[ ]	[ ]	Your cost estimate for pest control inspection?	$_____
[ ]	[ ]	Who usually pays pest control inspection fees?	_____
[ ]	[ ]	Your cost estimate for physical inspection fee?	$_____
[ ]	[ ]	Who usually pays physical inspection fees?	_____
[ ]	[ ]	Your cost estimate for points?	$_____
[ ]	[ ]	Your cost estimate for a prepayment penalty?	$_____
[ ]	[ ]	Your cost estimate for a reconveyance deed?	$_____
[ ]	[ ]	Your cost estimate for recording fee?	$_____

REAL ESTATE PROFESSIONAL QUESTIONS WORKSHEET

Ask Ans. Questions
          Negotiate (*continued*)
[ ] [ ]   Your cost estimate for satisfaction of mortgage? $_____
[ ] [ ]   Your cost estimate for subescrow fee? $_____
[ ] [ ]   Your cost estimate for title search fee? $_____
[ ] [ ]   Your cost estimate for title insurance? $_____
[ ] [ ]   Your cost estimate for the transfer fee? $_____
[ ] [ ]   Your cost estimate for transfer tax? $_____
[ ] [ ]   From what date might prorations be calculated?   _____
[ ] [ ]   _____

[ ] [ ]   _____

[ ] [ ]   _____

[ ] [ ]   _____

          Close
[ ] [ ]   What are the results of the preliminary title report?
          _____

[ ] [ ]   Which of the items on the report might prevent closing?
          _____

[ ] [ ]   How do you recommend I handle these items?
          _____

[ ] [ ]   _____

[ ] [ ]   _____

          Wrap Up
[ ] [ ]   _____

[ ] [ ]   _____

[ ] [ ]   _____

CHAPTER 5
Disclose!

As protection for real estate buyers, laws in some states require sellers to make known things that were previously unknown and that might not be evident. Wherever you live, you can protect yourself by making complete and accurate disclosures.

Step 1: Understand Your Disclosure Responsibilities

Ask closing or escrow personnel, your real estate attorney, or any real estate attorney licensed in your state whether a real estate disclosure statement is required by law on home sales in your state. Laws usually require disclosure for real property improved with specified numbers of dwelling units, often one to four units.

Who?

If your state has a real estate disclosure statement law, chances are you will have to disclose. Ask about the exceptions that apply in your state. The most common exceptions include

- Transfers from one co-owner to one or more other co-owners.
- Transfers to a spouse or to a direct blood relative.
- Transfers between spouses in connection with a dissolution of marriage or similar proceeding.
- Transfers by a fiduciary (person holding a position of trust) while administering a decedent's (deceased person's) estate, guardianship, conservatorship, or trust.

What?

For a real estate disclosure statement to be valid, laws usually require you to disclose

1. Information that you know about the property.
2. Information that you, a reasonable homeowner, would be able to find out about the property by making an proper effort.
3. A fair approximation based on the best information available to you listed as such. *If* you don't know *and* you can't find out by making a reasonable effort, state that you are making an approximation. Intentionally or carelessly made errors or omissions can create problems because they can
    - Be used as a defense if and when buyers refuse to carry out their contractual obligations to buy your home.
    - Be the basis for buyers' action to cancel the contract.
    - Make you liable to the buyers' court action for damages.

How?

You may obtain all information for the disclosure yourself. Consider having a licensed home inspector conduct a physical inspection. A physical inspection is a good source of thorough information of areas covered in real estate disclosure statements. A physical inspection is usually the most cost-effective way to obtain facts about your home's structural integrity. Providing a report as part of your disclosure usually limits your liability.

When you hire an inspector, consider

1. Hiring a inspector who
   - Is a trained general contractor, engineer, or architect.
   - Is licensed by a home inspection trade organization.
   - Is knowledgeable about local properties and problems.
   - Has no vested interest in the property, including being someone you would hire to repair any defects.
2. Requiring the inspector to provide you with a detailed written report. Ask the inspector to include items that
   - Are in good condition.
   - Need repair or replacement.
   - Are not currently problems but may need repair or replacement in the next few years—for example, a roof.

When?

Time your transfer disclosure so that you meet any legal requirements and protect yourself further.

Legal Requirements

To legally protect yourself, consider

1. Delivery of a detailed disclosure statement about the property as soon as possible before the transfer of title.
2. The law that buyers may cancel within the periods of time specified by your state if you deliver the disclosure after signing a purchase offer. In California, for example, buyers may cancel within three days after personal delivery or five days after the postmarked date, if you mail the statement.

Recommendations

To protect yourself and avoid the time and expense of tying up your property with buyers who do not want the property in its present condition, consider

1. Preparing a transfer disclosure type statement *before* you put your home on the market.
2. Giving a copy of this disclosure to any prospective buyers who express a serious interest in your property.
3. Having any prospective buyers to whom you give a disclosure sign a written form acknowledging receipt of the disclosure.

Step 2: Prepare Your Disclosure Statement

Use the sample Real Estate Transfer Disclosure Statement to help you understand the wording of disclosure statements. The statement shown accompanies, as appropriate, an explanation of anticipated responses, possible choices and their probable conse-

REAL ESTATE TRANSFER DISCLOSURE STATEMENT
(CALIFORNIA CIVIL CODE 1102, ET SEQ.)
CALIFORNIA ASSOCIATION OF REALTORS® (CAR) STANDARD FORM

THIS DISCLOSURE STATEMENT CONCERNS THE REAL PROPERTY SITUATED IN THE CITY OF_____
_____, COUNTY OF_____, STATE OF CALIFORNIA,
DESCRIBED AS_____.
THIS STATEMENT IS A DISCLOSURE OF THE CONDITION OF THE ABOVE DESCRIBED PROPERTY IN COMPLIANCE
WITH SECTION 1102 OF THE CIVIL CODE AS OF _____, 19_____. IT IS NOT A WARRANTY
OF ANY KIND BY THE SELLER(S) OR ANY AGENT(S) REPRESENTING ANY PRINCIPAL(S) IN THIS TRANSACTION,
AND IS NOT A SUBSTITUTE FOR ANY INSPECTIONS OR WARRANTIES THE PRINCIPAL(S) MAY WISH TO OBTAIN.

I
COORDINATION WITH OTHER DISCLOSURE FORMS

This Real Estate Transfer Disclosure Statement is made pursuant to Section 1102 of the Civil Code. Other statutes require disclosures, depending upon the details of the particular real estate transaction (for example: special study zone and purchase-money liens on residential property).

Substituted Disclosures: The following disclosures have or will be in connection with this real estate transfer, and are intended to satisfy the disclosure obligations on this form, where the subject matter is the same:_____
_____
_____

(LIST ALL SUBSTITUTED DISCLOSURE FORMS TO BE USED IN CONNECTION WITH THIS TRANSACTION)

II
SELLER'S INFORMATION

The Seller discloses the following information with the knowledge that even though this is not a warranty, prospective Buyers may rely on this information in deciding whether and on what terms to purchase the subject property. Seller hereby authorizes any agent(s) representing any principal(s) in this transaction to provide a copy of this statement to any person or entity in connection with any actual or anticipated sale of the property.

THE FOLLOWING ARE REPRESENTATIONS MADE BY THE SELLER(S) AND ARE NOT THE REPRESENTATIONS OF THE AGENT(S), IF ANY. THIS INFORMATION IS A DISCLOSURE AND IS NOT INTENDED TO BE PART OF ANY CONTRACT BETWEEN THE BUYER AND SELLER.

Seller ☐ is   ☐ is not occupying the property.

A. The subject property has the items checked below (read across):

☐ Range	☐ Oven	☐ Microwave
☐ Dishwasher	☐ Trash Compactor	☐ Garbage Disposal
☐ Washer/Dryer Hookups	☐ Window Screens	☐ Rain Gutters
☐ Burglar Alarms	☐ Smoke Detector(s)	☐ Fire Alarm
☐ T.V. Antenna	☐ Satellite Dish	☐ Intercom
☐ Central Heating	☐ Central Air Conditioning	☐ Evaporator Cooler(s)
☐ Wall/Window Air Conditioning	☐ Sprinklers	☐ Public Sewer System
☐ Septic Tank	☐ Sump Pump	☐ Water Softener
☐ Patio/Decking	☐ Built-in Barbeque	☐ Gazebo
☐ Sauna	☐ Pool	☐ Spa ☐ Hot Tub
☐ Security Gate(s)	☐ Garage Door Opener(s)	☐ Number of Remote Controls_____
Garage: ☐ Attached	☐ Not Attached	☐ Carport
Pool/Spa Heater: ☐ Gas	☐ Solar	☐ Electric
Water Heater: ☐ Gas	☐ Solar	☐ Electric
Water Supply: ☐ City	☐ Well	☐ Private Utility ☐ Other_____
Gas Supply: ☐ Utility	☐ Bottled	

Exhaust Fan(s) in_____ 220 Volt Wiring in_____
Fireplace(s) in_____ ☐ Gas Starter
☐ Roof(s): Type:_____Age:_____(approx.)
☐ Other:_____
Are there, to the best of your (Seller's) knowledge, any of the above that are not in operating condition? ☐ Yes ☐ No If yes, then describe. (Attach additional sheets if necessary.):_____
_____
_____

B. Are you (Seller) aware of any significant defects/malfunctions in any of the following? ☐ Yes ☐ No If yes, check appropriate space(s) below.
☐ Interior Walls ☐ Ceilings ☐ Floors ☐ Exterior Walls ☐ Insulation ☐ Roof(s) ☐ Windows ☐ Doors ☐ Foundation ☐ Slab(s)
☐ Driveways ☐ Sidewalks ☐ Walls/Fences ☐ Electrical Systems ☐ Plumbing/Sewers/Septics ☐ Other Structural Components
(Describe: _____
_____
_____)

If any of the above is checked, explain. (Attach additional sheets if necessary): _____
_____
_____

Buyer and Seller acknowledge receipt of copy of this page, which constitutes Page 1 of 2 Pages.
Buyer's Initials (_____) (_____) Seller's Initials (_____) (_____)

┌─ OFFICE USE ONLY ─┐
Reviewed by Broker or Designee _____
Date _____

EQUAL HOUSING OPPORTUNITY

REAL ESTATE TRANSFER DISCLOSURE STATEMENT (TDS-14 PAGE 1 OF 2)

C. Are you (Seller) aware of any of the following:

1. Substances, materials, or products which may be an environmental hazard such as, but not limited to, asbestos, formaldehyde, radon gas, lead-based paint, fuel or chemical storage tanks, and contaminated soil or water on the subject property. . . . . ☐ Yes ☐ No
2. Features of the property shared in common with adjoining landowners, such as walls, fences, and driveways, whose use or responsibility for maintenance may have an effect on the subject property. ☐ Yes ☐ No
3. Any encroachments, easements or similar matters that may affect your interest in the subject property. . . . . ☐ Yes ☐ No
4. Room additions, structural modifications, or other alterations or repairs made without necessary permits. . . . . . . ☐ Yes ☐ No
5. Room additions, structural modifications, or other alterations or repairs not in compliance with building codes. . . . ☐ Yes ☐ No
6. Landfill (compacted or otherwise) on the property or any portion thereof. . . . . ☐ Yes ☐ No
7. Any settling from any cause, or slippage, sliding, or other soil problems. . . . . ☐ Yes ☐ No
8. Flooding, drainage or grading problems. . . . . ☐ Yes ☐ No
9. Major damage to the property or any of the structures from fire, earthquake, floods, or landslides. . . . . ☐ Yes ☐ No
10. Any zoning violations, nonconforming uses, violations of "setback" requirements. . . . . ☐ Yes ☐ No
11. Neighborhood noise problems or other nuisances. . . . . ☐ Yes ☐ No
12. CC&R's or other deed restrictions or obligations. . . . . ☐ Yes ☐ No
13. Homeowners' Association which has any authority over the subject property. . . . . ☐ Yes ☐ No
14. Any "common area" (facilities such as pools, tennis courts, walkways, or other areas co-owned in undivided interest with others). . . . . ☐ Yes ☐ No
15. Any notices of abatement or citations against the property. . . . . ☐ Yes ☐ No
16. Any lawsuits against the seller threatening to or affecting this real property. . . . . ☐ Yes ☐ No

If the answer to any of these is yes, explain. (Attach additional sheets if necessary.): _____

_____

_____

Seller certifies that the information herein is true and correct to the best of the Seller's knowledge as of the date signed by the Seller.

Seller_____ Date_____

Seller_____ Date_____

III
AGENT'S INSPECTION DISCLOSURE

(To be completed only if the seller is represented by an agent in this transaction.)
THE UNDERSIGNED, BASED ON THE ABOVE INQUIRY OF THE SELLER(S) AS TO THE CONDITION OF THE PROPERTY AND BASED ON A REASONABLY COMPETENT AND DILIGENT VISUAL INSPECTION OF THE ACCESSIBLE AREAS OF THE PROPERTY IN CONJUNCTION WITH THAT INQUIRY, STATES THE FOLLOWING:

_____

_____

Agent (Broker
Representing Seller)_____ By_____ Date_____
　　　　　　　　　　(PLEASE PRINT)　　　　　(ASSOCIATE LICENSEE OR BROKER-SIGNATURE)

IV
AGENT'S INSPECTION DISCLOSURE

(To be completed only if the agent who has obtained the offer is other than the agent above.)
THE UNDERSIGNED, BASED ON A REASONABLY COMPETENT AND DILIGENT VISUAL INSPECTION OF THE ACCESSIBLE AREAS OF THE PROPERTY, STATES THE FOLLOWING:

_____

_____

Agent (Broker
obtaining the Offer)_____ By_____ Date_____
　　　　　　　　　(PLEASE PRINT)　　　　　(ASSOCIATE LICENSEE OR BROKER-SIGNATURE)

V
BUYER(S) AND SELLER(S) MAY WISH TO OBTAIN PROFESSIONAL ADVICE AND/OR INSPECTIONS OF THE PROPERTY AND TO PROVIDE FOR APPROPRIATE PROVISIONS IN A CONTRACT BETWEEN BUYER AND SELLER(S) WITH RESPECT TO ANY ADVICE/INSPECTIONS/DEFECTS.

I/WE ACKNOWLEDGE RECEIPT OF A COPY OF THIS STATEMENT.

Seller_____ Date_____   Buyer_____ Date_____

Seller_____ Date_____   Buyer_____ Date_____

Agent (Broker
Representing Seller)_____ By_____ Date_____
　　　　　　　　　　(PLEASE PRINT)　　　　　(ASSOCIATE LICENSEE OR BROKER-SIGNATURE)

Agent (Broker
obtaining the Offer)_____ By_____ Date_____
　　　　　　　　　(PLEASE PRINT)　　　　　(ASSOCIATE LICENSEE OR BROKER-SIGNATURE)

A REAL ESTATE BROKER IS QUALIFIED TO ADVISE ON REAL ESTATE. IF YOU DESIRE LEGAL ADVICE, CONSULT YOUR ATTORNEY.

Page 2 of _____ Pages.

───── OFFICE USE ONLY ─────
Reviewed by Broker or Designee _____
Date _____

REAL ESTATE TRANSFER DISCLOSURE STATEMENT (TDS-14 PAGE 2 OF 2)

quences, and recommendations. If the question is inappropriate, enter the words **not applicable**.

Many variations of disclosure statements exist. The sample here represents the most up-to-date form available in California at the time this book was written. The California Association of Realtors® produces this statement.

Completing Part I: Coordination with Other Disclosure Forms

Although the Real Estate Transfer Disclosure Statement may be the only form needed, other laws in your state or town may require other disclosures. Use of other disclosures depends upon your state laws and details of your real estate contract. Your closing agent or escrow officer should let you know what other forms are required, if any.

Substituted Disclosures

The blanks at the end of Part I of the disclosure require you to list all disclosure forms that were or will be made about this transfer. They are intended to satisfy the disclosure requirements of this form.

Completing Part II: Seller's Information

Completing Section A: Items on the Subject Property

Section A of Part II lists many items your property may contain. Check off the ones included for the buyers' information.

Exhaust Fans and 220-Volt Wiring. Exhaust fans are usually in kitchens and bathrooms. 220-volt wiring is generally in kitchens, laundry areas, garages or workshops, and wherever water heaters are located.

Roof Type. Common roofs include composition shingle, concrete shake, gravel, rock, shake, tile, and wood shingle.

Items Not in Operating Condition. For questions of whether any of the items checked are not in operating condition, enter **Yes** if you know of even one item that does not operate. If you are not sure whether some item is operable, check the item thoroughly before filling in the disclosure. Enter **No** only if none of the items are inoperable.

Completing Section B: Defects and Malfunctions in Structural Components

To limit your liability while you describe any structural faults the property may have, follow these steps for Section B:

1. Read entire list before indicating whether or not you are aware of any serious defects or malfunctions.
2. Enter **Yes** if even *one* item has a problem. Indicate which item(s) has (have) the difficulty on the blank lines at the foot of the page.
3. Enter **No** only if *all* items have no significant defects or malfunctions.

Interior Walls. Defects might include sizable cracks or holes and/or water damage indicated by stains or peeling.

Ceilings. Defects might include sizable cracks or holes and/or water damage indicated by stains or peeling.

Floors. Defects might include unevenness, sizable cracks or holes, badly stained carpeting, and/or finish of hardwood floors in need of significant refinishing.

Exterior Walls. Defects might include sizable holes or vertical cracks; excessive softness indicating possible decay or pest damage; paint peeling, curling, or cracking suggesting possible moisture in walls; eroding mortar; and/or missing caulk around doors and windows.

Insulation. Defects might include inadequate insulation in ceiling, walls, and floors and/or insufficient weather-stripping around doors and windows.

Roof(s). Defects might include leaks, bare spots, and/or loose, rusted, or gaping flashing on all roofs; curling up at edges of asbestos (composition) or wooden shingles; washing away of rock and gravel roofing; cracked, loose, and missing pieces on concrete shake, tile, and slate roofs; and/or rust on tin roofs.

Foundations. Defects might include sizable vertical V-shaped cracks and/or eroding mortar.

Slabs. Defects might include sizable cracks and holes.

Driveways. Defects might include sizable cracks, holes, and/or areas of buckling or, if driveway is not paved, deep ruts and/or gravel washing away.

Sidewalks. Defects might include sizable cracks, holes, and/or areas of buckling.

Walls/Fences. Defects might include sizable holes and missing mortar in walls and missing or decaying sections in walls or fences.

Electrical System. Defects or malfunctions might be indicated by brownouts or tripping a circuit breaker when many appliances operate, inadequate electrical outlets (at least one for approximately every 12 linear feet of wall), and/or inadequate 220-volt wiring for major appliances.

Plumbing/Sewer/Septic. Defects or malfunctions might be indicated by frozen or broken main water shut-off valve; water or sewer pipes that are encrusted or corroded; stains or wetness on inappropriate surfaces near the connection of fixtures or equipment to water and/or sewer lines; inoperable, cracked, loose, or slowly draining fixture or equipment; no sink or toilet shut-off valves; cracked lid on septic tank; or strong odor in area of septic tank field bed.

Completing Section C: Environmental Hazards, Zoning Problems, Legal Actions, and Structural Damage

Section C on the second page of the disclosure lists possible complications resulting from items such as environmental hazards, soil problems, floods, or landslides; violations of zoning regulations; other parties with authority over the property; and legal encumbrances.

- Indicate any items listed of which you are aware.
- If you are not sure whether any of these problems exist, make a reasonable effort to find out and report the information.
- If you cannot find out by making a reasonable effort, approximate and note that you made an approximation.

1. Substance, materials, or products which may be an environmental hazard. Asbestos, formaldehyde, radon gas, and lead-based paint, and contaminated soil or water and other items can affect people's health. These items may be difficult or impossible to detect without special knowledge or tests. If you have had inspections performed for these items report the results of these tests as well as the presence of any fuel or chemical storage tanks on the property.

2. Features of the property shared in common with adjoining landowners, such as fences, walls, and driveways. Buyers need to know what items they will share with adjacent properties to avoid disagreements with neighbors over ownership and to arrange for maintenance.

3. Any encroachments, easements, or similar matters that may affect your interest in the subject property. An encroachment is the construction of a structure wholly or partly on land belonging to someone else. An easement is the right to use another's land. An easement can be valid even if unidentified, unlocated, not mentioned in the deed, and not recorded.

4. Room additions, structural modifications, or other alterations or repairs made without necessary permits. Permits are usually issued by the city or county building inspection departments with authority from the applicable building code.

If you do not know the answer to this question, consider

- Requesting copies of regulations regarding projects for which the city or county issues permits.
- Preparing a list of additions, modifications, and other alterations or major repairs for your home.
- Requesting the applicable department also tell you what permits have been issued on your property.
- Comparing the list of permits issued with the list of projects to discover what work has been done without a permit. Permits are required by building codes for most types of home construction.

When you reveal that work was done without a permit, buyers may decide to accept the situation *or* may require you to certify that construction conforms to local building codes, as a condition of sale.

To certify the conformance, you can obtain an existing or as built permit from the building inspection department. If construction was major, you may need to hire a professional, such as an engineer or architect, to submit drawings and certification of proper construction for the intended use.

5. Room additions, structural modifications, or other alterations or repairs not in compliance with building codes. Building codes are regulations by governments giving requirements and standards for structures constructed within their jurisdiction. When you reveal work was done that does not comply with these codes, buyers may decide to

- Not buy your home.
- Buy your home as is.
- Request you to bring the work up to code before they buy your home.

6. Landfill (compacted or otherwise) on the property or any portion thereof. Landfill is soil moved onto the site from another location. *Compacted* means compressed.

7. Any settling from any cause, or slippage, sliding, or other soil problems. Settling means sinking, then coming to rest in one place. *Slippage* is the small downward movement of a soil mass out of its previous position. *Sliding* is the large downward movement of a soil mass out of its previous position.

8. Flooding, drainage, or grading problems.

- Check structures for signs of damage.
- Be aware that flooding and drainage problems may be evident only after a rain or prolonged watering.

9. Major damage to the property or any of the structures from fire, earthquake, floods, or landslides. Major damage, although generally immediately visible, must be reported as part of a full disclosure.

10. Any zoning violations, non-conforming uses, violations of "setback" requirements. Zoning violations involve breaking laws concerning specific uses of land and buildings. *Non-conforming uses* are preexisting uses of land allowed to continue although a current ordinance excluding that use has been enacted for that area. *Violations of "setback" requirements* are breaking laws that prohibit the erection of a building within a certain distance of the curb.

11. Neighborhood noise problems or other nuisances. Neighborhood noise problems often include noisy animals, vehicles, and neighbors. Other nuisances might include animals that roam loose or are confined to an area that is not kept clean, creating odor and pest problems.

12. CC&R's or other deed restrictions or obligations. CC&Rs (covenants, conditions, and restrictions) are conditions that govern property use. Subdivisions or communities in which some areas are owned in common (planned development projects) usually have CC&Rs enforced by a homeowner's association.

Covenants are agreements or promises contained in and conveyed by a deed. They are pledges for the performance or nonperformance of certain acts or the use or nonuse of a property. A covenant is inseparable from the property or transfer of that property.

Conditions are stipulations (provisions) or qualifications in a deed, which if violated or not performed, defeat (nullify) the deed. Then title reverts back to the original owner (grantor).

Restrictions are covenants in a deed that list actions the owner must take or cannot take on or with his or her property.

13. Homeowners' Association which has any authority over the subject property. A *homeowner's association* is an organized group of homeowners whose members help to make and enforce the rules of their community, subdivision, planned development project, condominium, or co-op. If a homeowner's association has control over your property, be prepared to give the buyers the appropriate documents. Laws may require that the association provide you with documents within a certain time period of your written request. The association may often charge you a reasonable amount for preparing these documents. Documents include

- Governing documents of the association, including bylaws and CC&Rs.
- The most recent financial statement of the association.
- A written statement of any unpaid assessments against the property.

14. Any "common area" (facilities such as pools, tennis courts, walkways, or other areas co-owned in undivided interest with others). Common areas create extra expense and liability for buyers to consider.

15. Any notices of abatement or citations against the property. These legal notices and orders either require you to discontinue or take some action, for other people's good. A *notice of abatement* is a notice to decrease or cease unlawful or unreasonable annoyance that inconveniences, hurts, or damages others or creates a repeated or continuing disturbance of another's right. Notices may be issued for excessive noise or health hazards.

A *citation* is a legal order to appear before a judge on a specified date. The person receiving this order is required to do the listed action or show why he or she should not do it. These orders may be issued for reasons similar to those for notices of abatement, particularly if you do not act on the notices.

16. Any lawsuits against the seller threatening to or affecting the property. Lawsuits or the threat of lawsuits may affect whether a buyer decides to purchase your property.

Completing Parts III and IV

Insert the words **not applicable** here.

Completing Part V

Have the buyers sign a copy of this disclosure for your files.

If you decide to provide suitable clauses in a contract that enable you to handle recommendations, inspections, and/or defects, these clauses might include

- Buyers accepting all items in "as is" condition.
- You agreeing to share the cost of listed repairs or replacements with buyers.
- You agreeing to make listed repairs or replacements at your own cost.

Now that you have completed your disclosure statement to inform buyers about aspects of your home they might otherwise not notice, you are ready to prepare your home for marketing. Your marketing preparation might include making improvements and/or repairs and handling attractiveness items. These actions are the topics of Chapter 6.

CHAPTER 6
Prepare Property

Marketing your home includes several related activities, including preparing your home for sale, advertising, and showing your home. How you carry out these activities can influence how quickly your home sells and for what price.

Start marketing by preparing your home to be shown for sale. Homes that have well-thought-out improvements, are in good repair, and are attractive are generally easiest to sell. The sections of this chapter regarding improvements, repairs, and attractiveness each contain information and an accompanying worksheet to aid you in deciding what to do and how to go about doing it.

Step 1: Make Necessary Improvements

The improvements you make to your home generally add to its value, if the remodeling is well done and not an over-improvement. The percentage by which the improvement adds to the value of your home depends on the nature of the improvement and your location. Some improvements are considered more desirable than others depending upon the area of the country, the city, and even the neighborhood in which you live.

Improvements

If you have not made or do not plan to make any improvements, consider proceeding directly to Step 2, regarding repairs. If you are considering making an improvement, be aware that almost any remodeling will cost more and take longer than you estimate. Most renovations will also probably be less cost effective than you estimate.

The following list is intended to give you a general idea of the cost effectiveness of various renovations. The listed improvements are in descending order, with the remodeling generally yielding the greatest percentage of return listed first and those usually yielding the least listed last. Because the same improvement may be considered more desirable in one geographical area than another, we do not quote specific percentages or ranges. Check with local contractors or building associations for the order and the approximate percentage of value added in your area.

Kitchen	Updates and enlargements are usually most cost effective, over-improvement is not.
Bathrooms	Updates or additions are generally most cost effective; again, over-improvement is not.

Landscaping	A moderate amount of neat-appearing landscaping is usually cost effective. Large amounts of landscaping may not be cost effective because of the amount of maintenance work they represent to many buyers.
Carpeting	Generally most cost effective if you choose carpet of moderate quality in a neutral color and pattern.
Family Rooms	A location in main living area without reducing other valuable space such as a garage is usually best.
Energy-Saving Equipment	Storm windows are most cost effective in areas where they substantially reduce heating and cooling costs. Roof and attic fans are most cost effective in warm and hot areas. Storm doors are usually not cost effective.
Bedrooms	A well-located extra bedroom in a two- or three-bedroom home is generally most cost effective. Extra bedrooms in larger homes may even decrease the salability.
Central Air-conditioning	Central air is most cost effective in areas with warm summers and only then where extra ducting need not be installed.
Garages and Carports	Garages are usually more cost effective in colder climates, near the coast, and in more expensive homes. Carports are usually more cost effective in warmer areas and less expensive homes.
Wallpaper	Usually most cost effective if of moderate quality in neutral colors and patterns.
Swimming Pools	Can be somewhat cost effective in warm or expensive areas. Many buyers do not like the trouble and cost of maintenance or the possible hazard of a pool.
Garage Conversions	Creating a room from a garage is usually not very cost effective, because the conversion makes the house appear strange from the exterior and is often poorly located in relation to the rest of the house.

Completing the Capital Improvements Worksheet

Use the Capital Improvements Worksheet included in Chapter 2 to make an inventory of improvements you made on your home. Items on the list have previously been considered tax deductible. Consider

- Making improvements only if necessary *and* cost effective.
- Reading the information concerning capital improvements later in this chapter before you decide what projects to undertake.
- Checking with your accountant or tax preparer for the current tax status of these improvements.

Step 2: Perform Repairs That Sell Your Home

Repairing obvious problems generally makes your property salable to a greater number of buyers. If your home has obvious damage that needs repair *and* you are able to fix it at a reasonable cost, repairs are usually very cost effective.

Repairs

Do not attempt to conceal problems by making poor or cosmetic repairs. You may be required to make extensive disclosures to buyers regarding your property. Intentionally or carelessly made errors or omissions in the disclosure may leave you liable to buyers for actual damages. The information your state may require you to disclose includes

- Facts that you know about the property.
- Details you, as a reasonable homeowner, should know about the property.
- A reasonable approximation of facts based on the best information available to you, listed as such (if you do not know and cannot find out by making a reasonable effort).

If you do not contemplate making repairs, proceed directly to Step 3, regarding attractiveness. If you plan to hire professional help in making repairs, consider reading Step 4 regarding contracting before you decide on a contractor.

Completing the Repairs Worksheet

Use the Repairs Worksheet to help you restore your property to a sound condition by

1. Taking the worksheet to each area mentioned and checking off only those areas that you feel need repair work.
2. Reading the completed list and deciding who will be responsible for ensuring that each task is accomplished.
3. Indicating beside each task the date by which you want the repair accomplished.
4. Indicating beside each task whom you need to contact for the repair and his or her telephone number. If you are repairing the item yourself, indicate the materials you need.
5. Indicating a cost estimate for the repair.
6. Checking off each item as it is completed in the Did column.

Step 3: Enhance Your Home's Attractiveness

Most projects you do to enhance your home's attractiveness are like frosting on a cake. Remember, however, attractiveness is in the eyes, nose, and ears of the beholder.

Completing the Attractiveness Worksheet

Use the Attractiveness Worksheet to ensure that you handle items that enhance your property's appeal to potential buyers by

1. Taking the worksheet to each area mentioned and checking off only those items you feel need cosmetic work.
2. Reading the completed list and deciding which member of the household is responsible for seeing that each item is accomplished.
3. Indicating by each item by what date you feel it should be accomplished.
4. Indicating beside each item whom you need to contact and the company's telephone number or the materials you need if you will do the job yourself.
5. Indicating an estimate, as you obtain it, of how much you expect each item to cost.
6. Checking off each item in the Did column as it is completed.

Step 4: Understand Contracting Out Work

If you have a contractor perform work on your home, consider taking actions to reduce the number of problems you have as well as saving you time and money. Such preventive actions include

1. Learning about the work to be done. The more you know about any job, the better your chances are of getting a job well done.

REPAIRS WORKSHEET

Name:_____

Address:_____

To Be Done					Call to repair/	Estimate
Do	Did	By	Date	Job	telephone number or material needed	
				Lawn		
[ ]	[ ]	___	___	Bare spots replanted	_____	_____
[ ]	[ ]	___	___	Lawn fertilized	_____	_____
[ ]	[ ]	___	___	Other _____	_____	_____
				Plantings		
[ ]	[ ]	___	___	Dead plants removed	_____	_____
[ ]	[ ]	___	___	Dead plants replaced	_____	_____
[ ]	[ ]	___	___	Dead limbs removed	_____	_____
[ ]	[ ]	___	___	Other _____	_____	_____
				Driveway and Walks		
[ ]	[ ]	___	___	Holes patched	_____	_____
[ ]	[ ]	___	___	Concrete repaired	_____	_____
[ ]	[ ]	___	___	Asphalt sealed	_____	_____
[ ]	[ ]	___	___	Gravel smoothed	_____	_____
[ ]	[ ]	___	___	Other _____	_____	_____
				Walls and Fences		
[ ]	[ ]	___	___	Sections repaired	_____	_____
[ ]	[ ]	___	___	Sections painted	_____	_____
[ ]	[ ]	___	___	Termite and rot free	_____	_____
[ ]	[ ]	___	___	Other _____	_____	_____
				Patios and Decks		
[ ]	[ ]	___	___	Smooth surface	_____	_____
[ ]	[ ]	___	___	Stained or painted	_____	_____
[ ]	[ ]	___	___	Termite and rot free	_____	_____
[ ]	[ ]	___	___	Railings sturdy	_____	_____
[ ]	[ ]	___	___	Other _____	_____	_____
				Pools and Spas		
[ ]	[ ]	___	___	Free of algae	_____	_____
[ ]	[ ]	___	___	Motor works	_____	_____
[ ]	[ ]	___	___	Filter works	_____	_____
[ ]	[ ]	___	___	Pool cleaner works	_____	_____
[ ]	[ ]	___	___	Cover in good repair	_____	_____
[ ]	[ ]	___	___	Other _____	_____	_____
					Subtotal #1	_____

REPAIRS WORKSHEET

	To Be Done				Call to repair/ telephone number or material needed	Estimate
Do	Did	By	Date	Job		

Septic Tanks/Leach Lines

[ ] [ ] ___ ___ Drain away from house _____ _____
[ ] [ ] ___ ___ Area dry and odorless _____ _____
[ ] [ ] ___ ___ Other _____ _____ _____

Roof

[ ] [ ] ___ ___ Missing parts replaced _____ _____
[ ] [ ] ___ ___ Broken parts repaired _____ _____
[ ] [ ] ___ ___ Flashing leak free _____ _____
[ ] [ ] ___ ___ TV antenna repaired _____ _____
[ ] [ ] ___ ___ Other _____ _____ _____

Gutters

[ ] [ ] ___ ___ Sections present _____ _____
[ ] [ ] ___ ___ Sections cleaned _____ _____
[ ] [ ] ___ ___ Sections repaired _____ _____
[ ] [ ] ___ ___ Drains away from house _____ _____
[ ] [ ] ___ ___ Other _____ _____ _____

Siding, Walls, and Foundation

[ ] [ ] ___ ___ Missing parts replaced _____ _____
[ ] [ ] ___ ___ Damaged parts repaired _____ _____
[ ] [ ] ___ ___ Emblems removed _____ _____
[ ] [ ] ___ ___ House numbers checked _____ _____
[ ] [ ] ___ ___ Paint _____ _____
[ ] [ ] ___ ___ Cracks repaired _____ _____
[ ] [ ] ___ ___ Bricks all present _____ _____
[ ] [ ] ___ ___ Loose mortar repaired _____ _____
[ ] [ ] ___ ___ Other _____ _____ _____

Windows

[ ] [ ] ___ ___ Awnings hung properly _____ _____
[ ] [ ] ___ ___ Awnings in good repair _____ _____
[ ] [ ] ___ ___ Shutters hung properly _____ _____
[ ] [ ] ___ ___ Shutters in good repair _____ _____
[ ] [ ] ___ ___ Screens present _____ _____
[ ] [ ] ___ ___ Screens without holes _____ _____
[ ] [ ] ___ ___ Panes in good repair _____ _____
[ ] [ ] ___ ___ Sashes painted _____ _____
[ ] [ ] ___ ___ Storm windows secure _____ _____
[ ] [ ] ___ ___ Storm windows caulked _____ _____
[ ] [ ] ___ ___ Other _____ _____ _____

Subtotal #2   _____

REPAIRS WORKSHEET

				Job	Call to repair/ telephone number or material needed	Estimate
To Be Done						
Do	**Did**	**By**	**Date**			

Chimney

Do	Did	By	Date	Job	Call to repair / material	Estimate
[ ]	[ ]	___	___	Straight	_____	_____
[ ]	[ ]	___	___	Bricks all present	_____	_____
[ ]	[ ]	___	___	Bricks mortared tight	_____	_____
[ ]	[ ]	___	___	Other _____	_____	_____

Entrance

Do	Did	By	Date	Job	Call to repair / material	Estimate
[ ]	[ ]	___	___	Ceiling painted	_____	_____
[ ]	[ ]	___	___	Lights work	_____	_____
[ ]	[ ]	___	___	Walls repaired	_____	_____
[ ]	[ ]	___	___	Walls painted	_____	_____
[ ]	[ ]	___	___	Steps repaired	_____	_____
[ ]	[ ]	___	___	Steps painted	_____	_____
[ ]	[ ]	___	___	Doorbell works	_____	_____
[ ]	[ ]	___	___	Door painted or oiled	_____	_____
[ ]	[ ]	___	___	Doors work	_____	_____
[ ]	[ ]	___	___	Woodwork painted	_____	_____
[ ]	[ ]	___	___	Windows work freely	_____	_____
[ ]	[ ]	___	___	Rugs or mats secure	_____	_____
[ ]	[ ]	___	___	Floors repaired	_____	_____
[ ]	[ ]	___	___	Closets repaired	_____	_____
[ ]	[ ]	___	___	Closets painted	_____	_____
[ ]	[ ]	___	___	Other _____	_____	_____

Living Room

Do	Did	By	Date	Job	Call to repair / material	Estimate
[ ]	[ ]	___	___	Ceiling painted	_____	_____
[ ]	[ ]	___	___	Lights work	_____	_____
[ ]	[ ]	___	___	Lights cleaned	_____	_____
[ ]	[ ]	___	___	Walls repaired	_____	_____
[ ]	[ ]	___	___	Walls painted	_____	_____
[ ]	[ ]	___	___	Wallpaper tight	_____	_____
[ ]	[ ]	___	___	Windows work easily	_____	_____
[ ]	[ ]	___	___	Window covering clean	_____	_____
[ ]	[ ]	___	___	Drapery hardware works	_____	_____
[ ]	[ ]	___	___	Woodwork painted	_____	_____
[ ]	[ ]	___	___	Doors painted or oiled	_____	_____
[ ]	[ ]	___	___	Door hardware repaired	_____	_____
[ ]	[ ]	___	___	Heater works	_____	_____
[ ]	[ ]	___	___	Fireplace repaired	_____	_____
[ ]	[ ]	___	___	Floor repaired	_____	_____

Subtotal #3 _____

REPAIRS WORKSHEET

To Be Done						
Do	**Did**	**By**	**Date**	**Job**	**Call to repair/ telephone number or material needed**	**Estimate**
				Living Room (*continued*)		
[ ]	[ ]	___	___	Carpet repaired	_____	_____
[ ]	[ ]	___	___	Furniture repaired	_____	_____
[ ]	[ ]	___	___	Other _____	_____	_____
				Dining Room		
[ ]	[ ]	___	___	Lights work	_____	_____
[ ]	[ ]	___	___	Walls repaired	_____	_____
[ ]	[ ]	___	___	Walls painted	_____	_____
[ ]	[ ]	___	___	Wallpaper tight	_____	_____
[ ]	[ ]	___	___	Windows work easily	_____	_____
[ ]	[ ]	___	___	Window cover repaired	_____	_____
[ ]	[ ]	___	___	Drapery hardware works	_____	_____
[ ]	[ ]	___	___	Woodwork painted	_____	_____
[ ]	[ ]	___	___	Doors painted or oiled	_____	_____
[ ]	[ ]	___	___	Door hardware repaired	_____	_____
[ ]	[ ]	___	___	Heater works	_____	_____
[ ]	[ ]	___	___	Floor repaired	_____	_____
[ ]	[ ]	___	___	Carpet repaired	_____	_____
[ ]	[ ]	___	___	Furniture repaired	_____	_____
[ ]	[ ]	___	___	Other _____	_____	_____
				Family Room		
[ ]	[ ]	___	___	Ceiling painted	_____	_____
[ ]	[ ]	___	___	Lights work	_____	_____
[ ]	[ ]	___	___	Walls repaired	_____	_____
[ ]	[ ]	___	___	Walls painted	_____	_____
[ ]	[ ]	___	___	Wallpaper tight	_____	_____
[ ]	[ ]	___	___	Windows work easily	_____	_____
[ ]	[ ]	___	___	Window cover repaired	_____	_____
[ ]	[ ]	___	___	Drapery hardware works	_____	_____
[ ]	[ ]	___	___	Woodwork painted	_____	_____
[ ]	[ ]	___	___	Doors painted or oiled	_____	_____
[ ]	[ ]	___	___	Door hardware repaired	_____	_____
[ ]	[ ]	___	___	Heater works	_____	_____
[ ]	[ ]	___	___	Fireplace repaired	_____	_____
[ ]	[ ]	___	___	Floor repaired	_____	_____
[ ]	[ ]	___	___	Carpet repaired	_____	_____
[ ]	[ ]	___	___	Furniture repaired	_____	_____
[ ]	[ ]	___	___	Other _____	_____	_____
					Subtotal #4	_____

REPAIRS WORKSHEET

To Do	Did	To Be Done By	Date	Job	Call to repair/ telephone number or material needed	Estimate
				Kitchen		
[ ]	[ ]	___	___	Ceiling painted	_____	_____
[ ]	[ ]	___	___	Lights work	_____	_____
[ ]	[ ]	___	___	Walls painted	_____	_____
[ ]	[ ]	___	___	Wallpaper repaired	_____	_____
[ ]	[ ]	___	___	Windows work easily	_____	_____
[ ]	[ ]	___	___	Window cover repaired	_____	_____
[ ]	[ ]	___	___	Doors painted	_____	_____
[ ]	[ ]	___	___	Door hardware repaired	_____	_____
[ ]	[ ]	___	___	Heater works	_____	_____
[ ]	[ ]	___	___	Counters repaired	_____	_____
[ ]	[ ]	___	___	Disposal works	_____	_____
[ ]	[ ]	___	___	Stove works	_____	_____
[ ]	[ ]	___	___	Hood works	_____	_____
[ ]	[ ]	___	___	Oven works	_____	_____
[ ]	[ ]	___	___	Microwave works	_____	_____
[ ]	[ ]	___	___	Trash compactor works	_____	_____
[ ]	[ ]	___	___	Cupboards repaired	_____	_____
[ ]	[ ]	___	___	Floor repaired	_____	_____
[ ]	[ ]	___	___	Carpet repaired	_____	_____
[ ]	[ ]	___	___	Other _____	_____	_____
				Den		
[ ]	[ ]	___	___	Ceiling painted	_____	_____
[ ]	[ ]	___	___	Lights work	_____	_____
[ ]	[ ]	___	___	Walls repaired	_____	_____
[ ]	[ ]	___	___	Walls painted	_____	_____
[ ]	[ ]	___	___	Wallpaper tight	_____	_____
[ ]	[ ]	___	___	Windows work easily	_____	_____
[ ]	[ ]	___	___	Window cover repaired	_____	_____
[ ]	[ ]	___	___	Drapery hardware works	_____	_____
[ ]	[ ]	___	___	Woodwork painted	_____	_____
[ ]	[ ]	___	___	Doors painted or oiled	_____	_____
[ ]	[ ]	___	___	Door hardware repaired	_____	_____
[ ]	[ ]	___	___	Heater works	_____	_____
[ ]	[ ]	___	___	Fireplace repaired	_____	_____
[ ]	[ ]	___	___	Floor repaired	_____	_____
[ ]	[ ]	___	___	Carpet repaired	_____	_____
[ ]	[ ]	___	___	Furniture repaired	_____	_____
[ ]	[ ]	___	___	Other _____	_____	_____

Subtotal #5 _____

REPAIRS WORKSHEET

To Be Done					
Do	Did	By	Date	Job	Call to repair/ telephone number or material needed	Estimate

Bedroom #1 (Master Bedroom)

[ ] [ ] ___ ___ Ceiling painted _____ _____
[ ] [ ] ___ ___ Lights work _____ _____
[ ] [ ] ___ ___ Walls repaired _____ _____
[ ] [ ] ___ ___ Walls painted _____ _____
[ ] [ ] ___ ___ Wallpaper tight _____ _____
[ ] [ ] ___ ___ Windows work easily _____ _____
[ ] [ ] ___ ___ Window cover repaired _____ _____
[ ] [ ] ___ ___ Drapery hardware works _____ _____
[ ] [ ] ___ ___ Woodwork painted _____ _____
[ ] [ ] ___ ___ Doors painted or oiled _____ _____
[ ] [ ] ___ ___ Door hardware repaired _____ _____
[ ] [ ] ___ ___ Heater works _____ _____
[ ] [ ] ___ ___ Fireplace repaired _____ _____
[ ] [ ] ___ ___ Floor repaired _____ _____
[ ] [ ] ___ ___ Carpet repaired _____ _____
[ ] [ ] ___ ___ Furniture repaired _____ _____
[ ] [ ] ___ ___ Other _____

Bedroom #2

[ ] [ ] ___ ___ Ceiling painted _____ _____
[ ] [ ] ___ ___ Lights work _____ _____
[ ] [ ] ___ ___ Walls repaired _____ _____
[ ] [ ] ___ ___ Walls painted _____ _____
[ ] [ ] ___ ___ Wallpaper tight _____ _____
[ ] [ ] ___ ___ Windows work easily _____ _____
[ ] [ ] ___ ___ Window cover repaired _____ _____
[ ] [ ] ___ ___ Drapery hardware works _____ _____
[ ] [ ] ___ ___ Woodwork painted _____ _____
[ ] [ ] ___ ___ Doors painted or oiled _____ _____
[ ] [ ] ___ ___ Door hardware repaired _____ _____
[ ] [ ] ___ ___ Heater works _____ _____
[ ] [ ] ___ ___ Fireplace repaired _____ _____
[ ] [ ] ___ ___ Floor repaired _____ _____
[ ] [ ] ___ ___ Carpet repaired _____ _____
[ ] [ ] ___ ___ Furniture repaired _____ _____
[ ] [ ] ___ ___ Other _____

Subtotal #6 _____

REPAIRS WORKSHEET

To Be Done		Job	Call to repair/ telephone number or material needed	Estimate
Do Did By Date				
		Bedroom #3		
[ ] [ ] ___ ___		Ceiling painted	_____	___
[ ] [ ] ___ ___		Lights work	_____	___
[ ] [ ] ___ ___		Walls repaired	_____	___
[ ] [ ] ___ ___		Walls painted	_____	___
[ ] [ ] ___ ___		Wallpaper tight	_____	___
[ ] [ ] ___ ___		Windows work easily	_____	___
[ ] [ ] ___ ___		Window cover repaired	_____	___
[ ] [ ] ___ ___		Drapery hardware works	_____	___
[ ] [ ] ___ ___		Woodwork painted	_____	___
[ ] [ ] ___ ___		Doors painted or oiled	_____	___
[ ] [ ] ___ ___		Door hardware repaired	_____	___
[ ] [ ] ___ ___		Heater works	_____	___
[ ] [ ] ___ ___		Fireplace repaired	_____	___
[ ] [ ] ___ ___		Floor repaired	_____	___
[ ] [ ] ___ ___		Carpet repaired	_____	___
[ ] [ ] ___ ___		Furniture repaired	_____	___
[ ] [ ] ___ ___		Other _____	_____	___
		Bedroom #4		
[ ] [ ] ___ ___		Ceiling painted	_____	___
[ ] [ ] ___ ___		Lights work	_____	___
[ ] [ ] ___ ___		Walls repaired	_____	___
[ ] [ ] ___ ___		Walls painted	_____	___
[ ] [ ] ___ ___		Wallpaper tight	_____	___
[ ] [ ] ___ ___		Windows work easily	_____	___
[ ] [ ] ___ ___		Window cover repaired	_____	___
[ ] [ ] ___ ___		Drapery hardware works	_____	___
[ ] [ ] ___ ___		Woodwork painted	_____	___
[ ] [ ] ___ ___		Doors painted or oiled	_____	___
[ ] [ ] ___ ___		Door hardware repaired	_____	___
[ ] [ ] ___ ___		Heater works	_____	___
[ ] [ ] ___ ___		Fireplace repaired	_____	___
[ ] [ ] ___ ___		Floor repaired	_____	___
[ ] [ ] ___ ___		Carpet repaired	_____	___
[ ] [ ] ___ ___		Furniture repaired	_____	___
[ ] [ ] ___ ___		Other _____	_____	___
			Subtotal #7	___

REPAIRS WORKSHEET

To Be Done				Job	Call to repair/ telephone number or material needed	Estimate
Do	Did	By	Date			

Bedroom #5

Do	Did	By	Date	Job		
[ ]	[ ]	___	___	Ceiling painted		
[ ]	[ ]	___	___	Lights work		
[ ]	[ ]	___	___	Walls repaired		
[ ]	[ ]	___	___	Walls painted		
[ ]	[ ]	___	___	Wallpaper tight		
[ ]	[ ]	___	___	Windows work easily		
[ ]	[ ]	___	___	Window cover repaired		
[ ]	[ ]	___	___	Drapery hardware works		
[ ]	[ ]	___	___	Woodwork painted		
[ ]	[ ]	___	___	Doors painted or oiled		
[ ]	[ ]	___	___	Door hardware repaired		
[ ]	[ ]	___	___	Heater works		
[ ]	[ ]	___	___	Fireplace repaired		
[ ]	[ ]	___	___	Floor repaired		
[ ]	[ ]	___	___	Carpet repaired		
[ ]	[ ]	___	___	Furniture repaired		
[ ]	[ ]	___	___	Other _____		

Bathroom #1 (Master Bath)

Do	Did	By	Date	Job		
[ ]	[ ]	___	___	Ceiling painted		
[ ]	[ ]	___	___	Lights work		
[ ]	[ ]	___	___	Exhaust fan works		
[ ]	[ ]	___	___	Heater works		
[ ]	[ ]	___	___	Walls repaired		
[ ]	[ ]	___	___	Walls painted		
[ ]	[ ]	___	___	Wallpaper tight		
[ ]	[ ]	___	___	Woodwork painted		
[ ]	[ ]	___	___	Doors painted or oiled		
[ ]	[ ]	___	___	Door hardware repaired		
[ ]	[ ]	___	___	Cabinet hardware works		
[ ]	[ ]	___	___	Tiles repaired & caulked		
[ ]	[ ]	___	___	Sink fixtures work		
[ ]	[ ]	___	___	Toilet works		
[ ]	[ ]	___	___	Bath fixtures work		
[ ]	[ ]	___	___	Floor repaired		
[ ]	[ ]	___	___	Carpet repaired		
[ ]	[ ]	___	___	Other _____		

Subtotal #8 _____

REPAIRS WORKSHEET

					Call to repair/	Estimate
To Be Done					**telephone number**	
Do	**Did**	**By**	**Date**	**Job**	**or material needed**	

Bathroom #2

Do	Did	By	Date	Job
[ ]	[ ]	___	___	Ceiling painted
[ ]	[ ]	___	___	Lights work
[ ]	[ ]	___	___	Exhaust fan works
[ ]	[ ]	___	___	Heater works
[ ]	[ ]	___	___	Walls repaired
[ ]	[ ]	___	___	Walls painted
[ ]	[ ]	___	___	Wallpaper tight
[ ]	[ ]	___	___	Woodwork painted
[ ]	[ ]	___	___	Doors painted or oiled
[ ]	[ ]	___	___	Door hardware repaired
[ ]	[ ]	___	___	Cabinet hardware works
[ ]	[ ]	___	___	Tiles repaired & caulked
[ ]	[ ]	___	___	Sink fixtures work
[ ]	[ ]	___	___	Toilet works
[ ]	[ ]	___	___	Bath fixtures work
[ ]	[ ]	___	___	Floor repaired
[ ]	[ ]	___	___	Carpet repaired
[ ]	[ ]	___	___	Other _____

Bathroom #3

Do	Did	By	Date	Job
[ ]	[ ]	___	___	Ceiling painted
[ ]	[ ]	___	___	Lights work
[ ]	[ ]	___	___	Exhaust fan works
[ ]	[ ]	___	___	Heater works
[ ]	[ ]	___	___	Walls repaired
[ ]	[ ]	___	___	Walls painted
[ ]	[ ]	___	___	Wallpaper tight
[ ]	[ ]	___	___	Woodwork painted
[ ]	[ ]	___	___	Doors painted or oiled
[ ]	[ ]	___	___	Door hardware repaired
[ ]	[ ]	___	___	Cabinet hardware works
[ ]	[ ]	___	___	Tiles repaired & caulked
[ ]	[ ]	___	___	Sink fixtures work
[ ]	[ ]	___	___	Toilet works
[ ]	[ ]	___	___	Bath fixtures work
[ ]	[ ]	___	___	Floor clean & waxed
[ ]	[ ]	___	___	Carpet clean & secure
[ ]	[ ]	___	___	Clutter free
[ ]	[ ]	___	___	Other _____

Subtotal #9 _____

REPAIRS WORKSHEET

To Be Done					Call to repair/	Estimate
Do	Did	By	Date	Job	telephone number or material needed	

Hall and Stairs

[ ] [ ] ___ ___	Ceiling painted	_____	_____
[ ] [ ] ___ ___	Lights work	_____	_____
[ ] [ ] ___ ___	Walls repaired	_____	_____
[ ] [ ] ___ ___	Walls painted	_____	_____
[ ] [ ] ___ ___	Wallpaper tight	_____	_____
[ ] [ ] ___ ___	Windows work easily	_____	_____
[ ] [ ] ___ ___	Window cover repaired	_____	_____
[ ] [ ] ___ ___	Drapery hardware works	_____	_____
[ ] [ ] ___ ___	Woodwork painted	_____	_____
[ ] [ ] ___ ___	Doors painted or oiled	_____	_____
[ ] [ ] ___ ___	Door hardware repaired	_____	_____
[ ] [ ] ___ ___	Other _____	_____	_____

Utility Room

[ ] [ ] ___ ___	Ceiling painted	_____	_____
[ ] [ ] ___ ___	Lights work	_____	_____
[ ] [ ] ___ ___	Walls repaired	_____	_____
[ ] [ ] ___ ___	Walls painted	_____	_____
[ ] [ ] ___ ___	Windows work easily	_____	_____
[ ] [ ] ___ ___	Window cover repaired	_____	_____
[ ] [ ] ___ ___	Drapery hardware works	_____	_____
[ ] [ ] ___ ___	Woodwork painted	_____	_____
[ ] [ ] ___ ___	Doors painted or oiled	_____	_____
[ ] [ ] ___ ___	Doors work	_____	_____
[ ] [ ] ___ ___	Hardware operates	_____	_____
[ ] [ ] ___ ___	Washer operates	_____	_____
[ ] [ ] ___ ___	Dryer operates	_____	_____
[ ] [ ] ___ ___	Water heater operates	_____	_____
[ ] [ ] ___ ___	Floor repaired	_____	_____
[ ] [ ] ___ ___	Other _____	_____	_____

Utilities

[ ] [ ] ___ ___	Heater works	_____	_____
[ ] [ ] ___ ___	Air conditioner works	_____	_____
[ ] [ ] ___ ___	Smoke detectors work	_____	_____
[ ] [ ] ___ ___	Water softener works	_____	_____
[ ] [ ] ___ ___	Intercom works	_____	_____
[ ] [ ] ___ ___	Central vacuum works	_____	_____
[ ] [ ] ___ ___	Burglar alarm works	_____	_____
[ ] [ ] ___ ___	Other _____	_____	_____

Subtotal #10   _____

REPAIRS WORKSHEET

To Be Done				Job	Call to repair/ telephone number or material needed	Estimate
Do	Did	By	Date			
				Garage or Carport		
[ ]	[ ]	___	___	Clutter free	_____	_____
[ ]	[ ]	___	___	Roof free of leaks	_____	_____
[ ]	[ ]	___	___	Garage door balanced	_____	_____
[ ]	[ ]	___	___	Door opener works	_____	_____
[ ]	[ ]	___	___	Doors painted or oiled	_____	_____
[ ]	[ ]	___	___	Doors work	_____	_____
[ ]	[ ]	___	___	Windows work easily	_____	_____
[ ]	[ ]	___	___	Light fixtures work	_____	_____
[ ]	[ ]	___	___	Floor oil free	_____	_____
[ ]	[ ]	___	___	Other _____	_____	_____
				Attic		
[ ]	[ ]	___	___	Leak free	_____	_____
[ ]	[ ]	___	___	Ceiling repaired	_____	_____
[ ]	[ ]	___	___	Ceiling painted	_____	_____
[ ]	[ ]	___	___	Lights work	_____	_____
[ ]	[ ]	___	___	Walls repaired	_____	_____
[ ]	[ ]	___	___	Walls painted	_____	_____
[ ]	[ ]	___	___	Wallpaper tight	_____	_____
[ ]	[ ]	___	___	Windows work easily	_____	_____
[ ]	[ ]	___	___	Window repaired	_____	_____
[ ]	[ ]	___	___	Drapery hardware works	_____	_____
[ ]	[ ]	___	___	Woodwork painted	_____	_____
[ ]	[ ]	___	___	Doors painted or oiled	_____	_____
[ ]	[ ]	___	___	Door hardware repaired	_____	_____
[ ]	[ ]	___	___	Floor repaired	_____	_____
[ ]	[ ]	___	___	Carpet repaired	_____	_____
[ ]	[ ]	___	___	Furniture repaired	_____	_____
[ ]	[ ]	___	___	Other _____	_____	_____
				Basement		
[ ]	[ ]	___	___	Ceiling repaired	_____	_____
[ ]	[ ]	___	___	Ceiling painted	_____	_____
[ ]	[ ]	___	___	Lights work	_____	_____
[ ]	[ ]	___	___	Walls repaired	_____	_____
[ ]	[ ]	___	___	Walls painted	_____	_____
[ ]	[ ]	___	___	Windows repaired	_____	_____
[ ]	[ ]	___	___	Window cover repaired	_____	_____
					Subtotal #11	_____

REPAIRS WORKSHEET

To Be Done						
Do	Did	By	Date	Job	Call to repair/ telephone number or material needed	Estimate

Basement (*continued*)

Do	Did	By	Date	Job	Call to repair/material	Estimate
[ ]	[ ]	____	____	Drapery hardware works	_____	_____
[ ]	[ ]	____	____	Woodwork painted	_____	_____
[ ]	[ ]	____	____	Doors painted or oiled	_____	_____
[ ]	[ ]	____	____	Door hardware repaired	_____	_____
[ ]	[ ]	____	____	Floor drain works	_____	_____
[ ]	[ ]	____	____	Sump pump operates	_____	_____
[ ]	[ ]	____	____	Floor clean & waxed	_____	_____
[ ]	[ ]	____	____	Carpet clean & secure	_____	_____
[ ]	[ ]	____	____	Furniture repaired	_____	_____
[ ]	[ ]	____	____	Other _____	_____	_____

Subtotal #12   _____

Subtotal #1   _____
Subtotal #2   _____
Subtotal #3   _____
Subtotal #4   _____
Subtotal #5   _____
Subtotal #6   _____
Subtotal #7   _____
Subtotal #8   _____
Subtotal #9   _____
Subtotal #10   _____
Subtotal #11   _____
Subtotal #12   _____

TOTAL $ _____

ATTRACTIVENESS WORKSHEET

Name:_____

Address:_____

		To Be Done				
Do	**Did**	**By**	**Date**	**Job**	**Material needed**	**Estimate**

Lawn and plantings

[ ] [ ] ___ ___   Lawn mowed and raked _____ _____

[ ] [ ] ___ ___   Lawn edged   _____ _____

[ ] [ ] ___ ___   Shrubs trimmed   _____ _____

[ ] [ ] ___ ___   Plantings watered   _____ _____

[ ] [ ] ___ ___   Toys picked up   _____ _____

[ ] [ ] ___ ___   Pet messes removed   _____ _____

[ ] [ ] ___ ___   Hoses rolled   _____ _____

[ ] [ ] ___ ___   Other _____   _____ _____

Garages and carports

[ ] [ ] ___ ___   Swept   _____ _____

[ ] [ ] ___ ___   Orderly   _____ _____

[ ] [ ] ___ ___   Other _____   _____ _____

Patios and decks

[ ] [ ] ___ ___   Swept   _____ _____

[ ] [ ] ___ ___   Orderly   _____ _____

[ ] [ ] ___ ___   Other _____   _____ _____

Pools and spas

[ ] [ ] ___ ___   Vacuumed   _____ _____

[ ] [ ] ___ ___   Chlorinated   _____ _____

[ ] [ ] ___ ___   Other _____   _____ _____

Entrance

[ ] [ ] ___ ___   Clutter free   _____ _____

[ ] [ ] ___ ___   Lights clean   _____ _____

[ ] [ ] ___ ___   Walls clean   _____ _____

[ ] [ ] ___ ___   Windows & sills clean _____ _____

[ ] [ ] ___ ___   Steps swept   _____ _____

[ ] [ ] ___ ___   Door clean   _____ _____

[ ] [ ] ___ ___   Hardware polished   _____ _____

[ ] [ ] ___ ___   Woodwork clean   _____ _____

[ ] [ ] ___ ___   Windows clean   _____ _____

[ ] [ ] ___ ___   Rugs or mats vacuumed _____ _____

[ ] [ ] ___ ___   Floors clean & waxed _____ _____

[ ] [ ] ___ ___   Other _____   _____ _____

Subtotal #1   _____

ATTRACTIVENESS WORKSHEET

	To Be Done					
Do	Did	By	Date	Job	Material needed	Estimate

Living Room

Do	Did	By	Date	Job	Material needed	Estimate
[ ]	[ ]	___	___	Clutter free	_____	_____
[ ]	[ ]	___	___	Lights clean	_____	_____
[ ]	[ ]	___	___	Walls clean	_____	_____
[ ]	[ ]	___	___	Windows clean	_____	_____
[ ]	[ ]	___	___	Windows & sills clean	_____	_____
[ ]	[ ]	___	___	Woodwork clean	_____	_____
[ ]	[ ]	___	___	Hardware polished	_____	_____
[ ]	[ ]	___	___	Fireplace clean	_____	_____
[ ]	[ ]	___	___	Floor clean & waxed	_____	_____
[ ]	[ ]	___	___	Carpet vacuumed	_____	_____
[ ]	[ ]	___	___	Furniture clean	_____	_____
[ ]	[ ]	___	___	Furniture arrangement	_____	_____
[ ]	[ ]	___	___	Other _____	_____	_____

Dining Room

Do	Did	By	Date	Job	Material needed	Estimate
[ ]	[ ]	___	___	Clutter free	_____	_____
[ ]	[ ]	___	___	Lights clean	_____	_____
[ ]	[ ]	___	___	Walls painted	_____	_____
[ ]	[ ]	___	___	Windows & sills clean	_____	_____
[ ]	[ ]	___	___	Woodwork clean	_____	_____
[ ]	[ ]	___	___	Hardware polished	_____	_____
[ ]	[ ]	___	___	Floor clean	_____	_____
[ ]	[ ]	___	___	Carpet vacuumed	_____	_____
[ ]	[ ]	___	___	Furniture clean	_____	_____
[ ]	[ ]	___	___	Furniture arrangement	_____	_____
[ ]	[ ]	___	___	Other _____	_____	_____

Family Room

Do	Did	By	Date	Job	Material needed	Estimate
[ ]	[ ]	___	___	Clutter free	_____	_____
[ ]	[ ]	___	___	Lights clean	_____	_____
[ ]	[ ]	___	___	Walls clean	_____	_____
[ ]	[ ]	___	___	Windows & sills clean	_____	_____
[ ]	[ ]	___	___	Woodwork clean	_____	_____
[ ]	[ ]	___	___	Hardware polished	_____	_____
[ ]	[ ]	___	___	Fireplace clean	_____	_____
[ ]	[ ]	___	___	Floor clean & waxed	_____	_____
[ ]	[ ]	___	___	Carpet vacuumed	_____	_____
[ ]	[ ]	___	___	Furniture clean	_____	_____
[ ]	[ ]	___	___	Furniture arrangement	_____	_____
[ ]	[ ]	___	___	Other _____	_____	_____

Subtotal #2   _____

ATTRACTIVENESS WORKSHEET

To Be Done Do Did By Date	Job	Material needed	Estimate
	Kitchen		
[ ] [ ] ___ ___	Clutter free	_____	_____
[ ] [ ] ___ ___	Lights clean	_____	_____
[ ] [ ] ___ ___	Walls clean	_____	_____
[ ] [ ] ___ ___	Windows & sills clean	_____	_____
[ ] [ ] ___ ___	Counters clutter free	_____	_____
[ ] [ ] ___ ___	Disposal clean	_____	_____
[ ] [ ] ___ ___	Stove clean	_____	_____
[ ] [ ] ___ ___	Hood clean	_____	_____
[ ] [ ] ___ ___	Oven clean	_____	_____
[ ] [ ] ___ ___	Microwave clean	_____	_____
[ ] [ ] ___ ___	Cupboards orderly	_____	_____
[ ] [ ] ___ ___	Floor cleaned & waxed	_____	_____
[ ] [ ] ___ ___	Carpet vacuumed	_____	_____
[ ] [ ] ___ ___	Other _____	_____	_____
	Den		
[ ] [ ] ___ ___	Clutter free	_____	_____
[ ] [ ] ___ ___	Lights clean	_____	_____
[ ] [ ] ___ ___	Walls clean	_____	_____
[ ] [ ] ___ ___	Windows & sills clean	_____	_____
[ ] [ ] ___ ___	Woodwork clean	_____	_____
[ ] [ ] ___ ___	Hardware polished	_____	_____
[ ] [ ] ___ ___	Floor clean & waxed	_____	_____
[ ] [ ] ___ ___	Carpet vacuumed	_____	_____
[ ] [ ] ___ ___	Furniture clean	_____	_____
[ ] [ ] ___ ___	Furniture arrangement	_____	_____
[ ] [ ] ___ ___	Other _____	_____	_____
	Bedroom #1 (Master Bedroom)		
[ ] [ ] ___ ___	Clutter free	_____	_____
[ ] [ ] ___ ___	Lights clean	_____	_____
[ ] [ ] ___ ___	Walls clean	_____	_____
[ ] [ ] ___ ___	Windows & sills clean	_____	_____
[ ] [ ] ___ ___	Woodwork clean	_____	_____
[ ] [ ] ___ ___	Hardware polished	_____	_____
[ ] [ ] ___ ___	Floor clean & waxed	_____	_____
[ ] [ ] ___ ___	Carpet vacuumed	_____	_____
[ ] [ ] ___ ___	Furniture clean	_____	_____
[ ] [ ] ___ ___	Furniture arrangement	_____	_____
[ ] [ ] ___ ___	Other _____		
		Subtotal #3	_____

ATTRACTIVENESS WORKSHEET

	To Be Done			Job	Material needed	Estimate
Do	Did	By	Date			

Bedroom #2

Do	Did	By	Date	Job	Material needed	Estimate
[ ]	[ ]	___	___	Clutter free		
[ ]	[ ]	___	___	Lights clean		
[ ]	[ ]	___	___	Walls clean		
[ ]	[ ]	___	___	Windows & sills clean		
[ ]	[ ]	___	___	Woodwork clean		
[ ]	[ ]	___	___	Hardware polished		
[ ]	[ ]	___	___	Floor clean & waxed		
[ ]	[ ]	___	___	Carpet vacuumed		
[ ]	[ ]	___	___	Furniture clean		
[ ]	[ ]	___	___	Furniture arrangement		
[ ]	[ ]	___	___	Other _____		

Bedroom #3

Do	Did	By	Date	Job	Material needed	Estimate
[ ]	[ ]	___	___	Clutter free		
[ ]	[ ]	___	___	Lights clean		
[ ]	[ ]	___	___	Walls clean		
[ ]	[ ]	___	___	Windows & sills clean		
[ ]	[ ]	___	___	Woodwork clean		
[ ]	[ ]	___	___	Hardware polished		
[ ]	[ ]	___	___	Floor clean & waxed		
[ ]	[ ]	___	___	Carpet vacuumed		
[ ]	[ ]	___	___	Furniture clean		
[ ]	[ ]	___	___	Furniture arrangement		
[ ]	[ ]	___	___	Other _____		

Bedroom #4

Do	Did	By	Date	Job	Material needed	Estimate
[ ]	[ ]	___	___	Clutter free		
[ ]	[ ]	___	___	Lights clean		
[ ]	[ ]	___	___	Walls clean		
[ ]	[ ]	___	___	Windows & sills clean		
[ ]	[ ]	___	___	Woodwork clean		
[ ]	[ ]	___	___	Hardware polished		
[ ]	[ ]	___	___	Floor clean & waxed		
[ ]	[ ]	___	___	Carpet vacuumed		
[ ]	[ ]	___	___	Furniture clean		
[ ]	[ ]	___	___	Furniture arrangement		
[ ]	[ ]	___	___	Other _____		

Subtotal #4 _____

ATTRACTIVENESS WORKSHEET

		To Be Done				
Do	Did	By	Date	Job	Material needed	Estimate

Bedroom #5

Do	Did	By	Date	Job	Material needed	Estimate
[ ]	[ ]	___	___	Clutter free	_____	_____
[ ]	[ ]	___	___	Lights clean	_____	_____
[ ]	[ ]	___	___	Walls clean	_____	_____
[ ]	[ ]	___	___	Windows & sills clean	_____	_____
[ ]	[ ]	___	___	Woodwork clean	_____	_____
[ ]	[ ]	___	___	Hardware polished	_____	_____
[ ]	[ ]	___	___	Floor clean & waxed	_____	_____
[ ]	[ ]	___	___	Carpet vacuumed	_____	_____
[ ]	[ ]	___	___	Furniture clean	_____	_____
[ ]	[ ]	___	___	Furniture arrangement	_____	_____
[ ]	[ ]	___	___	Other _____	_____	_____

Bathroom #1 (Master Bath)

Do	Did	By	Date	Job	Material needed	Estimate
[ ]	[ ]	___	___	Clutter free	_____	_____
[ ]	[ ]	___	___	Lights clean	_____	_____
[ ]	[ ]	___	___	Walls & trim clean	_____	_____
[ ]	[ ]	___	___	Windows & sills clean	_____	_____
[ ]	[ ]	___	___	Hardware polished	_____	_____
[ ]	[ ]	___	___	Tile joints clean	_____	_____
[ ]	[ ]	___	___	Sink fixtures clean	_____	_____
[ ]	[ ]	___	___	Toilet clean	_____	_____
[ ]	[ ]	___	___	Bath fixtures clean	_____	_____
[ ]	[ ]	___	___	Floor clean & waxed	_____	_____
[ ]	[ ]	___	___	Carpet vacuumed	_____	_____
[ ]	[ ]	___	___	Other _____	_____	_____

Bathroom #2

Do	Did	By	Date	Job	Material needed	Estimate
[ ]	[ ]	___	___	Clutter free	_____	_____
[ ]	[ ]	___	___	Lights clean	_____	_____
[ ]	[ ]	___	___	Walls & trim clean	_____	_____
[ ]	[ ]	___	___	Windows & sills clean	_____	_____
[ ]	[ ]	___	___	Hardware polished	_____	_____
[ ]	[ ]	___	___	Tile joints clean	_____	_____
[ ]	[ ]	___	___	Sink fixtures clean	_____	_____
[ ]	[ ]	___	___	Toilet clean	_____	_____
[ ]	[ ]	___	___	Bath fixtures clean	_____	_____
[ ]	[ ]	___	___	Floor clean & waxed	_____	_____
[ ]	[ ]	___	___	Carpet vacuumed	_____	_____
[ ]	[ ]	___	___	Other _____	_____	_____

Subtotal #5   _____

ATTRACTIVENESS WORKSHEET

To Be Done					
Do Did By Date	Job	Material needed	Estimate

Bathroom #3

[ ] [ ] ___ ___ Clutter free

[ ] [ ] ___ ___ Lights clean

[ ] [ ] ___ ___ Walls & trim clean

[ ] [ ] ___ ___ Windows & sills clean

[ ] [ ] ___ ___ Hardware polished

[ ] [ ] ___ ___ Tile joints clean

[ ] [ ] ___ ___ Sink fixtures clean

[ ] [ ] ___ ___ Toilet clean

[ ] [ ] ___ ___ Bath fixtures clean

[ ] [ ] ___ ___ Floor clean & waxed

[ ] [ ] ___ ___ Carpet vacuumed

[ ] [ ] ___ ___ Other _____

Hall and Stairs

[ ] [ ] ___ ___ Clutter free

[ ] [ ] ___ ___ Lights clean

[ ] [ ] ___ ___ Walls clean

[ ] [ ] ___ ___ Windows & sills clean

[ ] [ ] ___ ___ Woodwork clean

[ ] [ ] ___ ___ Hardware polished

[ ] [ ] ___ ___ Floor clean & waxed

[ ] [ ] ___ ___ Carpet vacuumed

[ ] [ ] ___ ___ Furniture clean

[ ] [ ] ___ ___ Furniture arrangement

[ ] [ ] ___ ___ Other _____

Utility Room

[ ] [ ] ___ ___ Clutter free

[ ] [ ] ___ ___ Lights clean

[ ] [ ] ___ ___ Walls & trim clean

[ ] [ ] ___ ___ Windows & sills clean

[ ] [ ] ___ ___ Hardware polished

[ ] [ ] ___ ___ Washer clean

[ ] [ ] ___ ___ Dryer clean

[ ] [ ] ___ ___ Floor clean & waxed

[ ] [ ] ___ ___ Furniture clean

[ ] [ ] ___ ___ Furniture arrangement

[ ] [ ] ___ ___ Other _____

Subtotal #6 _____

ATTRACTIVENESS WORKSHEET

		To Be Done				
Do	Did	By	Date	Job	Material needed	Estimate

Garage or Carport

Do	Did	By	Date	Job	Material needed	Estimate
[ ]	[ ]	___	___	Clutter free	_____	_____
[ ]	[ ]	___	___	Lights clean	_____	_____
[ ]	[ ]	___	___	Walls & trim clean	_____	_____
[ ]	[ ]	___	___	Windows & sills clean	_____	_____
[ ]	[ ]	___	___	Hardware polished	_____	_____
[ ]	[ ]	___	___	Other _____	_____	_____

Attic

Do	Did	By	Date	Job	Material needed	Estimate
[ ]	[ ]	___	___	Clutter free	_____	_____
[ ]	[ ]	___	___	Lights clean	_____	_____
[ ]	[ ]	___	___	Walls & trim clean	_____	_____
[ ]	[ ]	___	___	Windows & sills clean	_____	_____
[ ]	[ ]	___	___	Hardware polished	_____	_____
[ ]	[ ]	___	___	Floor clean & waxed	_____	_____
[ ]	[ ]	___	___	Carpet vacuumed	_____	_____
[ ]	[ ]	___	___	Furniture clean	_____	_____
[ ]	[ ]	___	___	Furniture arrangement	_____	_____
[ ]	[ ]	___	___	Other _____	_____	_____

Basement

Do	Did	By	Date	Job	Material needed	Estimate
[ ]	[ ]	___	___	Clutter free	_____	_____
[ ]	[ ]	___	___	Lights clean	_____	_____
[ ]	[ ]	___	___	Walls & trim clean	_____	_____
[ ]	[ ]	___	___	Windows & sills clean	_____	_____
[ ]	[ ]	___	___	Hardware polished	_____	_____
[ ]	[ ]	___	___	Floor clean & waxed	_____	_____
[ ]	[ ]	___	___	Furniture clean	_____	_____
[ ]	[ ]	___	___	Furniture arrangement	_____	_____
[ ]	[ ]	___	___	Other _____	_____	_____

Subtotal #7	_____
Subtotal #1	_____
Subtotal #2	_____
Subtotal #3	_____
Subtotal #4	_____
Subtotal #5	_____
Subtotal #6	_____
Subtotal #7	_____
TOTAL	$ _____

2. Asking for recommendations. Ask others to recommend someone who they know does good work or, preferably, someone who did similar work for them satisfactorily, including
   - Friends, neighbors, and relatives who own property.
   - Real estate professionals.
   - Contractors who work in related fields.
   - Subcontractors who are not dependent on those contractors for their livelihood.
3. Ask pertinent questions. When you initially contact a contractor, ask
   - The address of his or her established place of business
   - What licenses he or she has, including contractor's license and business licenses.
   - Whether he or she is bonded.
   - How long he or she has been in business.
   - References where you can inspect his or her work.
   - List of subcontractors and suppliers.
4. Obtain at least three estimates from competing contractors. If the estimates vary substantially, get more estimates.
5. Choose two contractors.
6. Talk with contractor's contacts, including
   - Contractor's references. Ask to inspect the work.
   - Subcontractors and suppliers. Find what reputation the contractor has regarding the quality of work and paying debts when they are due.
   - State licensing board. Ask if contractor's license is valid and the nature of the work for which the license applies.
   - Government agencies issuing business licenses and permits and checking work. Ask about contractor's reputation.
   - Bonding company. Ask whether contractor is bonded against liens.
7. Choose your contractor.
8. Prepare the contract. Prepare a specific and detailed written agreement with your contractor, including
   - Names, addresses, and license numbers. Include the contractor's name, business address, and state license number, as well as your name and the address where the work will be performed.
   - Description of the work. Include sketches, plans, and blueprints, as well as a list of products and materials, including brand names and model numbers.
   - Dates. Include starting date, 20-day notice date, and completion date. The 20-day notice is a clause stating that failure to begin work within 20 days of the stated starting date is a violation of the contract and makes the entire contract null and void at your discretion.
   - Cost. List the cost of the entire job including interest and service charges.
   - Payment schedule. Include a plan of how much you will pay and when. Consider paying in stages of about 20 percent in each installment at the beginning, the end, and as specified portions of the work are completed. With staged payments, a contractor is less likely to delay or abandon your job.
   - Permits and licenses. List permits and licenses and who takes responsibility for obtaining them.
   - Guarantees. List guarantees and warranties of material and/or workmanship.

- Changes in work. Incorporate a clause worded to allow your written request for changes without annulling the entire contract.
- Cleanup. Include a statement that the contractor is responsible for cleaning all debris resulting from the job and removing all excess materials.
- Owner's rights and responsibilities. Include a clause describing your rights and responsibilities.
- Mechanic's lien laws. Incorporate a statement describing your state's mechanic's lien law. This law usually allows any contractor, subcontractor, supplier, laborer, or other person who helped to improve your property but has not been paid for his or her work or supplies the right to enforce a claim (lien) against your property. Even if you have paid a contractor in full, if he or she has not paid subcontractors, suppliers, or laborers, they may have a valid claim against your property. If you cannot afford to pay these claims, your property could be sold by a court officer after a court hearing and the proceeds of the sale used to satisfy the debt.
- Cancellation. Include a clause stating that you have three days after signing the contract in which to cancel it.
- Insurance. Incorporate a statement that the contractor is responsible for worker's compensation and liability insurance for his or her workers, subcontractors, and suppliers.
- Work stoppage. Include a clause giving the contractor the right to stop work if you do not make the required payments.
- Completion bond. Make the statement that the contractor will supply a bond. This bond ensures that if the contractor does not complete the project, an insurance company will pay for the rest of the work to be done.
- Arbitration. Incorporate a clause providing for arbitration in the case of contract disputes. Arbitration is the process of taking a dispute to an unbiased third party who holds a hearing at which you both have an opportunity to speak and who then issues an opinion.
- Unconditional lien release (waiver of liens). Make the statement that the contractor will provide you with an unconditional lien release after the job is complete and you have made the final payments. With this document the contractor waives and releases all his or her mechanic's lien rights, stop notice rights, notice to withhold rights, bond rights, and any and all claims against your property. Without this release you could end up paying twice for the work.
- Bankruptcy. Include a clause stating that if the contractor goes bankrupt you are not liable for the contractor's debts.

9. Read the contract thoroughly and understand it well before you sign it.
   - Do not sign estimates. Estimates may be worded in a manner that makes them binding contracts.
   - Do not make separate agreements with subcontractors or suppliers without checking with your contractor.
10. Ensure the quality of the work by
    - Being home as much as possible while the contractor is working.
    - Checking the work as it is done.
    - Informing the contractor of problems with the work immediately and in writing.
11. Obtain a detailed signed receipt stating the amount paid and what the payment was for each time you pay.

12. Sign the certificate of completion and make the final payment only *after*
    - Work is finished to your satisfaction and according to the terms of the contract.
    - All subcontractors, suppliers, and workers are paid.
13. Make final payment.
14. Keep a copy of all documents about the work.

After you finish preparing for marketing so you can obtain the most money in your pocket when you sell your home, you are now ready to advertise your home for sale.

CHAPTER 7
Advertise!

An advertising adage says that 50 percent of all advertising is effective and 50 percent is ineffective. Unfortunately, no one knows for sure which 50 percent is which!

The most important element in successfully marketing your home is giving it the widest possible exposure. As you read this chapter, decide how best to advertise for most productive exposure. You will pay for advertising whether you purchase advertising space or not, due to such circumstances as

- Making payments on your home for a longer time.
- Having to spend time, effort, and money to maintain your property in top condition to show to prospective buyers.
- Uncertainty and delays in not being able to plan your move.

Step 1: Understand Advertising Basics

Identify the Target Market

Identify the audience that is likely to be interested in purchasing your property. The following categories of property indicate the buyers who are most likely to purchase your type of property.

Suburban Property
- Smaller homes—First time buyers, young couples without children or with few children, single or divorced persons, older couples, and retirees.
- Larger homes—Buyers who are trading up, large or growing families, and executives.
- Vacation homes—Executives with families and successful young couples as a vacation home; older persons and retirees as their only home.

Urban Property
- Smaller homes or condominiums—First time buyers, single or divorced persons, successful young people, and executives for a house in town.
- Larger homes or condominiums—Buyers who are trading up, successful young couples, and corporations for the periodic use of their executives.

Learn About Laws

Understand and comply with laws regarding discrimination and disclosure in advertising.

Discrimination

Discrimination is the arbitrary selection of certain types of persons from a larger group and the giving to or withholding from these persons certain advantages. Treating other persons unfairly or denying them normal privileges are both forms of discrimination. Housing discrimination on the basis of race, color, religion, sex, marital status, national origin, or ancestry is illegal under the federal Civil Rights Act of 1968. Check laws in your area. Laws in many areas prohibit

- Discriminating on the basis of sexual preference.
- Asking buyers about their race, color, religion, sex, marital status, national origin, ancestry, or sexual preferences.
- Indicating any preferences for or against any such factor.
- Discriminating against anyone who has previously opposed your prior discriminatory procedures.

Disclosure

Disclosure, or making known things previously unknown, is also required by federal and state laws. For your own protection

- State only correct information in your advertising.
- If some items of information you list are estimates, state that they are approximations.
- Understand that if you make intentional or careless errors or omissions, you may be violating disclosure laws.

Understand Types of Advertising

Advertising your home for sale encompasses all forms of attracting attention including signs, newspapers, newsletters, flyers, bulletin boards, and telling friends and co-workers. Planning for productive handling of telephone inquiries is also part of effective advertising.

Signs

Signs, one of the most productive forms of real estate advertising, usually work best when they suggest quality, care, and concern.

ADVANTAGES
- Signs are relatively inexpensive.
- They let neighbors know you are selling your property.
- They reach people familiar with the neighborhood. (These persons are a good source of referrals, because they like and can afford property in the area.)

DISADVANTAGES
- Even if you have a telephone number and the message "By Appointment Only," people may still ring your doorbell and ask to see your home.
- When signs remain in place for a long period, it becomes obvious that you have not been able to sell your home.

Effective Signs. Productive signs are usually
- Rectangular in shape and approximately 18 by 24 inches.
- Visible against landscaping or building.
- Simple and easy to read.
- Capable of being read from a car moving in either direction along a street at a normal speed.

Size and Placement. Laws in some cities and restrictions in some subdivisions may limit size and/or placement of signs. Consider

1. Checking with your city for any applicable laws.
2. Examining a copy of your subdivision covenants, conditions, and restrictions (CC&Rs) for sign regulations.
3. Asking permission of property owners before putting signs on their property. (Requests can keep you on good terms with other residents and allow you to tell them about your home sale.)
4. Placing your signs where they will be safe for the readers while you follow local laws and customs.

Types of Signs. Two types of signs are generally used by owners who sell their homes themselves: For Sale by Owner signs and Open House signs.

For Sale by Owner signs say you are selling your home yourself. The preferred wording is *For Sale by Owner,* followed by a blank area on which you can write your telephone number with chalk or marking pen, and then by the words *By Appointment Only.* These signs are easy to read and yet give the necessary information. The requirement for an appointment usually does not discourage serious buyers, but rather prevents the curious from dropping by unexpectedly or at inconvenient times.

Open House signs let the public know that your home is open for viewing. Area open houses, discussed later in this chapter, require no signs and are more likely to be instrumental in selling your home.

Placement of Signs. The following are tips for placing the For Sale by Owner signs:

1. Place signs in your yard so that they are visible from both directions from any streets that border your property.
2. Leave these signs in place at all times for maximum effect, except when you will be away for several days or more.
3. Take signs down if you have no one to at least answer calls.

If you decide to hold a open house for the public, you should know about small and large Open House signs. Attach a small Open House sign to the same pole as your large For Sale by Owner sign when you hold an open house. Consider using a large sign that states simply Open House and then has two blank areas to be filled in with chalk or marking pen. Put your street address in the first blank and your telephone number in the second.

To place Open House signs for maximum exposure:

1. Put signs on both corners of your block, usually on the same side of the street as your home.
2. Place a sign at the nearest major intersection or major street near your home— the closer to your home, the better.

Flags

Use flags to draw attention to your signs. Use flags especially if you must place a sign where it is difficult to see or where it competes with other signs.

Newspapers

The type of advertising you do in a newspaper and type of newspaper you choose depends upon the kind of house you have and the effect you desire. Classified and display advertisements are different in effectiveness, rates, and composition.

Classified Advertisements. Classifieds are the easier of the two types to write, cheaper, and function better for most homes.

- *Effectiveness* of these ads is greatest when you use several small ads stressing different advantages of your home. In this way you reach more types of people than a single large advertisement.

- *Rates* for these ads are usually inexpensive. Ask newspapers for their schedule of rates. Note what special rates apply to what number of insertions and what number of consecutive insertions.
- *Composition* of an ad can make a difference in buyers' responses. Use copies of the Ad Grid to compose your classified ad. Compose several ads using the following suggestions to draw attention to your ad:
  o Employ LARGE, specific headlines. Use CAPITAL LETTERS. Be concise. Use two- to three-word headlines.
  o Describe the property's key features, using attractive words.
  o Make each advertisement brief but use descriptive *whole* words and phrases. (Abbreviations are often difficult to understand.)
  o Emphasize the benefits your home has for the buyer and that it is an unbeatable value.

			C	O	M	P	L	E	T	E	L	Y		R	E	M	O	D	E	L	E	D		/			
O	p	e	n	,		a	i	r	y	,		l	a	r	g	e		c	o	r	n	e	r		l	o	t	,
h	u	g	e		m	a	s	t	e	r		s	u	i	t	e	,		3	B	R		2	B	A		
$	2	0	0	,	0	0	0		C	a	l	l		O	w	n	e	r		9	4	2	-	2	4	5	5

2	4	6	8	10	12	14	16	18	20	22	24	26	28	30

- Surround the ad with blank (white) space to make it easier to read and stand out from other ads.
- Include information in the approximate order listed here. Change the order to list most attractive features first or support the headline.
  1. List of best features
  2. Number of bedrooms and baths
  3. Price
  4. Terms
  5. Demand for action ("Phone today for an appointment!")
  6. For Sale by Owner
  7. Telephone number
- Do not exaggerate.
- Omit your address so that buyers call you to get further information; in this way you can screen callers over the telephone, be ready for buyers when they arrive in order to show your home to best advantage, and discourage theft while you are not at home.

Select the best two or three advertisements and set them aside. Rewrite the best ads after you have set them aside for a period of time, preferably overnight.

Place the advertisement under the appropriate heading in the classified section, usually under Homes for Sale in the city or area where your home is located.

If you decide to run an ad for several weeks, consider running at least two versions on alternate weeks. Buyers are less likely to decide something is wrong with your property because it has not sold.

Display Advertisements. Display ads may be effective in special situations.

- *Effectiveness* of these larger advertisements is greatest for immense and unique homes or for special promotions.
- *Rates* are generally expensive, and usually you must pay in advance. Sometimes special rates are offered for a combination of classified and display advertisements.
- *Composition* is similar to that for a classified ad. Explain in more detail about the special features of your property. Newspapers will often help you compose display ads, usually at no charge.
- *Lead times* vary among newspapers. Ask newspaper representatives the length of their lead time as well as their policies on canceling an ad. Many newspapers have a two- to three-day lead time between placing the order and running the ad. Generally you must pay a penalty or forfeit your whole payment if you cancel during the lead time.

Types of Newspapers. Effectiveness and rates vary depending upon the type of newspaper in which you advertise. *General circulation dailies* are usually effective for reaching the most people at the lowest rate per person. *Local dailies* are often especially good for attracting people who want another home in the same area or who are considering moving into a specific area. *Weeklies* are generally not very effective unless they are the only newspaper in a rural area. *Special interest* papers are generally like newsletters. They may be effective if your home has unique features of interest to persons with similar special interests.

To avoid charges of discrimination, run an ad in a newspaper of general circulation every time you run an advertisement in one of limited circulation.

Newsletters

Groups with special interests usually receive newsletters.

- *Effectiveness* of newsletters depends on whether your home has unique features important to persons with special interests.

- *Rates* and costs vary, but newsletter ads are usually fairly inexpensive.
- *Composition* of the ad may be handled as for newspapers. Newsletters may have both classified and display advertisements. Check with newsletter staff for specific requirements.
- *Lead times* depend on how often newsletter is published. Check with newsletter staff for schedule.

Magazines

Effectiveness, rates, composition, and lead times of real estate advertisements in magazines vary greatly, depending upon the nature of the magazine. Inexpensive formats are often published weekly on inexpensive paper. Expensive formats are usually published less often, printed on more expensive paper, and usually contain pictures (sometimes in color).

For magazines devoted to shoppers in general, the most effective are usually those in which the advertisements are classified and you can target your ad to the locality you desire by selecting areas by zip code.

- *Effectiveness* of magazines in selling your home varies with the magazine format and the nature of the home. Inexpensive formats of classified ads to make ads easy to locate can be cost effective for moderately priced homes. Some magazines devoted solely to real estate may allow or require a photograph. If you use a photograph, be sure it compliments your home so that potential buyers will get a good impression. Expensive formats are usually not cost effective except for unique and expensive homes.
- *Rates* vary by format also. Inexpensive formats have prices that may range from inexpensive to expensive, depending upon the publication. Usually they are costlier if a photograph is required. Expensive formats have costs that are usually quite high. Some may require expensive color photographs.
- *Composition* depends upon type of magazine. Check with magazine staff for details. Some publications require photographs processed by special methods.
- *Lead time* varies depending upon how often the magazine is published. Check with magazine staff for details.

Flyers

Flyers are leaflets for mass distribution. They should accurately describe your property. They are relatively inexpensive and easily distributed. If information such as your asking price changes, you have to print new flyers. Used indiscriminately, flyers may create litter.

- *Effectiveness* of flyers depends on several factors. Choose the methods that work best for you.
  - Give buyers who have just viewed your property flyers as they leave so that they have information regarding your property. (If you give them flyers before you show them the property, they may not pay full attention during the tour.)
  - Give flyers to the neighbors after they have viewed your home when you hold an area open house.
  - Post them on bulletin boards at strategic locations.
  - Mail flyers to the Chamber of Commerce, which often gets inquiries about properties for sale in the area.
- *Composition* of your flyer varies with your locale, the market, and price of the property. Review the sample Home for Sale Flyer, explained here. It lists some of the most commonly used descriptions for relevant sections. In some cases it

may be appropriate to list more than one option, for example, Exterior: Brick and frame.

Community: Name of city, town, or area where your property is located.

Nearest major cross streets: Names of major streets that cross nearest to your property to enable a buyer to find your property easily.

Approximate square feet: Number of square feet of living area. Living area usually *excludes* the garage unless garage is finished and converted into a usable room in the house.

Style: Bungalow, Cape Cod, Colonial, Contemporary, Dutch Colonial, Ranch, Spanish, Split Level, Traditional, Tudor.

Exterior: Adobe, Aluminum siding, Block, Brick, Brick veneer, Frame, Stone, Stucco, Wood.

Roof: Composition shingle, Concrete shake, Gravel, Rock, Shake, Slate, Tile, Wood shingle.

Age: Approximate age of your home.

Lot size: Approximate square feet of lot size.

Lot character: Corner, Cul-de-sac, Irregular, Pie-shaped, Rectangular, Square.

View: Bay, Canyon, City, Golf course, Green belt, Lagoon, Lake, Mountains, Ocean, Panoramic, Trees, Valley.

Stories: Enter number of stories.

Floors: Hardwood, metal, slab, wood.

Living room, Dining room, Family room, Bedrooms 1-5, and *Den:* Approximate square feet.

Extra room: Room purpose (breakfast, library, office, sewing, sitting, storage) and approximate square feet.

Fireplace: Room or rooms that have fireplaces, nature of the fireplace (brick, metal, stone, freestanding), and any amenities (gas starter, gas log).

Garage: Number of vehicles for which garage was constructed and that it can comfortably fit (1, 2, 3) and the placement (attached or detached). If you have a carport, enter carport in this space and the number of vehicles it can accommodate (1, 2, 3).

Garage door opener: Yes if you have it on all garage doors or on which door you have the opener, if it is only on one (single, double).

Laundry: Location (garage, inside, room) and utilities available in that area (electric, gas, propane).

Patio: Nature (covered, deck, enclosed, gazebo, porch, screened) and construction (brick, concrete, flagstone, wood).

Pool: Nature (above ground, gunite, vinyl liner). If heated, enter heated and source of heat (diesel, electric, gas, propane, solar). If unheated, enter unheated.

Spa: Nature (above ground, gunite, hot tub, Jacuzzi). If heated, enter heated and source of heat (diesel, electric, gas, propane, solar). If unheated, enter unheated.

Sauna: Location.

Television: Nature of reception equipment (antenna, cable, dish).

Fence: Nature of fence (brick wall, chain link, split rail, stock, wood) and coverage (front, rear, side, total).

Sewer: Nature of system (seepage pit, septic tank, sewer) and conditions it meets (available, approved, bond, needs percolation test, paid for).

Water: Source (public, private, well) and any modifying factors (filtered, softener).

HOME FOR SALE FLYER

Center   1 picture
Or use   2 pictures

Community:_____   Cross streets:_____
Approx. square feet:_____   Bedrooms:_____   Bathrooms:_____
Address:_____
Telephone number:_____
Style:_____   Price: $_____
Exterior:_____   Financing: ☐ 1st   ☐ 2nd
Roof:_____   Payment: _____   _____
Age:_____   Lender: _____   _____
Lot size:_____   Due date: _____   _____
Lot shape:_____   Take over: _____   _____
View:_____   Interest %: _____   _____
Stories:_____
Living room: Approx. ____×____ feet   Possession date:_____
Dining room: Approx. ____×____ feet
Kitchen: Approx. ____×____ feet   ☐Planned Development ☐Condominium
Family room: Approx. ____×____ feet   Homeowner's fees: $_____/month
Bedroom 1:   Approx. ____×____ feet   Maintenance: $_____/month
Bedroom 2:   Approx. ____×____ feet   Water: $_____/month
Bedroom 3:   Approx. ____×____ feet   Trash: $_____/month
Bedroom 4:   Approx. ____×____ feet   Insurance: $_____/month
Bedroom 5:   Approx. ____×____ feet   Recreation room:_____
Den: Approx. ____×____ feet   Pool:_____
Fireplace:_____   Spa:_____
Garage:_____   Tennis:_____
Laundry:_____   Golf:_____
Patio:_____
Pool:_____   Schools
Spa:_____   Elementary:_____
Television:_____   Junior high:_____
Fence:_____   High:_____
Sewer:_____
Septic:_____   Notes:_____
Sprinklers:_____   _____
Water Heater:_____   _____
Heating:_____   _____
Air Cond.:_____   _____
Stove:_____   _____
Oven:_____   _____
Microwave:_____   _____
Dishwasher:_____   _____
Disposal:_____   _____
Trash compactor:_____   _____

Sprinklers: If present, location (front, partial, rear, total).

Water heater: Source of heat (electric, gas, propane, solar).

Heating: Type and nature (baseboard, floor, forced air [electric, gas, propane], heat pump, radiant [electric, fluid], solar, wall [electric, gas]).

Air conditioning: Nature (evaporative cooler, forced air [electric, gas], heat pump) and location (central, window).

Stove: Source of heat (electric, gas, propane).

Oven: Number of ovens (single, double) and nature (electric, gas, propane, self-cleaning).

Microwave: Pertinent information (built-in, not included).

Smoke detector: Number (1, 2) and type (battery, electric).

Dishwasher: Pertinent information (built-in, not included).

Disposal: Yes if there is one, no if there is not.

Trash compactor: Pertinent information (built-in, not included).

Price: Amount you are asking for your property.

Financing: First loan (mortgage or trust deed) and/or second.

Payment: Payment amount and period to which it applies.

Lender: Name of the organization or person who made the loan.

Due date: When the loan balance is payable.

Take over: Yes if loan can be taken over by buyers, no if not.

Interest %: Percentage rate. If variable, so note.

Possession date: Date that buyers may take possession.

[ ] Planned Development [ ] Condominium: Check if appropriate.

Homeowner's fees, Maintenance, Water, Trash, Insurance: Amounts, if applicable.

Recreation room, Pool, Spa: Yes if present, no if not.

Tennis: Yes and number of courts if present, no if not.

Golf: Yes and number of holes if present, no if not.

Schools: Names of nearest schools in whose districts your property is located.

Notes: Items that have not been covered before or that you wish to describe in greater detail.

Bulletin Boards

Bulletin boards in locations frequented by people you think might be interested in purchasing your property are good places to post flyers. Such areas could include local community centers, athletic clubs, social clubs, churches, colleges and universities, and the club house of a planned unit development. Be sure to get permission from whoever is in charge before posting your flyer in any of these sites.

Using flyers on bulletin boards is a relatively inexpensive form of advertisement. Getting permission from the proper authority before posting a flyer on the bulletin board can be time consuming.

Co-workers, Friends, and Neighbors

Let your co-workers, friends, and neighbors know that your home is for sale.

1. Encourage people to tell others about your home.
2. Give acquaintances a flyer describing your property.
3. Invite acquaintances to your area open house.

Open Houses

Inviting your neighbors to view your open house is more effective than a public open house and is also safer.

Area Open House. Neighbors usually already know that your home is for sale. They are more likely to recommend your home to others after they see what your property has to offer. If you decide to hold an area open house, consider

1. Preparing your area open house announcement indicating you
   a. Are inviting your neighbors to an area open house to view your property, which is for sale.
   b. Will be serving refreshments during the open house.
   c. Will pay a fee (indicate the amount) at the closing to the person who refers the buyers to you.
2. Making enough copies to distribute these invitations for several blocks around your property.
3. Distributing invitations to the houses you choose.
4. Having the viewers sign a guest register as they enter.

Public Open House. Public open houses often attract many people who are not serious buyers or cannot afford your property. Real estate professionals generally hold public open houses primarily to gain potential clients. Real estate professionals seldom sell a property as the result of a public open house.

Multiple Listing Service (MLS)

The MLS is a service to which real estate brokers belong in order to share their listings and commissions with fellow members of the service. As of this writing, only real estate brokers may make submissions to the MLS. Some brokers will submit your home to an MLS for a nominal fee.

See Chapter 4 for more details about how to maximize the benefits real estate professionals can offer as you sell your property yourself, as well as other possible interactions you may have with real estate professionals.

Step 2: Plan Your Advertising Budget

Plan and keep in mind how much you are willing to spend on advertising.

Advertising Budget Information

As a basic budget for selling your home yourself, consider the following:
- For Sale by Owner signs at a one-time cost of $50 to $100.
- Classified advertisements in local papers at approximately $100 per week.
- Flyers at $100 to $300, depending on the nature and number required.

Completing the Advertising Budget Worksheet

Prepare an advertising budget for the sale of your home on the Advertising Budget Worksheet.

Step 3: Prepare Telephone Response

Because the more calls you receive the greater chance you have of selling your property, consider

ADVERTISING BUDGET WORKSHEET

Address:_____

Name:_____ Date:_____

ADVERTISEMENT	PUBLICATION	NUMBER	PRICE	SUBTOTAL
Signs				
For Sale by				
Owner		_____	_____	_____
Open House		_____	_____	_____
Flags		_____	_____	_____
Newspaper Ads				
Classified				
Ad #1	_____	_____	_____	_____
Ad #2	_____	_____	_____	_____
Ad #3	_____	_____	_____	_____
Ad #4	_____	_____	_____	_____
Ad #5	_____	_____	_____	_____
Ad #6	_____	_____	_____	_____
Display				
Ad #1	_____	_____	_____	_____
Ad #2	_____	_____	_____	_____
Newsletter Ads				
Ad #1	_____	_____	_____	_____
Ad #2	_____	_____	_____	_____
Magazine Ads				
Ad #1	_____	_____	_____	_____
Ad #2	_____	_____	_____	_____
Flyers				
Pictures		_____	_____	_____
Paper		_____	_____	_____
Printing		_____	_____	_____
Distribution		_____	_____	_____
Open Houses				
Announcements		_____	_____	_____
Signs (see above)		_____	_____	_____
TOTAL				$ _____

- Remaining at the telephone number you list on your advertisements as much as possible.
- Listing a time (for example, evenings) and a telephone number when and where you can be reached, if you are not available the whole day.
- Asking your employer before listing your work number on advertisements.

Telephone Register

A telephone register is a listing of information regarding telephone calls you receive.

Understand Use of Telephone Register

A telephone register, which you fill out during each call, can be a valuable source of information regarding

- The advertising method that triggered each call, which helps you determine the most effective methods.
- Who called and his or her telephone number, which allows you to get in touch with callers again, if necessary.
- With whom and for when you made appointments.
- Callers' remarks, which may be helpful in addressing callers' interests and concerns when you show them your home.

Prepare Telephone Register

Consider using the Telephone Register in conjunction with the suggested telephone screening conversation by

1. Copying several Telephone Register sheets.
2. Placing the sheets in a binder or folder.
3. Keeping the binder or folder near the telephone.
4. Entering the pertinent information as you are speaking to each prospective buyer.

Telephone Screening Conversation

To obtain necessary information from potential buyers without overselling your home, consider using a conversation similar to the one described here. Remember, your goal is to make an appointment with buyers to show your property.

In Person

Manage the in-person telephone conversation as follows:

1. Speak the wording given in **bold** typeface.
2. Do not speak the words in parentheses ( ). They are for your information only.
3. Allow the caller time to respond before continuing with the next remark or question.
4. Write information received in the Telephone Register.

Hello! My name is _____ . **To whom am I speaking?** (Listen)
Thank you for calling. Where did you hear about my property? (Listen)
What particularly interested you about my advertisement? (Listen)
My property is in the _____ **section of** _____ (city). **Where do you live?** (Listen)
The property has _____ **bedrooms,** _____ **baths, and approximately**
_____ **square feet of living space. Do you have a home now?** (Listen)
This property also has (list important features)

_____ , _____ ,

TELEPHONE REGISTER

Date	Ad Method	Name	Telephone Number	Appointment Date	Time	Remarks

_____, _____,
and _____. (Listen)
The price of our home is $_____. **Are you looking for a home like this?**
(Listen. If caller says no, thank him or her for calling. If callers say yes, proceed.)
When may I set up an appointment for you to see the house? (Listen. Whether caller
or you suggest a meeting time, continue.)
That time sounds fine to me, but I must check with _____(my
husband, my wife, others in my family) **to be sure that we have no conflicts. I will call
you back within the next** _____ **minutes. May I have your name and number?**
(Listen, say goodbye, then check for conflicts. Even if you do not need to check for
conflicts, follow this step, because people are more likely to give you the information
under these conditions. Call the person back and set up an appointment.

By Answering Machine

Although using an answering machine is less preferable than responding to the
telephone in person, an answering machine is still a very effective tool in marketing
your property. If you do not already own an answering machine, consider buying or
renting one. It allows you to be away from home and still receive calls from prospective
buyers as well as to screen your calls. Consider using a message similar to this:

Thank you for calling. You have reached _____ (your telephone number). **Our
home is for sale. It is in the** _____ **section of** _____.
Our home has _____ **bedrooms,** _____ **baths, and approximately**
_____ **square feet of living space. Our home also has**
_____, _____,
_____, _____,
and _____.
The price of our home is $_____. **If you would like to see the property,
please leave your name and number as well as any questions you may have at the sound
of the tone. We will return your call as soon as possible. Thank you.**

Step 4: Implement Your Advertising Plans

Put your advertising plans into action, now that you understand advertising basics,
have planned your budget, and have prepared your telephone response.

The response to your advertising depends on local market conditions, your pricing
your home correctly, and the scope of your advertising. Repetition is the key to successful advertising. Plan on a minimum 30-day advertising campaign. It only takes
one buyer seeing your ads to successfully sell your home yourself.

After you implement your advertising plans you are ready to take the steps necessary to show your home to prospective buyers.

CHAPTER 8
Show Your Home Successfully

Showing your home successfully includes safeguarding your property, protecting viewers, making finishing touches, managing the home tour, selling your home, and completing the sale.

Step 1: Safeguard Your Property

Take steps to protect your property and yourself. Consider these precautions:
1. Hiding valuables.
   - Hide anything that might be broken or easily taken.
   - Conceal large valuables such as fine china, silver, pieces of art, and your other prized possessions.
   - Avoid mentioning what valuables you have. Persons looking for a home to buy will not be interested.
2. Have all viewers sign the guest register to
   - Enable you to get the viewer's name, address, and telephone number so that you may make follow-up contact.
   - Let you see the effectiveness of your advertising.
     - Inquire of each person who views your home specifically where he or she learned about your house.
     - Tally the number of persons learning about your home from each source.
   - Discourage a would-be thief.
3. Accompany anyone viewing your home.
   - Make appointments to show your home.
   - Have family or friends aid you during an open house. Tell them to ask buyers who arrive while you are showing your home to wait for the next tour.
   - Have everyone enter and leave by one door to control the flow of traffic.
   - Invite buyers who return to view your home for a second time to view it unaccompanied.
     - Buyers are not inhibited by your presence.
     - Buyers have freedom to explore your home and study how your property would fit their needs.
     - You stay in one room or step outside.

       ○ You stay in the area so you are available to answer questions buyers may have.

4. Decline to discuss your lifestyle or schedule with viewers. People really interested in buying your home will not be interested in your lifestyle or schedule.

Step 2: Protect Viewers

Protect your viewers from possible injury and yourself from possible lawsuits.

1. Make walking safe by
   - Putting down rubber mats or other nonslip surfacing on slick areas.
   - Tacking down mats or throw rugs that might slip.
   - Putting away items over which viewers might trip.
2. Lock up anything potentially dangerous that children might discover, including
   - Household chemicals, such as cleaning compounds, medicines, toiletries, painting supplies, and gardening chemicals.
   - Dangerous instruments, such as guns and knives.
3. Childproof your yard, including decks, patios, pools, spas, and hot tubs.
4. Secure pets, even ones that have always been friendly.
   - Lock them in an enclosure if they are usually quiet.
   - Arrange for them to stay with a neighbor or in a kennel if they are likely to be noisy.
5. Arrange with a neighbor to accompany you or keep an eye out, if you feel uneasy showing your home to a man or a couple.

Step 3: Make Finishing Touches

Finishing touches can make a difference when you sell your home. They convey to buyers the idea that you care about the home and find it a wonderful place to live.

If you used the Repair Worksheet and Attractiveness Worksheet, all that is needed for you to show your home to best advantage are the finishing touches, which you can review on the Finishing Touches Checklist.

1. Look successful. When people shop for property, they also shop for lifestyle. Usually wearing tasteful, casual attire is most appropriate.
2. Make sure property is orderly.
3. Make walking safe. Put away anything viewers might trip over or slip on.
4. Secure pets.
5. Arrange for children to be away or stay with neighbors or friends while you show your home.
6. Create quiet or pleasing sounds. Turn off all appliances as well as radio, television, and stereo except for possible soft background music.
7. Make sure that the air temperature is in a pleasant range.
8. Turn on lights.
9. Open window coverings such as drapes, curtains, or shades.
10. Display the benefits of your property, as appropriate. Light the fireplace if it is cold outside or turn on air conditioning if it is hot outside.
11. Create pleasing visual images. Use such items as vases of flowers, a bowl of fruit, and reading material that might interest typical buyers of your home.
12. Create pleasing smells.

- Refrain from cooking strong-smelling food before showing your home.
- Eliminate smoke odor with activated charcoal placed in inconspicuous areas.
- Be sure that pet areas are clean.
- Bake bread or cookies or brew a pot of coffee.
- Put a drop of vanilla on foil in a warm oven.
- Simmer water and citrus peels with spices such as allspice, nutmeg, and/ or cinnamon.

13. Check bathrooms for tidiness just before viewers arrive. Close the toilet lid.

Step 4: Manage Home Tour

To manage the home tour to show your home to its best advantage, consider
  1. Planning the tour to emphasize the best features of your home.
     Show the best features at the beginning or end of tour.
  2. Having viewers sign a guest register. Copy the Guest Register form and put the copies in a notebook for viewers to sign.
  3. Accompanying viewers at all times, remembering to
     - Give viewers adequate time to see your home.
     - Stay with viewers and guide them to the strong points, but do not hover.

FINISHING TOUCHES CHECKLIST

Name:_____Date:_____
Address:_____

Instructions

1. Make copies of this checklist.
2. Use a fresh copy every time you handle the finishing touches.

Checklist

Do	Did	Action
[ ]	[ ]	Dress to look successful.
[ ]	[ ]	Property orderly.
[ ]	[ ]	Walking made safe.
[ ]	[ ]	Pets secured.
[ ]	[ ]	Children away.
[ ]	[ ]	Quiet or pleasing sounds created.
[ ]	[ ]	Air temperature pleasant.
[ ]	[ ]	Lights on.
[ ]	[ ]	Window coverings open.
[ ]	[ ]	Benefits (fireplace, air conditioner, etc.) displayed.
[ ]	[ ]	Pleasing visual images (flowers, fruit, etc.) set out.
[ ]	[ ]	Pleasing smells (bad eliminated, good created).
[ ]	[ ]	Bathrooms checked.

GUEST REGISTER

NAME   ADDRESS   TELEPHONE

_____   _____   _____

_____   _____   _____

_____   _____   _____

_____   _____   _____

_____   _____   _____

_____   _____   _____

_____   _____   _____

_____   _____   _____

_____   _____   _____

_____   _____   _____

_____   _____   _____

_____   _____   _____

_____   _____   _____

_____   _____   _____

_____   _____   _____

_____   _____   _____

- Refrain from intruding in conversations viewers have among themselves.
- Listen carefully and with sincere interest.
- Ask only a few questions. Do not pry.

4. Refraining from negotiating during the tour. You can bargain more effectively later.

Step 5: Sell Your Home

While you are showing prospective buyers your property, you may be more effective if you use low-key sales techniques. Read the methods listed here several times but don't try to memorize them.

1. Know the area. Be able to talk intelligently with buyers about such items as
   - Climate, terrain, and environmental hazards.
   - Age distribution in neighborhood and town planning.
   - Schools, including location and quality.
   - Services and utilities.
   - Recreation facilities and neighborhood improvements.
   - Traffic, transportation, parking, and noise levels.
   - Tax base, zoning, and assessments.
   - Crime rate in the area, plus police and fire protection.
   - Health care facilities and hospitals.
   - Churches and other places of worship.
2. Know your property. It gives you credibility and inspires buyers' confidence. Be able to talk intelligently about
   - Brand names and capacities of major systems and appliances.
   - Insulation, including ceiling, walls, and windows.
   - Utility costs and property taxes.
3. Be polite and friendly in a reserved manner.
   - Be relaxed and confident to give buyers confidence in you and in themselves.
   - Avoid an argument with the viewers. You may win the argument and lose the sale.
4. Answer all questions honestly, briefly, and confidently.
   - Do not exaggerate.
   - If you are selling because of some distress situation (divorce, job loss, illness), keep your reasons for selling to yourself. This way, they cannot be used against you in the negotiation process.
5. If you do not know the answer to a question, tell buyers that you don't know. Inform buyers that you will be happy to find out the answer and let them know. Then be sure to do so.
6. Appeal to buyers' needs.
   - Let most of the outstanding features that meet the buyers' needs speak for themselves.
   - Sell the benefits as a way of life for the buyer (not the features) in a brief manner. Do not oversell.
7. Handle buyers' objections.
   - Objections may be a sign that buyers are seriously interested in your home.
   - Try to understand buyers' objections by putting yourself in the buyers' place.
   - After empathizing with viewers

○ Agree briefly that the objection is valid. Tell how you handled it so it was not a disadvantage.
○ You can also acknowledge that the objection is valid, then explain why it is minor compared to the other qualities of your home.
○ A third alternative is to agree by nodding your head, then change the subject, if the objection depends on personal taste or if you found no way to surmount it.

8. Consider inviting buyers who are viewing your home for the second time to do so unaccompanied by you.
   • Unaccompanied buyers have freedom to explore your home to study how your property would fit their needs.
   • You stay in one room or step outside.
   • You stay in the area so you are available to answer any questions buyers may have.

Step 6: Complete the Sale

Restating the good points of your home is of no use if viewers are already interested in buying it. When viewers make statements that sound as if they might be seriously interested in purchasing your home, *stop selling and start completing the sale!*

1. Ask buyers whether they are interested in submitting an offer.
2. Ask buyers when you can schedule an appointment for them to present an offer to you.
3. Request that buyers submit an offer to you that
   • Is in writing.
   • Covers all important issues.
   • Is accompanied by a personal or cashier's check made out to an acceptable closing or escrow agent.
4. Ask buyers if the company or person you would like to use for the closing is acceptable to them.
5. Give buyers a copy of appropriate documents you prepared.
   • A copy of your disclosure statement.
   • Copies of all inspection reports issued in the last two years concerning the condition of your home.
6. Request that buyers contact a lender and be prequalified for a home loan. Explain that
   • Buyers' prequalification aids in making a decision regarding the offer, if buyers do not have all cash.
   • A lender can issue a written guarantee to finance buyers' home purchase in a specified price range, at a specified interest rate (or within a range), and for a specified period of time.
   • A lender can issue a written guarantee for a short-term bridge or gap loan to buyers who are simultaneously selling one house and trying to buy another.
7. Ask whether buyers feel comfortable preparing an offer. If not, you might
   • Give buyers a copy of the purchase contract to read.
   • Suggest that buyers write down on a separate sheet of paper the way they intend to fill out the form.

- Suggest that you will write the offer with the buyers when you get together the next time.

8. Read the section of Chapter 9 dealing with reevaluating your goals *before* you set up an appointment to negotiate the sale of your property.

9. Read all of Section III of this book before you start to negotiate.

10. When you get an offer
    - Proceed to read Section III of this book.
    - Continue to show your property until you have made an agreement. This agreement should include a signed offer and a check.

Now that you have shown your home successfully, you are ready to prepare for negotiation. Preparing for negotiation includes reevaluating your goals, preparing a preliminary estimate of proceeds, setting up the offer presentation, managing the offer presentation, and being aware of the possibility of revocation of the offer.

CHAPTER 9
Prepare for Negotiation

Prepare for negotiation by reevaluating your goals, scheduling an offer presentation, managing the offer presentation, and being aware of the possibility of a revocation of the offer by buyers.

Step 1: Reevaluate Your Goals

Reevaluate your goals before you begin negotiations with prospective buyers. You have several advantages when you understand the consequences of each decision and make choices based on that understanding.

Types of goals to have clear in your mind include
- Knowledge of the minimum price you will accept.
- Awareness of the type of terms to which you will agree.
- Items to be on the alert for in negotiating.

Consider Price and Terms

Consider both the price and your acceptable terms when you negotiate. The following chart indicates that *if*
- Seller and buyers are both primarily interested in price, they rarely sign a contract.
- A seller is primarily concerned with terms and buyers are mainly concerned with price, they generally sign a contract.
- A seller is primarily concerned with price and buyers are mainly concerned with terms, they usually sign a contract.
- Seller and buyers both have the greatest concern about terms, they generally reach an agreement, too.

		SELLER	
		Price	Terms
BUYER	Price	No agreement	Agreement
	Terms	Agreement	Agreement

Prepare Negotiating Goals Worksheet

The Negotiating Goals Worksheet helps to make your priorities in negotiating the sale of your home clear to you.
1. Write out all of the goals you wish to achieve relating to negotiating the sale of your home.

NEGOTIATING GOALS WORKSHEET
Number   Goal

_____   _____
_____   _____
_____   _____
_____   _____
_____   _____
_____   _____
_____   _____
_____   _____
_____   _____
_____   _____
_____   _____
_____   _____
_____   _____

PRIORITIZED NEGOTIATING GOALS WORKSHEET
Number   Goals

_____   _____
_____   _____
_____   _____
_____   _____
_____   _____
_____   _____
_____   _____
_____   _____
_____   _____
_____   _____
_____   _____
_____   _____
_____   _____

2. Prioritize the goals you listed above by placing a number to the left of each goal. (Make the most important goal 1, the second most important goal 2, and so on.)
3. Rewrite your goals in their order of importance. This prioritized goals list provides you with a reference as you negotiate the sale of your home.

Prepare Estimate of Proceeds Worksheet—Preliminary

To get a clear idea of how much you plan to receive from selling your home, prepare the Estimate of Proceeds Worksheet—Preliminary.

1. Enter the information requested at the top of each page.
2. Check the costs you intend to pay when you sell your home.
   - *Appraisal fee:* Cost for hiring an appraiser to determine the current market value of your property in order to make a loan to the buyers. Buyers usually pay.

ESTIMATE OF PROCEEDS WORKSHEET

[ ] <u>PRELIMINARY</u>   [ ] <u>WORKING</u>   [ ] <u>COUNTER OFFER</u>

Seller_____ Buyer_____
Property_____
Selling price_____ Type of financing_____
Date prepared_____ Proposed closing date_____

<u>ESTIMATED COSTS</u>

Pay Cost   Amount Notes
[ ] Appraisal fee $ _____
[ ] Assessments   _____ [ ] Prorate, $ from page 3
[ ] Assumption fee   _____
[ ] Attorney fees   _____
[ ] Beneficiary statement _____
[ ] Credit report   _____
[ ] Delinquent payments   _____
[ ] Demand fees   _____
[ ] Document preparation   _____
[ ] Drawing deed   _____
[ ] Escrow/closing fees   _____
[ ] Homeowner's insurance _____
[ ] Homeowner's assn. fee _____ [ ] Prorate, $ from page 3
[ ] Home warranty   _____
[ ] Impounds   _____ [ ] Prorate, $ from page 3
[ ] Interest   _____ [ ] Prorate, $ from page 3
[ ] Loan origination fee   _____
[ ] Loan tie-in fee   _____
[ ] Notary fee   _____
[ ] Pest control inspection _____
[ ] Pest control repair   _____
[ ] Physical inspection fee _____
[ ] Points   _____
[ ] Prepayment penalty   _____
[ ] Property taxes   _____ [ ] Prorate, $ from page 3
[ ] Reconveyance fee   _____
[ ] Recording fee   _____
[ ] Satisfaction of mort. _____
[ ] Subescrow fee   _____
[ ] Survey fee   _____
[ ] Title insurance   _____
[ ] Title search fee   _____
[ ] Transfer tax   _____
[ ] Other _____   _____
TOTAL EST. COSTS $ _____

ESTIMATE OF PROCEEDS WORKSHEET

Type of worksheet [ ] PRELIMINARY [ ] WORKING [ ] COUNTER OFFER

ESTIMATED ENCUMBRANCES

Pay Encumbrance	Amount	Notes
[ ] 1st loan	$ _____	_____
[ ] 2nd loan	_____	_____
[ ] 3rd loan	_____	_____
[ ] Improvement bonds	_____	_____
[ ] Liens	_____	_____
[ ] Other	_____	_____
TOTAL ENCUMBRANCES	$ _____	

ESTIMATED CREDITS

Pay Credits	Amount	Notes
[ ] Assessments	$ _____	_____
[ ] Bonds	_____	_____
[ ] Homeowner's assoc. dues	_____	_____
[ ] Impounds	_____	_____
[ ] Insurance	_____	_____
[ ] Interest	_____	_____
[ ] Property taxes	_____	_____
[ ] Rental payments	_____	_____
TOTAL EST. CREDITS	$ _____	

ESTIMATED DEBITS

	Amount	Notes
Total estimated costs	$ _____	From page 1
Total estimated encumbrances	_____	From page 2
TOTAL EST. DEBITS	$ _____	

CALCULATIONS

Proposed selling price	$	_____
Total estimated debits	−	_____
Subtotal	=	_____
Total estimated credit	+	_____
SELLER'S EST. PROCEEDS	=	_____
Note financed by you (seller)	−	_____
Seller's estimate of cash	=	
from sale	$	_____

ESTIMATE OF PROCEEDS WORKSHEET

Type of worksheet [ ] <u>PRELIMINARY</u> [ ] <u>WORKING</u> [ ] <u>COUNTER OFFER</u>

Item prorated_____

PRORATIONS
1. Assume a 30 day month and 360 day year for estimate purposes.
   a. To borrow days from Month column, subtract 1 month from Month column and add 30 days to Day column.
   b. To borrow months from Year column, subtract 1 year from Year column and add 12 months to Month column.
2. Seller does not pay costs for the day of the closing.
3. For items for which you have not paid, such as interest and property taxes, enter value on the proper line under the heading <u>Estimated Costs</u>.
4. For items for which you prepaid, such as insurance, taxes, and rents, enter value on the proper line under the heading <u>Estimated Credits</u>.

<u>Total days for which the payment applies</u>

	Year	Month	Day				
Ending	____	____	____	Year ____ × 360 =	____ days
-Starting	____	____	____	+ Month____ × 30 =	____ days
	____	____	____	+ Day ____ × 1 =	____ days

Total days (a)   ____

<u>Actual days for which the seller must pay</u>

	Year	Month	Day		
Ending	____	____	____	Year ____ × 360 =	____ days
-Starting	____	____	____	+ Month____ × 30 =	____ days
	____	____	____	+ Day ____ × 1 =	____ days

Actual days (b)   ____

<u>Payment per day</u>
Total payment required (c)	$_____
Total days (a)	+ _____
Payment per day (d)	= $_____

<u>Seller's payment required</u>
Payment per day (d)	$_____
Actual days (b)	× _____
Seller's payment (e)	= $_____

<u>Seller's credit for item that has been paid in advance</u>
Total payment required (c)	$_____
Seller's payment (e)	− $_____
Seller's credit for item	= $_____

- *Assessments:* Taxes or charges by a governmental body in addition to normal property taxes for a property owner's proportionate cost of specific improvements, such as schools, streets, and sewers. You and buyers usually pay your prorated share of assessments.

- *Assumption fee (transfer fee):* A charge for the work involved to transfer the mortgage from you to buyers. Buyers generally pay.

- *Attorney's fees (legal fees):* Charges by an attorney for legal advice and/or assistance. Whoever hires the attorney usually pays. If you hire an attorney to assist you with your home sale, you pay, unless you negotiate otherwise. If the matter is decided by a court of law, then the person against whose favor the case is decided must pay the fees.

- *Beneficiary statement:* A statement provided by a lender using a trust deed type of loan. On this statement a lender usually lists the remaining principal balance, interest payments, loan due dates, terms of payment, insurance data, taxes, assessments, and any other claims that do not appear on trust deed documents. Whoever handles the closing usually requires a beneficiary statement when buyers take over a trust deed. You generally pay.

- *Buyer's fees:* A term sometimes used to include a number of charges that are paid by buyers. See appraisal fee, assumption fee, credit report fee, points, loan origination fees, mortgage insurance fee, survey fee, and title insurance fee. Buyers usually pay.

- *Casualty insurance:* See homeowner's insurance.

- *Credit report:* Charge for a detailed report of buyers' credit history. Lenders usually require a credit report before making a loan to buyers. Lenders may include this charge as part of a loan fee. Buyers usually pay.

- *Defaults:* See delinquent payments.

- *Delinquent payments:* Failure to make loan payments when they are due. You usually pay.

- *Demand fee (demand for payoff charge):* A fee for a written request to a lender for the lender's demand for the payment of the loan in full and the supporting documents necessary for release of the lien against the property. Demands are used if you intend to pay off the existing loan in full. You usually pay.

- *Demand for payoff charge:* See demand fee.

- *Discount points:* See points.

- *Document preparation:* Charges for drawing up and preparing legal papers. The party that pays generally depends on the type of document being prepared. You typically pay for preparation of documents in favor of (to) the buyers.

- *Documentary transfer tax:* See transfer tax.

- *Drawing deed:* A fee for the preparation of a deed. The party that pays depends on the type of deed prepared. The party that benefits from the deed generally pays.

- *Closing/escrow fees:* Charges paid to the escrow holder or closing agent for handling the escrow or closing. Usually split evenly between you and the buyers.

- *Fire insurance:* See homeowner's insurance.

- *Geological inspection:* A charge for an investigation by a soils engineer for potential or actual geological problems, generally including but not limited to soil subsidence, fill, landslides, flooding, and earthquakes. Buyers usually pay.

- *Hazard insurance:* See homeowner's insurance.
- *Homeowner's insurance:* Insurance protection against stated specific hazards such as fire, hail, windstorms, earthquakes, floods, civil disturbances, explosions, riots, theft, and vandalism. Lenders usually require at least minimum coverage to protect their interest in a property. The lender's interest in the property is the balance of the loan that has not yet been paid. Buyers usually pay.
- *Home inspection fee:* See physical inspection fee.
- *Homeowner's association fees:* Monthly fees owners of homes pay to their homeowner's association. These dues can be for such items as maintenance, gardening, trash collection, outside lighting, pool, spa, and tennis courts. These dues are generally prorated.
- *Home protection plan:* See home warranty.
- *Home warranty (home protection plan):* Fee for insurance that the items listed in the contract (such as plumbing, wiring, water heater, and major appliances) are in working order for the specified length of time. Traditionally, you pay.
- *Impounds (reserve fund):* Funds held by the lender to assure payment in the future of recurring expenses. This money is generally held in a trust-type account. These expenses can include FHA mortgage premiums, insurance premiums, real estate taxes, and sewer and water taxes. Impounds are generally prorated. If you have prepaid these expenses, you should receive the excess at the close of escrow. If, however, you have not paid these expenses you will be charged for your portion of the costs.
- *Interest:* A charge or rate paid to a lender for borrowing money. Interest on existing loans is paid from the last monthly payment until the closing date. Interest is paid after the charge is incurred (in arrears). Interest on an existing loan is usually prorated.
- *Judgments:* Final determinations by a court of matters presented to it. A judgment is a general monetary obligation on all the property of the person who owes the money (debtor). This obligation applies in each county where an abstract of the court judgment was recorded. You, as the debtor, usually pay.
- *Legal fees:* See attorney's fees.
- *Loan discount fees:* See points.
- *Loan origination fee:* Lender's charge for arranging and processing a loan. The fee is usually based on a percentage of the loan. Buyers typically pay.
- *Loan tie-in fee:* A fee charged by whoever handles the closing or escrow for their work and liability in conforming to the lender's criteria for the buyers' new loan. Buyers generally pay.
- *Notary fee:* A charge paid to a notary public to guarantee signatures on some of the legal documents in the transaction. A notary public guarantees the signatures by demanding and receiving proof of a person's identity. The notary then attaches his or her name and seal to the document to notarize it. You typically pay fees on documents in favor of the buyers. Buyers generally pay notary charges on documents in favor of you and/or the lender.
- *Pest control inspection (structural pest control inspection fee, termite inspection fee):* The cost of the inspection of your property by a licensed pest control

inspector for infestation or infections by wood-destroying organisms. You generally pay. However, if you use a purchase contract similar to the one shown it provides that

- o If the report recommends inspection of inaccessible areas, buyers may request that the inspection be done at their own expense.
- o If no infestation, infection, or damage is found, buyers pay the cost of entry and closing the inaccessible areas.
- o If infestation, infection, or damage is found, you pay the cost of entry and closing of the inaccessible areas.

- *Pest control repair charge (structural pest control repair charge):* Cost of repairing any damage done by infestation or infection of property by wood-destroying organisms. You usually pay all charges, unless you negotiate or use a contract that states otherwise. Consider having a contract that provides that buyers pay for any work to correct conditions considered likely to lead to infestation or infection by wood-destroying organisms where there is no evidence of existing infestation or infection.
- *Physical inspection fee (home inspection fee):* A fee for a study of property's site, structures, systems, and appliances. Buyers usually pay.
- *Points (discount points, loan discount fee):* A one-time charge by the lender to adjust the yield on the loan to current market conditions or to adjust the rate on the loan to the level required by federal or state regulations. Each point is equal to one percent of the loan balance. This fee is treated as prepaid interest for tax purposes. Buyers usually pay; however, you are legally required to pay VA discount points.
- *Prepayment penalty:* The fine imposed on a borrower by a lender for the early payoff of a loan or any substantial part of a loan. You usually pay.
- *Property taxes (taxes):* The amount of the tax usually depends on the amount of the valuation of the property. You typically pay for property taxes that are due but which you have not yet paid.
- *Reconveyance fee:* A fee charged for the deed filed at the county recorder's office to record payment in full of a trust deed and transfer legal title from the trustee to you. You usually pay.
- *Recording fee:* Fee charged for the entry of your transaction into the official records at the county recorder's office. You usually pay for the recording of documents in favor of buyers. Buyers generally pay for the recording of documents in favor of the lender.
- *Reserve fund:* See impounds.
- *Satisfaction of mortgage:* A document signed by the holder of the mortgage that indicates you have paid your mortgage off in full. You generally pay.
- *Structural pest control inspection:* See pest control inspection.
- *Subescrow fee:* A fee charged by a title company for the firm's costs and liability when it handles money. You usually pay.
- *Survey fee:* Charge for a survey showing the exact location and boundaries of a property. Buyers usually pay.
- *Taxes:* See property taxes.
- *Tax stamp fee:* See transfer tax.
- *Termite inspection:* See pest control inspection.
- *Title examination fee:* See title search fee.
- *Title insurance:* A policy for protection against claims in the future based on circumstances in the past. This type of insurance is issued by the title

company on completion of the final title search. Title insurance coverage requirements vary depending on the need of the parties (seller, buyers, and lender) for a specific type of coverage, the amount of money each of the parties will pay for coverage, the type of property covered, complexity of the transaction, and exceptions and encumbrances to the title.

- ○ *Basic coverage:* All title insurance has basic coverage, including matters of public record such as encumbrances, liens, and judgments; forgery and fraud; lack of capacity (persons not being able to enter into a contract because they are minors or not of sound mind); and improper delivery (the deed has not met the criteria for proper delivery).

- ○ *Standard coverage insurance:* The regular investigation for standard insurance reveals only matters of record and the location of the improvements with respect to the lot line. These matters include access to public streets; defects in the title; charges, claims, or liens on the title; inability to sell the property due to unacceptable encumbrances on the title; vesting (interest that cannot be revoked) being other than stated. You or buyers may pay for standard coverage depending on what you negotiated or local customs. Standard owner's (joint protection) policy provides insurance to the buyers and the lender. Standard lender policy provides coverage for the lender only.

- ○ *Extended coverage insurance:* Extended coverage protects against numerous risks that are not a matter of record. This coverage usually requires a survey, which includes a thorough search, checking with government agencies, and on-site field work. Extended coverage policies generally cost considerably more than standard policies. These policies insure against all risks insured against by the standard policy *plus* claims not previously disclosed by examination of public record. Buyers usually pay for an extended coverage owner's policy.

- ○ *Special endorsements:* Special endorsements are clauses used to modify, expand, or delete the coverage of any policy.

- • *Title search fee (title examination fee):* A charge for the examination of information recorded on your property at the county recorder's office. This examination is to verify that the property has no outstanding claims or liens against it that could adversely affect buyers or lender. It also verifies that you can transfer clear legal title to the property. The party that pays traditionally depends on the customs in your area.

- • *Transfer tax (documentary transfer tax):* A tax that some states allow individual counties or cities to charge on the transfer of real property, including homes. This tax is often based on the amount of equity being transferred to the buyers. You typically pay.

- • *Other fees:* List fees you use that are not on the previous list.

3. Check the monetary encumbrances (claims or charges against a property) that exist against your property.
   - • First, second, or third loans (mortgages or trust deeds).
   - • Home equity line of credit. (Credit given by a lender based on the amount of equity the owner has in the property. The line of credit becomes a loan secured by a mortgage or trust deed when the borrower uses some or all of the credit.)
   - • Improvement bond (a debt secured by a government loan financing improvements within a district).

- Liens (charges against property for the payment of a debt or obligation).
- Other (such items as delinquent property taxes).

4. Check the expenses that you feel will be prorated. Prorations are adjustments to the amount owed by you and the buyers. These adjustments must be made because escrow rarely transfers title exactly corresponding to the paid-up dates of expenses, such as assessments, bonds, homeowner's association dues, impound accounts, insurance premiums, interest on existing loans, maintenance fees, property taxes, and rental payments. Buyers owe you for any time period after escrow closes for which you have already paid. You owe buyers for any time period before escrow closes for which you have not yet paid. For this estimate, base prorations on a 360-day year of 12 months, each containing 30 days.

5. Check which of the estimated credits you feel will be due to you. These items will be the prorations for which buyers owe you because you have already paid.

6. Obtain estimates for items you checked from sources listed.

   a. Costs
   - Appraisal fee—Local appraisers or lenders.
   - Assessments—Your property tax bill.
   - Assumption fee—The lender who made your home loan.
   - Attorney's fees—Local attorneys or the local bar association.
   - Beneficiary statement fee—The lender who made your home loan.
   - Credit report—Lender who made your home loan or other local lenders.
   - Delinquent payments—Lender who made your home loan.
   - Demand fee—Lender who made your home loan.
   - Document preparation fees—Whomever you want to handle closing, such as your lawyer, escrow or title company, or the escrow department of your bank.
   - Drawing deed—Whomever you want to do the closing, such as your lawyer, the escrow department of your bank, or an escrow or title company.
   - Escrow/closing fees—Whomever you want to do the closing, such as your lawyer, the escrow department of your bank, or an escrow company.
   - Geological inspection fee—Local soils engineering companies.
   - Homeowner's association fees—Your homeowner's association.
   - Homeowner's insurance—The company that currently insures your house.
   - Home warranty—Home warranty companies, represented locally.
   - Impounds—Lender who made your home loan.
   - Interest—Lender who made your home loan.
   - Judgments—Your title insurance company.
   - Loan origination fee—Local lenders.
   - Loan tie-in fee—Local escrow companies or the person whom you plan to have handle closing.
   - Notary fee—The person or company you plan to have handle closing or escrow.
   - Pest control inspection—Local pest control companies.
   - Pest control repair charge—Local pest control companies.
   - Physical inspection fee—Local home inspection companies.
   - Points—Local lenders.
   - Prepayment penalty—Lender who made your loan.
   - Property taxes—Your property tax bill.
   - Reconveyance fee—Trustee on your trust deed.

- Recording fee—Your county recorder or the person whom you want to handle the closing.
- Satisfaction of mortgage—Lender on your mortgage.
- Subescrow fee—Local title companies.
- Survey fee—Local survey companies.
- Title insurance—Local title insurance companies.
- Title search fee—Local title insurance companies.
- Transfer tax—Whomever you want to handle closing, such as your lawyer, the escrow department of your bank, or an escrow or title company.

  b. Encumbrances

- Loans, including home equity lines of credit—Lenders who made the loans.
- Improvement bonds—Your property tax bill or local title insurance companies.
- Liens other than loans—Local title insurance companies.

7. Add each column separately to obtain total estimated amounts for each column.
8. Add total estimated costs and total estimated encumbrances to obtain estimated debits.
9. Calculate your net proceeds from your proposed home sale.
   - a. Enter your proposed selling price.
   - b. Subtract total estimated debits.
   - c. Enter the subtotal.
   - d. Add the total estimated credits.
   - e. Obtain your estimate of proceeds from the proposed sale.
10. If you plan to finance a note for buyers and you want to estimate how much cash you might receive in that case,
    - a. Enter the amount you plan to finance.
    - b. Subtract the amount you plan to finance from your estimate of proceeds.
    - c. Enter the difference, which is the estimate of cash from such a sale.

Step 2: Set Up Offer Presentation

When?

Choose a time for an offer presentation when you are at your best, a time when

- You are rested, calm, and feeling well.
- You are able to have an offer presentation conference in a convenient and unhurried manner.
- You have reviewed not only what price and terms you will consider but also how to conduct the negotiation.

Where?

Have buyers present their offer at your clutter-free dining room or kitchen table. Maintain a quiet, business-like atmosphere in this area during the discussion.

How?

Consider

1. Informing everyone concerned about the exact location and time of the offer presentation.

2. After everyone arrives, introducing everyone who is present and explaining each of their roles in the offer presentation.
3. Insisting on seeing a written offer signed by buyers before you negotiate.
4. Giving buyers a copy of the disclosure statement and all inspection reports issued in the last two years on your home before they make the offer.

For multiple offers in a short time period, you might have buyers make offer presentations in the order that the buyers contacted you. Legally you can consider offers in any order in most areas. Maintaining the order may discourage hard feelings or unfounded charges by some potential buyers.

Step 3: Handle the Offer Presentation

Handle the offer presentation so that it works well for you.

Manage Offer Presentation

To manage the offer presentation to your best advantage,
1. Have buyers or their agent make the offer presentation.
2. Be aware of buyers' techniques. Some buyers may use a number of insidious but often powerful techniques to attempt to make you feel ill at ease and negotiate less effectively. If you recognize these techniques, you then may be able to avoid their pressure.
   - Buyers arrive late for your meeting.
     a. Remain calm if buyers are late. Becoming upset may cost you money.
     b. If buyers are more than 20 minutes late or you become upset, consider rescheduling the meeting for another mutually agreeable time.
   - Buyers make a telephone call when you are meeting.
     a. Request that they make the call after the meeting.
     b. Ask to set up the appointment for a time that would be more convenient for you both.
   - Buyers seem to care less about buying your home than you do about selling it; they appear disinterested.
     a. Remain objective.
     b. Be prepared to make a counter offer.
     c. Sign only agreements with which you are comfortable.
     d. Talk only to your consultants about the agreement you are negotiating. You will not be embarrassed if the agreement changes or does not go through.
     e. Spend money only after you receive it so you do not force yourself to accept detrimental changes.
   - Buyers make misleading or incorrect statements.
     a. Only believe what you hear if it is verified by someone without an interest in the transaction.
     b. Obtain a written copy of the statement signed by the buyers.
   - Buyers voice their opinions about things they feel are wrong with your property.
     a. Realize that buyers are trying to unnerve you and better their own bargaining position.
     b. Remain calm.

- Buyers make many notes.
  a. Understand that buyers may think that if they make many notes you may become nervous.
  b. Remain calm.
- Buyers may get too close to you for your comfort.
  a. Recognize that buyers may be trying to take your mind off the negotiations.
  b. If you are bothered, ask them to move away.
- Buyers may use statements that seem to sound authoritative or seem to put you down.
  a. Understand buyers are seldom authorities; they may be opinionated or trying to cover up their own ignorance.
  b. Ask questions, even if you fear buyers may think that you don't know the answers.
  c. Remember, the price or terms you get for your property may depend on your response.
- Buyers may try to pressure you into making an agreement at the last minute by appealing to your emotions using dramatic actions and words.
  a. Recognize that buyers may be attempting to play on your emotions.
  b. Tell buyers you need time to consider the offer.

3. Study each section of the offer carefully, particularly
   - The contingencies listed in the offer.
   - The time limits set by the buyers. Time limits should be adequate but not needlessly long.
4. Ask questions about each point covered in the contract that you are unsure of or do not understand.
5. Allow buyers or their agent to answer your questions and fully explain each point.
6. Inform buyers or their agent that you want time to consider the offer.
   a. Thank buyers courteously for their offer.
   b. Tell buyers you will consider their offer.
   c. Inform buyers you will let them know your decision within three business days (or an appropriate time limit under the circumstances). Consider never rejecting buyers' offer immediately.
   d. Take your time and prepare a counter offer.
   e. Remember that negotiation is a give and take process.
7. If you decide to negotiate, remember
   - Use logic to explain the soundness of your requests.
   - Compromise; exchange buyer's request for one of your own.
8. If you decide to accept buyers' offer
   - Accept a written offer *only* to prevent any questions as to when the contract was signed from arising later.
   - Sign your acceptance on the same form on which the offer was made.

Be Aware of Revocation Possibility

Be aware that an offer may be revoked (called back) in writing by buyers at any time before you communicate to buyers that you have accepted their offer.

After you have prepared for the negotiation, you are ready to study the contract in detail so that you understand it well.

CHAPTER 10
Understand Purchase Contracts

An important aspect of achieving your goals is your familiarity with the form you will be using. Your understanding of this form and ability to fill it in to accurately reflect your decisions are essential in saving you money and anxiety in your sale of your home.

Step 1: Learn About Contracts

Note that the following priorities exist in contracts in most states in the event of discrepancies or inconsistencies:
- Written words usually take precedence over printed and typed wording.
- Typed words generally take precedence over printed wording but not over written wording.
- Specific provisions in a contract usually supersede the general provisions.
- A real estate purchase contract normally takes precedence over escrow instructions, if the two do not agree.

Step 2: Understand Purchase Contract

A purchase contract is the basic agreement between you and buyers for their purchase of your home. Many variations of this form exist. Here we present the most up-to-date form available in California at the time we wrote this book. The form we present is the Real Estate Purchase Contract and Receipt for Deposit published by the California Association of Realtors.
1. Study the form presented, which gives you a comprehensive generic sampling of purchase contracts' contents.
2. Check with your consultants to obtain a copy of the type of purchase contract used in your area.
3. Query your consultants if you have questions regarding
   - Differences between the forms.
   - Applicability of sections you feel you might want to include in your contract.

The Real Estate Purchase Contract and Receipt for Deposit is shown. We explain, as appropriate, the form's expected responses, possible choices, and probable consequences, as well as give our recommendations.

REAL ESTATE PURCHASE CONTRACT AND RECEIPT FOR DEPOSIT

THIS IS MORE THAN A RECEIPT FOR MONEY. IT IS INTENDED TO BE A LEGALLY BINDING CONTRACT. READ IT CAREFULLY.
CALIFORNIA ASSOCIATION OF REALTORS® (CAR) STANDARD FORM

_____, California, _____, 19____

Received from _____

herein called Buyer, the sum of _____ Dollars $_____

evidenced by ☐ cash, ☐ cashier's check, ☐ personal check or ☐ _____ , payable to _____

_____ , to be held uncashed until acceptance of this offer as deposit on account of purchase price of

_____ Dollars $_____

for the purchase of property, situated in _____ , County of _____ California,

described as follows: _____

1. **FINANCING:** The obtaining of Buyer's financing is a contingency of this agreement.

   A. DEPOSIT upon acceptance, to be deposited into _____ $ _____

   B. INCREASED DEPOSIT within _____ days of acceptance to be deposited into _____ $ _____

   C. BALANCE OF DOWN PAYMENT to be deposited into _____ on or before _____ $ _____

   D. Buyer to apply, qualify for and obtain a NEW FIRST LOAN in the amount of . . . . $ _____

   payable monthly at approximately $_____ including interest at origination not to exceed _____%,

   ☐ fixed rate, ☐ other _____ all due _____ years from date of origination. Loan fee not to

   exceed _____ . Seller agrees to pay a maximum of _____ FHA/VA discount points.

   Additional terms _____

   _____

   E. Buyer ☐ to assume, ☐ to take title subject to an EXISTING FIRST LOAN with an approximate balance of . . . . $ _____

   in favor of _____ payable monthly at $_____ including interest at _____% ☐ fixed rate,

   ☐ other _____ . Fees not to exceed _____ .

   Disposition of impound account _____

   Additional terms _____

   F. Buyer to execute a NOTE SECURED BY a ☐ first, ☐ second, ☐ third DEED OF TRUST in the amount of . . . . $ _____

   IN FAVOR OF SELLER payable monthly at $_____ ☐ or more, including interest at _____% all due

   _____ years from date of origination, ☐ or upon sale or transfer of subject property. A late charge of _____

   _____ shall be due on any installment not paid within _____ days of the due date.

   ☐ Deed of Trust to contain a request for notice of default or sale for the benefit of Seller. Buyer ☐ will, ☐ will not execute a request

   for notice of delinquency. Additional terms _____

   _____

   G. Buyer ☐ to assume, ☐ to take title subject to an EXISTING SECOND LOAN with an approximate balance of . . . . $ _____

   in favor of _____ payable monthly at $_____ including interest at _____%

   ☐ fixed rate, ☐ other _____ . Buyer fees not to exceed _____

   Additional terms _____

   H. Buyer to apply, qualify for and obtain a NEW SECOND LOAN in the amount of . . . . $ _____

   payable monthly at approximately $_____ including interest at origination not to exceed _____% ☐ fixed rate,

   ☐ other _____ , all due _____ years from date of origination.

   Buyer's loan fee not to exceed _____ . Additional terms _____

   _____

   I. In the event Buyer assumes or takes title subject to an existing loan, Seller shall provide Buyer with copies of applicable notes and Deeds

   of Trust. A loan may contain a number of features which affect the loan, such as interest rate changes, monthly payment changes, balloon

   payments, etc. Buyer shall be allowed _____ calendar days after receipt of such copies to notify Seller in writing of disapproval.

   FAILURE TO NOTIFY SELLER IN WRITING SHALL CONCLUSIVELY BE CONSIDERED APPROVAL. Buyer's approval shall not be

   unreasonably withheld. Difference in existing loan balances shall be adjusted in ☐ Cash, ☐ Other _____

   _____

   J. Buyer agrees to act diligently and in good faith to obtain all applicable financing. _____

   _____

   _____

   K. ADDITIONAL FINANCING TERMS: _____

   _____

   _____

   _____

   L. TOTAL PURCHASE PRICE . . . . $ _____

2. **OCCUPANCY:** Buyer ☐ does, ☐ does not intend to occupy subject property as Buyer's primary residence.

3. **SUPPLEMENTS:** The ATTACHED supplements are incorporated herein:

   ☐ Interim Occupancy Agreement (CAR FORM IOA-11)   ☐ _____

   ☐ Residential Lease Agreement after Sale (CAR FORM RLAS-11)   ☐ _____

   ☐ VA and FHA Amendments (CAR FORM VA/FHA-11)   ☐ _____

4. **ESCROW:** Buyer and Seller shall deliver signed instructions to _____ the escrow holder, within _____ calendar days

   of acceptance of the offer which shall provide for closing within _____ calendar days of acceptance. Escrow fees to be paid as follows:

   _____

   _____

Buyer and Seller acknowledge receipt of copy of this page, which constitutes Page 1 of _____ Pages.

Buyer's Initials (_____) (_____)   Seller's Initials (_____) (_____)

THIS STANDARDIZED DOCUMENT FOR USE IN SIMPLE TRANSACTIONS HAS BEEN APPROVED BY THE CALIFORNIA ASSOCIATION OF REALTORS® IN FORM ONLY. NO REPRESENTATION IS MADE AS TO THE APPROVAL OF THE FORM OF ANY SUPPLEMENTS NOT CURRENTLY PUBLISHED BY THE CALIFORNIA ASSOCIATION OF REALTORS® OR THE LEGAL VALIDITY OR ADEQUACY OF ANY PROVISION IN ANY SPECIFIC TRANSACTION. IT SHOULD NOT BE USED IN COMPLEX TRANSACTIONS OR WITH EXTENSIVE RIDERS OR ADDITIONS.

A REAL ESTATE BROKER IS THE PERSON QUALIFIED TO ADVISE ON REAL ESTATE TRANSACTIONS. IF YOU DESIRE LEGAL OR TAX ADVICE, CONSULT AN APPROPRIATE PROFESSIONAL.

OFFICE USE ONLY
Reviewed by Broker or Designee _____
Date _____

Copyright © 1989, CALIFORNIA ASSOCIATION OF REALTORS®
525 South Virgil Avenue, Los Angeles, California 90020
REVISED 2/89

REAL ESTATE PURCHASE CONTRACT AND RECEIPT FOR DEPOSIT (DLF-14 PAGE 1 OF 4)

Subject Property Address: _____

5. TITLE: Title is to be free of liens, encumbrances, easements, restrictions, rights and conditions of record or known to Seller, other than the following: (a) Current property taxes, (b) covenants, conditions, restrictions, and public utility easements of record, if any, provided the same do not adversely affect the continued use of the property for the purposes for which it is presently being used, unless reasonably disapproved by Buyer in writing within _____ calendar days of receipt of a current preliminary report furnished at _____ expense, and (c) _____

Seller shall furnish Buyer at _____ expense a California Land Title Association policy issued by _____
_____ Company, showing title vested in Buyer subject only to the above. If Seller is unwilling or unable to eliminate any title matter disapproved by Buyer as above, Buyer may terminate this agreement. If Seller fails to deliver title as above, Buyer may terminate this agreement; in either case, the deposit shall be returned to Buyer.

6. VESTING: Unless otherwise designated in the escrow instructions of Buyer, title shall vest as follows: _____
_____.
(The manner of taking title may have significant legal and tax consequences. Therefore, give this matter serious consideration.)

7. PRORATIONS: Property taxes, payments on bonds and assessments assumed by Buyer, interest, rents, association dues, premiums on insurance acceptable to Buyer, and _____ shall be paid current and prorated as of ☐ the day of recordation of the deed; or ☐ _____. Bonds or assessments now a lien shall be ☐ paid current by Seller, payments not yet due to be assumed by Buyer; or ☐ paid in full by Seller, including payments not yet due; or ☐ _____. County Transfer tax shall be paid by _____. The _____ transfer tax or transfer fee shall be paid by _____. **PROPERTY WILL BE REASSESSED UPON CHANGE OF OWNERSHIP. THIS WILL AFFECT THE TAXES TO BE PAID.** A Supplemental tax bill will be issued, which shall be paid as follows: (a) for periods after close of escrow, by Buyer (or by final acquiring party if part of an exchange), and (b) for periods prior to close of escrow, by Seller. TAX BILLS ISSUED AFTER CLOSE OF ESCROW SHALL BE HANDLED DIRECTLY BETWEEN BUYER AND SELLER.

8. POSSESSION: Possession and occupancy shall be delivered to Buyer, ☐ on close of escrow, or ☐ not later than _____ days after close of escrow, or ☐ _____.

9. KEYS: Seller shall, when possession is available to Buyer, provide keys and/or means to operate all property locks, and alarms, if any.

10. PERSONAL PROPERTY: The following items of personal property, free of liens and without warranty of condition, are included: _____
_____

11. FIXTURES: All permanently installed fixtures and fittings that are attached to the property or for which special openings have been made are included in the purchase price, including electrical, light, plumbing and heating fixtures, built-in appliances, screens, awnings, shutters, all window coverings, attached floor coverings, TV antennas, air cooler or conditioner, garage door openers and controls, attached fireplace equipment, mailbox, trees and shrubs, and _____ except _____.

12. SMOKE DETECTOR(S): State law requires that residences be equipped with an operable smoke detector(s). Local law may have additional requirements. Seller shall deliver to Buyer a written statement of compliance in accordance with applicable state and local law prior to close of escrow.

13. TRANSFER DISCLOSURE: Unless exempt, Transferor (Seller), shall comply with Civil Code §§1102 et seq., by providing Transferee (Buyer) with a Real Estate Transfer Disclosure Statement: (a) ☐ Buyer has received and read a Real Estate Transfer Disclosure Statement; or (b) ☐ Seller shall provide Buyer with a Real Estate Transfer Disclosure Statement within _____ calendar days of acceptance of the offer after which Buyer shall have three (3) days after delivery to Buyer, in person, or five (5) days after delivery by deposit in the mail, to terminate this agreement by delivery of a written notice of termination to Seller or Seller's Agent.

14. TAX WITHHOLDING: Under the Foreign Investment in Real Property Tax Act (FIRPTA), IRC §1445, *every* Buyer of U.S. real property *must*, unless an exemption applies, deduct and withhold from Seller's proceeds 10% of the gross sales price. Under California Revenue and Taxation Code §§18805 and 26131, the Buyer must deduct and withhold an additional one-third of the amount required to be withheld under federal law. The primary FIRPTA exemptions are: No withholding is required if (a) Seller provides Buyer with an affidavit under penalty of perjury, that Seller is not a "foreign person," or (b) Seller provides Buyer with a "qualifying statement" issued by the Internal Revenue Service, or (c) Buyer purchases real property for use as a residence and the purchase price is $300,000 or less and Buyer or a member of Buyer's family has definite plans to reside at the property for at least 50% of the number of days it is in use during each of the first two twelve-month periods after transfer. Seller and Buyer agree to execute and deliver as directed any instrument, affidavit, or statement reasonably necessary to carry out those statutes and regulations promulgated thereunder.

15. MULTIPLE LISTING SERVICE: If Broker is a Participant of an Association/Board multiple listing service ("MLS"), the Broker is authorized to report the sale, its price, terms, and financing for the publication, dissemination, information, and use of the authorized Board members, MLS Participants and Subscribers.

16. ADDITIONAL TERMS AND CONDITIONS:
ONLY THE FOLLOWING PARAGRAPHS 'A' THROUGH 'K' *WHEN INITIALLED BY BOTH BUYER AND SELLER* ARE INCORPORATED IN THIS AGREEMENT.
Buyer's Initials   Seller's Initials
___/___   ___/___   **A. PHYSICAL AND GEOLOGICAL INSPECTION:** Buyer shall have the right, at Buyer's expense, to select a licensed contractor and/or other qualified professional(s), to make "Inspections" (including tests, surveys, other studies, inspections, and investigations) of the subject property, including but not limited to structural, plumbing, sewer/septic system, well, heating, electrical, built-in appliances, roof, soils, foundation, mechanical systems, pool, pool heater, pool filter, air conditioner, if any, possible environmental hazards such as asbestos, formaldehyde, radon gas and other substances/products, and geologic conditions. Buyer shall keep the subject property free and clear of any liens, indemnify and hold Seller harmless from all liability, claims, demands, damages, or costs, and repair all damages to the property arising from the "Inspections." All claimed defects concerning the condition of the property that adversely affect the continued use of the property for the purposes for which it is presently being used (☐ or as _____) shall be in writing, supported by written reports, if any, and delivered to Seller within _____ calendar days FOR "INSPECTIONS" OTHER THAN GEOLOGICAL, and/or within _____ calendar days FOR GEOLOGICAL "INSPECTIONS," of acceptance of the offer. Buyer shall furnish Seller copies, at no cost, of all reports concerning the property obtained by Buyer. When such reports disclose conditions or information unsatisfactory to the Buyer, which the Seller is unwilling or unable to correct, Buyer may cancel this agreement. Seller shall make the premises available for all Inspections. BUYER'S FAILURE TO NOTIFY SELLER IN WRITING SHALL CONCLUSIVELY BE CONSIDERED APPROVAL.
Buyer's Initials   Seller's Initials
___/___   ___/___   **B. CONDITION OF PROPERTY:** Seller warrants, through the date possession is made available to Buyer: (1) property and improvements, including landscaping, grounds and pool/spa, if any, shall be maintained in the same condition as upon the date of acceptance of the offer, and (2) the roof is free of all known leaks, and (3) built-in appliances, and water, sewer/septic, plumbing, heating, electrical, air conditioning, pool/spa systems, if any, are operative, and (4) Seller shall replace all broken and/or cracked glass; (5) _____.
Buyer's Initials   Seller's Initials
___/___   ___/___   **C. SELLER REPRESENTATION:** Seller warrants that Seller has no knowledge of any notice of violations of City, County, State, Federal, Building, Zoning, Fire, Health Codes or ordinances, or other governmental regulation filed or issued against the property. This warranty shall be effective until the date of close of escrow.

Buyer and Seller acknowledge receipt of copy of this page, which constitutes Page 2 of _____ Pages.
Buyer's Initials (_____) (_____)   Seller's Initials (_____) (_____)

OFFICE USE ONLY
Reviewed by Broker or Designee _____
Date _____

EQUAL HOUSING OPPORTUNITY

REAL ESTATE PURCHASE CONTRACT AND RECEIPT FOR DEPOSIT (DLF-14 PAGE 2 OF 4)

Subject Property Address _____

Buyer's Initials   Seller's Initials

_____ / _____   **D. PEST CONTROL:** (1) Within _____ calendar days of acceptance of the offer, Seller shall furnish Buyer at the expense of ☐ Buyer, ☐ Seller, a current written report of an inspection by _____, a licensed Structural Pest Control Operator, of the main building, ☐ detached garage(s) or carport(s), if any, and ☐ the following other structures on the property:

_____

(2) If requested by either Buyer or Seller, the report shall separately identify each recommendation for corrective measures as follows:

      "Section 1": Infestation or infection which is evident.

      "Section 2": Conditions that are present which are deemed likely to lead to infestation or infection.

(3) If no infestation or infection by wood destroying pests or organisms is found, the report shall include a written Certification as provided in Business and Professions Code § 8519(a) that on the date of inspection "no evidence of active infestation or infection was found."

(4) All work recommended to correct conditions described in "Section 1" shall be at the expense of ☐ Buyer, ☐ Seller.

(5) All work recommended to correct conditions described in "Section 2," if requested by Buyer, shall be at the expense of ☐ Buyer, ☐ Seller.

(6) The repairs shall be performed with good workmanship and materials of comparable quality and shall include repairs of leaking showers, replacement of tiles and other materials removed for repairs. It is understood that exact restoration of appearance or cosmetic items following all such repairs is not included.

(7) Funds for work agreed to be performed after close of escrow, shall be held in escrow and disbursed upon receipt of a written Certification as provided in Business and Professions Code § 8519(b) that the inspected property "is now free of evidence of active infestation or infection."

(8) Work to be performed at Seller's expense may be performed by Seller or through others, provided that (a) all required permits and final inspections are obtained, and (b) upon completion of repairs a written Certification is issued by a licensed Structural Pest Control Operator showing that the inspected property "is now free of evidence of active infestation or infection."

(9) If inspection of inaccessible areas is recommended by the report, Buyer has the option to accept and approve the report, or within _____ calendar days from receipt of the report to request in writing further inspection be made. BUYER'S FAILURE TO NOTIFY SELLER IN WRITING OF SUCH REQUEST SHALL CONCLUSIVELY BE CONSIDERED APPROVAL OF THE REPORT. If further inspection recommends "Section 1" and/or "Section 2" corrective measures, such work shall be at the expense of the party designated in subparagraph (4) and/or (5), respectively. If no infestation or infection is found, the cost of inspection, entry and closing of the inaccessible areas shall be at the expense of the Buyer.

(10) Other _____

_____ .

Buyer's Initials   Seller's Initials

_____ / _____   **E. FLOOD HAZARD AREA DISCLOSURE:** Buyer is informed that subject property is situated in a "Special Flood Hazard Area" as set forth on a Federal Emergency Management Agency (FEMA) "Flood Insurance Rate Map" (FIRM), or "Flood Hazard Boundary Map" (FHBM). The law provides that, as a condition of obtaining financing on most structures located in a "Special Flood Hazard Area," lenders require flood insurance where the property or its attachments are security for a loan.

The extent of coverage and the cost may vary. For further information consult the lender or insurance carrier. No representation or recommendation is made by the Seller and the Broker(s) in this transaction as to the legal effect or economic consequences of the National Flood Insurance Program and related legislation.

Buyer's Initials   Seller's Initials

_____ / _____   **F. SPECIAL STUDIES ZONE DISCLOSURE:** Buyer is informed that subject property is situated in a Special Studies Zone as designated under §§ 2621-2625, inclusive, of the California Public Resources Code; and, as such, the construction or development on this property of any structure for human occupancy may be subject to the findings of a geologic report prepared by a geologist registered in the State of California, unless such a report is waived by the City or County under the terms of that act.

Buyer is allowed _____ calendar days from acceptance of the offer to make further inquiries at appropriate governmental agencies concerning the use of the subject property under the terms of the Special Studies Zone Act and local building, zoning, fire, health, and safety codes. When such inquiries disclose conditions or information unsatisfactory to the Buyer, which the Seller is unwilling or unable to correct, Buyer may cancel this agreement. BUYER'S FAILURE TO NOTIFY SELLER IN WRITING SHALL CONCLUSIVELY BE CONSIDERED APPROVAL.

Buyer's Initials   Seller's Initials

_____ / _____   **G. ENERGY CONSERVATION RETROFIT:** If local ordinance requires that the property be brought in compliance with minimum energy.Conservation Standards as a condition of sale or transfer, ☐ Buyer, ☐ Seller shall comply with and pay for these requirements. Where permitted by law, Seller may, if obligated hereunder, satisfy the obligation by authorizing escrow to credit Buyer with sufficient funds to cover the cost of such retrofit.

Buyer's Initials   Seller's Initials

_____ / _____   **H. HOME PROTECTION PLAN:** Buyer and Seller have been informed that Home Protection Plans are available. Such plans may provide additional protection and benefit to a Seller or Buyer. The CALIFORNIA ASSOCIATION OF REALTORS® and the Broker(s) in this transaction do not endorse or approve any particular company or program:

a) ☐ A Buyer's coverage Home Protection Plan to be issued by _____

    Company, at a cost not to exceed $_____, to be paid by ☐ Buyer, ☐ Seller; or

b) ☐ Buyer and Seller elect not to purchase a Home Protection Plan.

Buyer's Initials   Seller's Initials

_____ / _____   **I. CONDOMINIUM/P.U.D.:** The subject of this transaction is a condominium/planned unit development (P.U.D.) designated as unit _____ and _____ parking space(s) and an undivided interest in community areas, and _____

_____ . The current monthly assessment charge by the homeowner's association or other governing body(s) is $_____ . As soon as practicable, Seller shall provide Buyer with copies of covenants, conditions and restrictions, articles of incorporation, by-laws, current rules and regulations, most current financial statements, and any other documents as required by law. Seller shall disclose in writing any known pending special assessment, claims, or litigation to Buyer. Buyer shall be allowed _____ calendar days from receipt to review these documents. If such documents disclose conditions or information unsatisfactory to Buyer, Buyer may cancel this agreement. BUYER'S FAILURE TO NOTIFY SELLER IN WRITING SHALL CONCLUSIVELY BE CONSIDERED APPROVAL.

Buyer's Initials   Seller's Initials

_____ / _____   **J. LIQUIDATED DAMAGES: If Buyer fails to complete said purchase as herein provided by reason of any default of Buyer, Seller shall be released from obligation to sell the property to Buyer and may proceed against Buyer upon any claim or remedy which he/she may have in law or equity; provided, however, that by initialling this paragraph Buyer and Seller agree that Seller shall retain the deposit as liquidated damages. If the described property is a dwelling with no more than four units, one of which the Buyer intends to occupy as his/her residence, Seller shall retain as liquidated damages the deposit actually paid, or an amount therefrom, not more than 3% of the purchase price and promptly return any excess to Buyer. Buyer and Seller agree to execute a similar liquidated damages provision, such as CALIFORNIA ASSOCIATION OF REALTORS® Receipt for Increased Deposit (RID-11), for any increased deposits. (Funds deposited in trust accounts or in escrow are not released automatically in the event of a dispute. Release of funds requires written agreement of the parties, judicial decision or arbitration.)**

Buyer and Seller acknowledge receipt of copy of this page, which constitutes Page 3 of _____ Pages.

Buyer's Initials (_____) (_____)   Seller's Initials (_____) (_____)

OFFICE USE ONLY

Reviewed by Broker or Designee _____

Date _____

REAL ESTATE PURCHASE CONTRACT AND RECEIPT FOR DEPOSIT (DLF-14 PAGE 3 OF 4)

Subject Property Address ____________________

K. ARBITRATION OF DISPUTES: Any dispute or claim in law or equity arising out of this contract or any resulting transaction shall be decided by neutral binding arbitration in accordance with the rules of the American Arbitration Association, and not by court action except as provided by California law for judicial review of arbitration proceedings. Judgment upon the award rendered by the arbitrator(s) may be entered in any court having jurisdiction thereof. The parties shall have the right to discovery in accordance with Code of Civil Procedure § 1283.05. The following matters are excluded from arbitration hereunder: (a) a judicial or non-judicial foreclosure or other action or proceeding to enforce a deed of trust, mortgage, or real property sales contract as defined in Civil Code § 2985, (b) an unlawful detainer action, (c) the filing or enforcement of a mechanic's lien, (d) any matter which is within the jurisdiction of a probate court, or (e) an action for bodily injury or wrongful death, or for latent or patent defects to which Code of Civil Procedure § 337.1 or § 337.15 applies. The filing of a judicial action to enable the recording of a notice of pending action, for order of attachment, receivership, injunction, or other provisional remedies, shall not constitute a waiver of the right to arbitrate under this provision.

Any dispute or claim by or against broker(s) and/or associate licensee(s) participating in this transaction shall be submitted to arbitration consistent with the provision above only if the broker(s) and/or associate licensee(s) making the claim or against whom the claim is made shall have agreed to submit it to arbitration consistent with this provision.

"NOTICE: BY INITIALLING IN THE SPACE BELOW YOU ARE AGREEING TO HAVE ANY DISPUTE ARISING OUT OF THE MATTERS INCLUDED IN THE 'ARBITRATION OF DISPUTES' PROVISION DECIDED BY NEUTRAL ARBITRATION AS PROVIDED BY CALIFORNIA LAW AND YOU ARE GIVING UP ANY RIGHTS YOU MIGHT POSSESS TO HAVE THE DISPUTE LITIGATED IN A COURT OR JURY TRIAL. BY INITIALLING IN THE SPACE BELOW YOU ARE GIVING UP YOUR JUDICIAL RIGHTS TO DISCOVERY AND APPEAL, UNLESS THOSE RIGHTS ARE SPECIFICALLY INCLUDED IN THE 'ARBITRATION OF DISPUTES' PROVISION. IF YOU REFUSE TO SUBMIT TO ARBITRATION AFTER AGREEING TO THIS PROVISION, YOU MAY BE COMPELLED TO ARBITRATE UNDER THE AUTHORITY OF THE CALIFORNIA CODE OF CIVIL PROCEDURE. YOUR AGREEMENT TO THIS ARBITRATION PROVISION IS VOLUNTARY."

"WE HAVE READ AND UNDERSTAND THE FOREGOING AND AGREE TO SUBMIT DISPUTES ARISING OUT OF THE MATTERS INCLUDED IN THE 'ARBITRATION OF DISPUTES' PROVISION TO NEUTRAL ARBITRATION."

Buyer's Initials ____/____ Seller's Initials ____/____

17. **OTHER TERMS AND CONDITIONS:** ____________________

18. **ATTORNEY'S FEES:** In any action, proceeding or arbitration arising out of this agreement, the prevailing party shall be entitled to reasonable attorney's fees and costs.
19. **ENTIRE CONTRACT:** Time is of the essence. All prior agreements between the parties are incorporated in this agreement which constitutes the entire contract. Its terms are intended by the parties as a final expression of their agreement with respect to such terms as are included herein and may not be contradicted by evidence of any prior agreement or contemporaneous oral agreement. The parties further intend that this agreement constitutes the complete and exclusive statement of its terms and that no extrinsic evidence whatsoever may be introduced in any judicial or arbitration proceeding, if any, involving this agreement.
20. **CAPTIONS:** The captions in this agreement are for convenience of reference only and are not intended as part of this agreement.
21. **AGENCY CONFIRMATION:** The following agency relationship(s) are hereby confirmed for this transaction:

LISTING AGENT: ____________________ (Print Firm Name) is the agent of (check one):

☐ the Seller exclusively; or ☐ both the Buyer and Seller

SELLING AGENT: ____________________ (Print Firm Name) (if not the same as Listing Agent) is the agent of (check one):

☐ the Buyer exclusively; or ☐ the Seller exclusively; or ☐ both the Buyer and Seller.

22. **AMENDMENTS: This agreement may not be amended, modified, altered or changed in any respect whatsoever except by a further agreement in writing executed by Buyer and Seller.**
23. **OFFER:** This constitutes an offer to purchase the described property. Unless acceptance is signed by Seller and a signed copy delivered in person, by mail, or facsimile, and received by Buyer at the address below, or by ____________________ who is authorized to receive it, on behalf of Buyer, within ________ calendar days of the date hereof, this offer shall be deemed revoked and the deposit shall be returned. Buyer has read and acknowledges receipt of a copy of this offer. This agreement and any supplement, addendum or modification relating hereto, including any photocopy or facsimile thereof, may be executed in two or more counterparts, all of which shall constitute one and the same writing.

REAL ESTATE BROKER ____________________ BUYER ____________________

By ____________________ BUYER ____________________

Address ____________________ Address ____________________

Telephone ____________________ Telephone ____________________

ACCEPTANCE

The undersigned Seller accepts and agrees to sell the property on the above terms and conditions and agrees to the above confirmation of agency relationships (☐ subject to attached counter offer).

Seller agrees to pay to Broker(s) ____________________

compensation for services as follows: ____________________.

Payable: (a) On recordation of the deed or other evidence of title, or (b) if completion of sale is prevented by default of Seller, upon Seller's default, or (c) if completion of sale is prevented by default of Buyer, only if and when Seller collects damages from Buyer, by suit or otherwise, and then in an amount not less than one-half of the damages recovered, but not to exceed the above fee, after first deducting title and escrow expenses and the expenses of collection, if any. Seller shall execute and deliver an escrow instruction irrevocably assigning the compensation for service in an amount equal to the compensation agreed to above. In any action, proceeding, or arbitration between Broker(s) and Seller arising out of this agreement, the prevailing party shall be entitled to reasonable attorney's fees and costs. The undersigned has read and acknowledges receipt of a copy of this agreement and authorizes Broker(s) to deliver a signed copy to Buyer.

Date ____________ Telephone ____________ SELLER ____________________

Address ____________________

SELLER ____________________

Real Estate Broker(s) agree to the foregoing.

Broker ____________ By ____________ Date ____________

Broker ____________ By ____________ Date ____________

Page 4 of ________ Pages.

OFFICE USE ONLY

Reviewed by Broker or Designee ________

Date ________

EQUAL HOUSING OPPORTUNITY

REAL ESTATE PURCHASE CONTRACT AND RECEIPT FOR DEPOSIT (DLF-14 PAGE 4 OF 4)

When you fill out a form, consider filling in each blank with either the specific information you desire to convey or with the words **not applicable** as appropriate, so that no information can be added later. The only spaces that should be left blank are those requiring signatures and dates. If you amend a contract later, make the changes on a separate sheet.

Completing the Contract Preliminaries

Sum
The sum of wording asks for an amount written as words.

Dollars
Dollars followed by the blank for the dollar amount requests an amount written as numbers.

Evidence of Payment
Payment may be evidenced in one or a combination of several ways.
- Cash—Count cash several times and give a receipt to the buyer. Obtain a receipt for the exact amount when you deposit it with the closing agent or escrow holder.
- Cashier's check—A bank's own check guaranteed to be good by that bank.
- Personal check—Buyers usually use a personal check for the initial deposit. Be aware that buyers may not have sufficient funds in their personal account when you try to cash their check.
- Jewelry, furniture, works of art, and so on—You may accept these items as partial or full deposit. We do not recommend them because they are difficult to identify, set a value on, and in some cases store.

Payable to
Consider asking buyers to make out a check to the closing agent or escrow holder (often a title or escrow company) on which you and buyers agree. This action should prevent any accusation by buyers that you have misused funds.

Completing Item 1: Financing
This contract depends on buyers obtaining financing.

A. Deposit
Wherever you live, consider requiring a deposit (earnest money) from buyers as evidence of their intention and ability to buy in exchange for tying up your property by signing a contract with buyers. In theory, if buyers default, they forfeit the deposit. Failing to make a good faith effort to remove contingencies or backing out of a contract without good reason are generally considered defaults.

In practice, because home purchase contracts usually contain contingency clauses, buyers seldom forfeit deposits to sellers. Sellers also seldom receive forfeited deposits because title and escrow companies rarely release deposit money without the written consent of both parties.

Still, we recommend deposits. Most buyers are much more likely to act in good faith to attempt to buy your property if they made a substantial deposit.

Deposited into. Consider choosing an escrow holder who handles many of these transactions each year to hold the deposit. This escrow holder is most likely to give you the best service and price. Institutional lenders such as banks and savings and loans often have escrow departments within their own organizations. Other escrow holders include attorneys and real estate brokers.

Amount of Deposit. The amount of the initial deposit is often $500 to $5000 or more, depending on the price of your home and the amount common in your area.

B. Increased Deposit

Depending on the amount of the initial deposit, buyers may increase the deposit by a specified date. Buyers usually increase a deposit to demonstrate that they are serious about wanting to purchase your home.

Time Limit. Usually, on or before 10 to 14 days after your acceptance is ample time for the buyers to increase the deposit.

Deposited into. Generally you designate **escrow** or **the closing agent** as the receiver of the funds.

Amount of Increased Deposit. The amount of the increased deposit, if any, depends on what you negotiate with the buyers. For example, the buyers may have some questions about your home. They will offer you a small initial deposit and agree to pay you the balance of a larger amount of deposit after certain conditions are met. These conditions might include a clear preliminary title report or a clear termite report.

C. Down Payment Balance

Down payment is the money you and buyers agree on or that a lender requires buyers to pay toward the purchase price before escrow can close. A deposit is generally part, but not all, of the down payment. Buyers usually pay the final amount of the down payment on or before a particular date *or* before the occurrence of a specified action such as the close of escrow.

If you will be carrying a loan from buyers or are remaining primarily or secondarily liable for the loan, consider weighing the advantages and disadvantages of different amounts of down payment. Decide a range of down payments within which you are comfortable selling your home. See Chapter 3 for more information regarding down payments.

Deposited into. Usually you designate **escrow** or **with the closing agent**.

Time Limit. Specified date or the occurrence of a certain action, such as the closing of escrow.

Amount of Down Payment Balance. The final amount of the down payment. This amount is often the sum needed to make the total deposit equal to 5 percent to 10 percent of the purchase price.

Example:

Price of house	$ 150,000
Percentage down payment	× .10
Total down payment needed	$ 15,000
Total down payment needed	$ 15,000
Less deposit	− 1,000
Less increased deposit	− 2,000
Balance of down payment	$ 12,000

D. New First Loan

Buyers will apply for, qualify for, and secure a new first loan (mortgage or trust deed). Buyers may need to obtain a new first loan for one of the following reasons:

- You currently have no first loan on your home.
- You or the lender are not willing for the buyer to assume or take title subject to an existing loan.

Loan Type. The buyers choose the type of loan they want to obtain in order to purchase your home.

- Fixed rate loan—A loan on which the percentage of interest remains at the same rate and payments of principal remain equal over the life of the loan.
- Adjustable rate loan—A loan that allows periodic adjustments in interest rate. This loan adjusts at a specified period of time based on a named index.

Loan Fee Maximum. Loan fees are one-time charges by lenders for initiating a loan. Buyers are usually willing to pay no more than a maximum of 3 percent of the loan amount in loan fees. Loan fees usually include points, appraisal costs, and charges for credit checks.

Discount Points. Each discount point is equal to 1 percent of the loan total. This fee is paid to the lender when the lender makes the loan. Federal regulations require the seller to pay VA discount points. Buyer or seller may pay FHA discount points, depending on what you negotiate.

Additional Terms. Consider including

- The stipulation that buyers must qualify for a loan within 10 days from the opening of escrow.
- The designation of who pays which loan fees. These fees generally include the costs for points (loan origination fees), an appraisal, and a credit check. See the discussion of these costs later in the chapter.
- If your house does not appraise at the value on which you and buyers agreed, you have several options:
  o Buyers may pay for the difference between the appraisal and the purchase price.
  o You both may renegotiate the price of the home.
  o You both may revoke (cancel) the contract.

E. Existing First Loan

If you will allow buyers to assume or take title subject to an existing first (most senior) loan, use this section.

Assuming and Taking Title Subject to. Be sure you understand the effects of allowing buyers to assume or take title subject to an existing first loan.

- Assume—Buyers take over primary responsibility for the payment of the existing loan and primary liability for any deficiency judgment arising from it. You become secondarily liable for the loan and for any deficiency judgment arising from it. A deficiency judgment makes an individual personally liable for the payoff of a remaining amount due because less than the full amount was obtained by foreclosure.
- Take title subject to—Buyers take over responsibility for payment on an existing loan without taking on the liability of a deficiency judgment. You remain primarily responsible for the loan and any deficiency judgment arising from it.

Approximate Balance. Give an estimate of the amount you owe on the first loan.

In Favor of. The party to whom the loan is in favor of is the lender on the first loan.

Interest Rate. The *current* rate of interest on the loan. For information about fixed rate and adjustable rate loans, see item 1D under Loan Type earlier in this chapter.

Loan Fee Maximum. Give the maximum loan fee. For information regarding loan fees, see item 1D under Loan Fee Maximum earlier in this chapter. For disposition of the impound account, indicate how you want the account handled. *Impound accounts* are trust accounts established by lenders to accumulate funds to meet certain debts.

These debts may include taxes, premiums on homeowner's insurance policies, and/or FHA mortgage insurance premiums. Lenders usually collect these funds along with note payments, then place funds in a trust account. The contents of impound accounts are generally prorated as of the close of escrow. You and buyers may negotiate another date if you wish.

Additional Terms. Indicate additional terms you want included. If you fill in this section, you should also fill in section I of this agreement.

F. Note Secured by a Deed of Trust in Favor of the Seller

You can act as a lender to carry back (hold) loans from buyers. These notes may be first, second, or even third loans. They may be mortgages or trust deeds depending on the type of loan used in your area. For details regarding seller carry back loans, see Chapter 3.

Deeds of Trust. If buyers plan to obtain money for the purchase as more than one loan, use this section for the most senior loan. Indicate the seniority of the loan (first, second, or third). Place information regarding any other notes secured by mortgages or trust deeds that you may make to buyers in an additional financing terms section of the agreement.

Interest Rate. For the interest rate on a loan in favor of the seller, consider checking with your escrow holder or title representative regarding federally required and assigned (imputed) interest rules before entering a percentage in this blank. Federally imputed interest rate rules are for federal income tax calculations only. If you do not charge a federally set minimum interest rate on a loan, the federal government taxes you as if you had charged the minimum. Consult your tax preparer or accountant for further details.

Due Date. Consider using this or a similar due-on-sale clause in a loan. It not only makes the loan due at a specific time but also gives you the right to call (demand payment of) all sums owed immediately due and payable if buyers sell or otherwise transfer title. You may then decide whether to continue the loan with the new owners or request the loan be paid off.

Late Charge. A late charge is often set at 5 to 10 percent of the usual payment by sellers. The charge is negotiable. The number of days following the due date after which a late charge will be added is negotiable. Sellers often request 5 to 15 days.

Request for Notice of Default or Sale. Making sure the loan (trust deed or mortgage) contains a notice of default or sale is for your benefit.

- If buyers default on loan, you will know to make the payments on the senior loan to protect your investment.
- If buyers sell the property, you will be notified so you can collect the money owed to you on the loan.

Request for Notice of Delinquency. Buyers have the choice of whether or not to execute (sign) a request for notice of delinquency, although they may ask for your advice. Advising buyers when their payment is late is more work for you. Informing buyers can be worth the effort if it helps remind buyers to make payments they forgot.

Additional Terms. If you checked **or upon sale or transfer of the subject property**, consider using a prepayment penalty, the fine imposed on buyers for repaying a loan early.

G. Existing Second Loan

If you are willing to have buyers assume or take title subject to an existing second loan, use this section. You can eliminate this contingency by

1. Obtaining lender's permission for buyers to assume your second loan or take title subject to your first loan.
2. Requiring buyers to prequalify with the lender to assume or take title subject to your second loan.

Information regarding the buyer assuming or taking title to an existing loan is the same as for an existing first loan, described earlier in item E.

In Favor of. The name of the lender on the second loan.

Interest Rate. Enter the *current* rate of interest on the loan, no matter what type of loan is involved.

Type of Loan. See item 1D under Type of Loan earlier in this chapter.

H. New Second Loan

Buyers may want or need a new second loan because
- Buyers do not have sufficient ready cash to pay up to the amount of the first loan.
- You or the lender would not be willing for buyers to assume or take title subject to the existing second loan.
- Buyers may be able to obtain a loan at a lower interest rate than the rate of the loan you currently have.

Type of Loan. See item 1D under Type of Loan earlier in this chapter.

Loan Fee. See item 1D under Loan Fee Maximum earlier in this chapter.

Additional Terms. See item 1D under Additional Terms earlier in this chapter.

I. Loan Copies and Balances

If buyers assume or take title subject to an existing loan, you must provide buyers with copies of documents that apply to that loan for the buyer to approve or disapprove.

Time Limit. Ten calendar days after buyers receive copies of documents that apply to the loan is considered ample time for buyers to notify you in writing of their disapproval.

Loan Balance Difference Adjustment. You and the buyers may agree on one or several methods to adjust (make up the difference) between estimated amount of the existing loan and the actual amount of the existing loan. These methods include the buyer paying cash for the difference, the lender changing the loan amount to include the difference, or you carrying back financing for the difference. See Chapter 3 regarding seller carry back financing.

J. Diligence and Good Faith

You must rely on buyers to act with diligence and good faith to obtain financing. Consider requiring buyers to prequalify for a loan(s) before you sign an agreement with them.

Time Limits. Thirty days after the opening of escrow is generally sufficient time for buyers to obtain all applicable financing.

K. Additional Financing Terms

Enter any other financing terms that are too lengthy to fit into another section or do not apply to other sections. These terms might include such items as
- *All Inclusive Trust Deed (AITD, Wraparound Mortgage, Overriding Deed of Trust):* A junior loan at one overall interest rate used to wrap existing mortgages or trust deeds into a package. The amount is sufficient to cover the existing loan and provide extra for you, the seller. You make payments on existing loan(s) from buyers' payments. You remain primarily responsible for the mortgages or trust deeds wrapped. See Chapter 3 for more details regarding these loans.

- *Seller Buy-down:* A loan in which the effective interest rate is bought down or reduced during the beginning years of the loan by your contributions. You are really paying buyers' interest in advance. This lower interest rate usually lasts two or three years. You may increase the price to cover this added cost. See Chapter 3 for more information.

Completing Item 2: Occupancy

Occupancy information is for lenders. Lenders offer a better rate on a property occupied by the owner.

Completing Item 3: Supplements

Supplements are contracts that are incorporated in an agreement, although they are not written on the same form as the agreement. Supplements listed include those described here.

Interim Occupancy Agreement

The interim occupancy agreement is a lease purchase agreement used in California to rent your home *to* the buyers *before* the sale. For more information on lease purchase agreements, see Chapter 12.

Residential Lease Agreement After Sale

A residential lease agreement after sale is a sale leaseback agreement used in California to lease your former home *from* the buyers *after* the sale. For more information on sale leaseback agreements, see Chapter 12.

VA and FHA Amendments

These amendments are on a form used in California describing financial arrangements when buyers are getting a new Veterans Administration (VA) or Federal Housing Administration (FHA) loan on the property.

Residential Lease Option

Although they are not printed on forms, consider using lease options and purchase option agreements under the appropriate circumstances. The lease option, or lease with an option to buy, is a combination lease, purchase contract, and option. Use a lease option type form if you and potential buyers make an agreement that includes
- You leasing your property to buyers for the specified rental payment.
- Buyers having the right and the option to purchase your home for the amount listed in the contract within the period of time agreed on by you and buyers.
- Buyers paying you a lease option fee if they do not purchase the property.
See Chapter 12 for further information.

Real Estate Purchase Option

A purchase option or option to buy is a combination purchase contract and option. Use a purchase option if you and buyers negotiate a contract in which buyers agree to
- Make the purchase within the listed period of time, *if* they decide to buy the property.
- Purchase the property for the amount listed and under the terms in the contract, *if* they decide to buy your home.

•ˈ Pay an option fee to you if they do not use the option.
See Chapter 12 for further information.

Completing Item 4: Escrow

Escrow is a process by which you and buyers deposit documents and/or money with a neutral third party. You both give instructions for the third party to hold and disburse documents and funds after certain listed conditions are met.

Delivery of Escrow Instructions

Lenders in many areas often require an escrow as a condition for making a loan. Institutional lenders, such as banks and savings and loans, have escrow departments within their own organizations. Other escrow holders include attorneys and real estate brokers. The choice of an escrow holder is negotiable between you and the buyers. Consider choosing an escrow holder who handles many of these transactions each year. That party is most likely to be competent.

Time Limit

The amount of time until closing depends on what steps are necessary.
- Within 45 to 60 days from your acceptance is usually considered sufficient time.
- For houses upon which new FHA or VA loans must be obtained, allow about 90 days after your acceptance of buyers' offer to close of escrow.
- For transactions that are all cash or in which the necessary inspections were performed before signing the contract, 20 days after your acceptance of buyer's offer may be all that is required.

Escrow Fees

Escrow fees are negotiable. You and buyers usually split this cost equally.

Completing Item 5: Title

Title insurance protects parties to the sale against claims in the future based on circumstances in the past.

Title insurance coverages vary depending on the needs of the parties (you, buyers, and lender) for a particular coverage, amount of money each is willing to pay, type of property covered, complexity of the transaction, and exceptions and encumbrances to the title. See Chapter 9 for further information regarding title insurance.

Time Limit

Within 10 calendar days of receipt of the current preliminary title report is usually ample time for buyers to disapprove the report in writing.

Expense

The party that traditionally pays title insurance fees depends on local customs in your area. Check with your local lender, title representative, or escrow officer if you are unsure.

Completing Item 6: Vesting

Vesting, the manner in which buyers hold title, may have significant legal and tax consequences. Each method of holding title has certain advantages and disadvantages, depending on the buyer's situation and objectives.

Vesting of Title

If buyers ask you how they should vest title, suggest they consult their attorney.

Completing Item 7: Prorations

Prorations distribute responsibility for payment of expenses of home ownership. This distribution is based on the percentage of an assessment or billing period during which you and buyers own the property. Prorations may be calculated as of any mutually agreeable date.

Items usually prorated include property taxes, insurance premiums, interest on loans, homeowner dues, and rents. Other items may be prorated if you and buyers agree.

Proration Date

Date options for prorations include but are not limited to the date the deed is recorded in the county recorder's office, the date of the close of escrow, or the date of possession (the date buyers may physically move into the property).

Bonds and Assessments

The party that pays bonds or assessments is negotiable. Generally you pay bonds or assessments that are now a lien while payments that are not yet due are assumed by buyers.

Although you may pay most bonds and assessments in full, including all payments not yet due, some liens must be assumed because they legally cannot be paid off. Liens that must be assumed are often treated as a credit to buyers in escrow or a reduction of the purchase price.

County Transfer Tax

Transfer tax or documentary transfer fee is a tax that some states allow individual counties and/or cities to place on the transferral of real property, including homes. Tax stamps, used in some areas, are a method of showing that a transfer tax has been paid. Buyers generally pay for tax stamps. These stamps are then attached to the deed to prove that the tax has been paid.

Whether buyers or sellers pay the tax is negotiable. You traditionally pay, although some states may have laws requiring buyers to pay in certain types of sales. Check with your escrow holder or attorney regarding the laws in your state.

Other Transfer Tax

In some states, counties and cities may each impose their own documentary transfer tax. Whether buyers or sellers pay the tax is negotiable. You typically pay this tax. Check with a closing agent, escrow holder, or attorney to see
- *If* there is a transfer tax or stamp tax required.
- The rate of taxation for each transfer tax required.
- What amount is considered to be taxable.

Completing Item 8: Possession

Possession means that buyers may physically move into the property.

Close of Escrow

Indicate whether you and buyers agree that buyers get possession at close of escrow. At close of escrow is the time title usually transfers to buyers. You can
- Move out of your home *before* close of escrow. The house is available for buyers to move into immediately after close of escrow, so that you do not owe buyers any money. You must make all payments on the home you are selling up to the close of escrow as well as paying for wherever you are staying in the meantime.

- Move out of your home *at* the close of escrow. In this way you are not paying for two places to stay. The exact date for the close of escrow is often difficult to determine. Even if a date is set, the date may change.

Not Later Than

At the close of escrow title usually transfers to buyers. You pay buyers rent from the day escrow closes until you actually move out. Rent is usually computed on a daily basis. The advantage is you are not paying for two places to stay. The disadvantage is the rent you pay is based on buyers' cost of ownership, which is usually more than your cost when it was your own home.

Three days after the close of escrow is usually sufficient time to allow you to move out.

Other Possession Arrangements

Avoid renting your home to buyers or even allowing them to move a few things into the house before escrow closes.

- Buyers have less incentive to complete escrow if they are living in your home. They may live in your home at less cost than they will pay after the purchase.
- Buyers may find many small things not to their liking and try to avoid purchasing your home.
- Buyers may be difficult to remove from your home if escrow should fail.

Completing Item 9: Keys

You must provide buyers keys and/or means to operate (such as combinations) all locks and alarms on the property on the possession date.

Completing Item 10: Personal Property

Personal property is considered items that are not permanently attached to your home or other structures on your property. Items of personal property that you list here you include in the sale of your home. These listed items are free of any liens against them (money owed or rights of others regarding the items). You do not guarantee the condition of the items you list.

Completing Item 11: Fixtures

Fixtures and fittings are considered items that are permanently attached to or for which special openings have been made in your home and its associated structures. They are included in the purchase price and are transferred with the home unless you and buyers agree to specifically exclude certain items.

Completing Item 12: Smoke Detector(s)

Laws in some states require a home to be equipped with at least one approved smoke detector in good working order. Local laws may contain added regulations regarding number, type, and placement of smoke detectors. In some cases you must deliver a written statement that you have complied with applicable local and state laws before escrow can close. Check with the escrow holder or your real estate attorney regarding applicable laws.

Completing Item 13: Transfer Disclosure

In some states when you sell your home you must provide buyers with a copy of real estate transfer disclosure unless the transfer is exempt. Check with your closing agent, escrow holder, or attorney to determine if you must meet disclosure requirements on the sale of your property and the nature of those requirements. You usually must disclose

- Information you know about the property.
- Information that you, a reasonable homeowner, should know about the property.
- A reasonable approximation based on the best information available to you that is listed as such.

Time Limit

Within 15 days is usually ample time for you to deliver a disclosure statement to buyers after you accept their purchase contract. If you do not provide a disclosure statement within the time indicated, buyers may have the right to end the purchase contract by delivering a written termination notice to you within the time limits shown.

Completing Item 14: Tax Withholding

A federal law ensuring that foreign nationals who sell property in the USA pay capital gains tax on their profit makes buyers responsible for the collection of those taxes.

Buyers may ask you to sign an affidavit stating that you are *not* a nonresident alien for the purposes of U.S. income taxation in order to comply with FIRPTA regulations. FIRPTA is the Foreign Investment in Real Property Tax Act. FIRPTA requires *buyers* to deduct and withhold 10 percent of the sales price to pay the tax *unless* an exemption applies.

See Chapter 17 for more details.

Completing Item 15: Multiple Listing Service

A multiple listing service (MLS) is an agency to which real estate brokers may belong to pool their listings and commissions with other real estate brokers. If a real estate broker is involved in the sale of your home *and* the broker participates in an MLS, the broker may act as indicated.

Completing Item 16: Additional Terms and Conditions

The original purpose of inspections was to protect property buyers. Sellers now order inspections more often because inspection reports can convince buyers that you have nothing to hide and also provide proof of disclosure often required by law. If one is not performed previous to the signing of the purchase contract, then

- Whoever requested the inspection hires the inspector.
- You cooperate by arranging for an inspector to enter the necessary areas within a reasonable length of time.
- If inspectors' reports disclose conditions or facts unacceptable to buyers that you are unwilling or unable to correct, buyers may cancel this agreement.

Although buyers may cancel, you and buyers may also negotiate who pays for which repairs, *or* you may reduce the price to buyers to account for some or all needed repairs. Some lenders may require that the amount of the price reduction be used to make the repairs before they allow escrow to close.

A. Physical and Geological Inspection

A *physical inspection* is an examination of the general physical condition of a property's site and structures. Inspection includes but is not limited to items listed. Consider having an inspection even if your state law does not require it, if you have not already done so.

A *geological inspection* is an investigation by a soils engineer for potential geological problems. This inspection is generally done only if a problem is expected or physical inspection shows a condition that requires more evaluation.

Providing a physical inspection report to buyers before you negotiate can prevent some items from becoming contingencies. Items buyers question if no inspection is done often become points to negotiate if you provide an inspection report. If buyers do not require a physical inspection, consider requesting and paying for one yourself. It

- Provides an excellent source of information for a real estate transfer disclosure form.
- Protects you from charges of trying to hide problems or potential problems, when you provide it to buyers in addition to a real estate transfer disclosure statement.
- Is generally less expensive than becoming involved in a lawsuit over even a minor issue.

At their own expense, buyers may choose a qualified professional(s) to inspect the property including, but not limited to, the listed aspects. Buyers agree to the following arising from the inspections:

- Keep property free and clear of any liens.
- Hold you harmless from all liability, claims, demands, damages, or costs.
- Repair all damages to the property resulting from the inspections.

For both physical and geological inspections, within 30 days after you accept buyers' offer, buyers may

- Write a list of problems that they claim to be defects in the condition of the property, which make it less usable for the purpose for which it is presently used or for which the property legally could be used.
- Support the list of problems with written reports.
- Deliver the list of problems and written reports to you.

Buyers may cancel this contract *if* they are not satisfied by data or conditions revealed by the reports *and* you are unwilling or unable to correct the problems.

B. Condition of Property

You guarantee through the date you make possession available to the buyers that

- You will maintain property and improvements in the same condition on the date you accepted buyers' offer.
- The roof is free of all known leaks, and all systems and built-in appliances operate.
- You will replace all broken and cracked glass.

C. Seller Representation

You guarantee that you have no knowledge of any notice of violations of any codes or ordinances or other regulations filed or issued against the property by any department of any governmental body. You will give notice if you gain such knowledge until date escrow closes.

D. Pest Control

Pest control inspections, sometimes called *structural pest control inspections* or *termite inspections,* are checks for other infestations or infections by other wood-destroying organisms in addition to termites. Most lenders require pest control inspections and reports. Some buyers may require this inspection even if a lender does not.

Time Limit. Within 30 days from the date you accept the buyers' offer is usually enough time for you to provide buyers with a current written pest control report.

Licensed Structural Pest Control Operators. Consider consulting your lender, title representative, or escrow officer for names of honest and competent structural pest control operators.

E. Flood Hazard Area Disclosure

This disclosure informs buyers that property is located in a region designated as a "Special Flood Hazard Area." Legally, for lenders to make a loan they must require flood insurance on a property or item attached to the property located within the zone *and* used as security for a loan.

Consult your lender, title representative, escrow officer, or insurance carrier for information whether your home is in an area where Flood Hazard Area Disclosure is required and have him or her inform you of the amount of insurance required.

F. Special Studies Zone Disclosure

This disclosure informs buyers that the property is located in an area designated as a Special Studies Zone by California law. Special Studies Zones affect primarily areas where there has been or is a possibility of serious earthquake destruction. Consult your lender, escrow officer, or title representative to determine whether your home is in an area where Special Studies Zone Disclosure or similar disclosure is required.

Time Limit. Thirty calendar days from the date of your acceptance is usually considered ample time during which buyers may make inquiries concerning Special Studies Zones.

G. Energy Conservation Retrofit

Energy conservation retrofit laws may require that property comply with local minimum energy conservation standards before property can be sold or title transferred. Consult your lender, title representative, or escrow officer to determine whether your home is situated in an area where an energy conservation retrofit is required.

Compliance and Payment. The party that complies and pays is negotiable. You generally both comply with and pay for the requirements. If you must pay for the retrofit, in places where the law permits you may pay the bill by authorizing escrow to give enough credit to buyers to cover the costs of the retrofit.

H. Home Protection Plan

A home protection plan or home warranty ensures that specified items such as plumbing, wiring, and major appliances are in working order for a specified length of time. You can purchase coverage separately for other home items, such as pools and spas. When something goes wrong with one of the covered items
- The new homeowner usually pays for a service call.
- The plan pays for the cost of the repair.
- Labor on a repair is often guaranteed for 30 days.
- Parts are often guaranteed for 90 days.

Issuing Company. Consult your lender, title representative, or escrow officer for names of providers of home protection plans:
1. Contact providers and obtain several sample policies.
2. Compare all policies carefully.
3. Choose a policy that insures all home components you wish to cover.

Payment. The party that pays is negotiable. Traditionally, either you pay or the costs are split evenly between you and buyers.

I. Condominium/PUD

Condominiums and planned unit developments (PUDs) are often subject to additional designations, fees, and regulations.

- *Condominium* is defined as an undivided ownership in common in a portion of a piece of real property (real estate) plus a separate interest in space in a building.
- *Planned unit development* is defined as a subdivision in which the lots are separately owned, but other areas such as green belts and recreation facilities are owned in common.

As soon as is practical you are to
1. Provide buyers with copies of
   a. Covenants, conditions, and restrictions (CC&Rs).
   b. Articles of incorporation, the basic document filed with the correct government agency when a association incorporates.
   c. Current rules and regulations.
   d. Most recent financial statement, the report summarizing the financial condition of the homeowner's association for a specified period.
   e. Any other documents required by law.
2. Disclose to buyers in writing any known
   a. Special assessments or taxes charged on a property for benefits given to that property.
   b. Claims, demands for money or property.
   c. Litigation, lawsuits.

Time Limit. Ten calendar days from the date buyers receive the listed documents from you is usually ample time for buyers to review documents and cancel this contract by notifying you if documents disclose information or conditions buyers find unsatisfactory.

J. Liquidated Damages

Liquidated damages consists of the money you may keep if buyers default or breach the contact. Defaults include failing to make a good faith effort to remove contingencies or welshing on the contract for no reason. If buyers default and fail to complete the purchase you are not obligated to sell the property to them *or* you may sue buyers for specific performance (to carry out their agreement).

Funds deposited in escrow or trust accounts are not automatically released if you and buyers disagree. Usually, both you and buyers must give written consent or there must be a judgment before escrow releases funds.

K. Arbitration

Arbitration is taking a controversy to an unbiased third person who issues a decision after a hearing at which you both may speak. If arbitration is binding, you both agree to abide by the person's decision. Consider opting for arbitration in most cases. Arbitration is almost always faster and less costly than a court of law. You cannot normally appeal an arbitrator's decision to another arbitrator or a court of law.

Clauses in a contract may provide that you and buyers
- Agree to neutral arbitration of all applicable disputes.
- Give up your right to court trial about these disputes.
- Affect your legal rights to discovery (disclosure of things previously unknown) and appeal (resort to a higher court to review the decision of a lower court).
- Admit you voluntarily agreed to the arbitration clause.

Completing Item 17: Other Terms and Conditions

Enter items in this section that
- Might not logically be included in any other section.
- Place conditions on a section that is already included but in which there is not sufficient space to insert those conditions. Be sure to
  1. List the section number, letter, and name designation, before listing the conditions.
  2. Indicate under the appropriate section to **See Section 17.**

Conditions you might consider including (and that are described elsewhere in this book) are beneficiary statements (demands), drawing of documents, judgments, and notary fees.

Completing Item 19: Entire Contract

Time is important. That is, some actions required by this contract cannot be taken until other actions required by the contract are performed.

Completing Item 20: Captions

Captions are headings, which are used to make it easier to locate items.

Completing Item 21: Agency Confirmation

Put **not applicable** in all spaces.

Completing Item 22: Amendments

After you have signed a contract, do not write on the form. The contract should not be changed except by *another agreement* in written form and signed by both you and buyers.

Completing Item 23: Offer

The offer is to buy the property described. The offer is considered revoked unless the listed conditions are met.

Time Limit

Five calendar days is usually considered sufficient time from the date of the offer that unless the following are done the offer will be considered revoked and you must return the deposit to the buyers.
1. You, the seller, sign the acceptance.
2. You deliver the signed copy of the contract to buyers or to the person authorized by buyers to receive it either in person or by mail.

Acceptance

If a real estate professional is involved in this transaction, that professional should fill out the contract.

Now that you have read and studied the purchase contract, you are ready to understand its implications. Such implications include the contingencies and the amount of money you expect to make from the sale of your home, which are the subjects of Chapter 11.

CHAPTER 11
Understand Implications of Contract

Understanding implications of any contract can help you to negotiate the best contract. Implications for real estate sales contracts can include the amount of proceeds you expect to receive, the contingencies you decide to allow, and the taxes you expect to pay.

Step 1: Understand Monetary Implications

To understand the monetary implications of any sales contract, calculate the expected results.

Estimate of Proceeds Worksheet—Working

In order to estimate the amount you will receive from selling your home, collect the following documents to use as you prepare the Estimate of Proceeds Worksheet—Working:

- Purchase contract buyers submitted to you.
- Estimate of Proceeds Worksheet—Preliminary that you completed in preparing for the negotiations. See Chapter 9.
- If you did not prepare the Estimate of Proceeds Worksheet—Preliminary, you may fill out the Estimate of Proceeds Worksheet—Working using the instructions here, starting with step 2.
  1. Using a copy of the Estimate of Proceeds Worksheet from Chapter 9, mark an X in the box marked Working.
  2. If the purchase contract lists a specific amount for an item for which you will pay, use that amount.
  3. Where the purchase contract lists no specific amount for an item for which you will pay, use the estimate you entered on the Estimate of Proceeds Worksheet—Preliminary.
  4. If you did not list the item on the preliminary estimate or did not prepare a preliminary estimate, check the source of cost information listed in Chapter 9 for the approximate cost of this item.

Other Monetary Implications

Understand that you may be charged for an item even though you do not list it. If you do not list who will pay the charge in the purchase contract, escrow generally assigns these costs according to local customs.

Step 2: Understand Contingencies

Understanding *contingencies*—the conditions on which a valid contract depends—is vital. Understanding contingencies allows you to know which conditions will work for you and how to handle these conditions.

Contingency Basics

A contingency provides that both you and buyers are released from all duties of the contract if a condition on which the contract depends fails to occur. A typical home purchase contract contains many of these conditions. Before you sell, consider how you want to deal with various contingencies that may occur. Such planning can aid you greatly in your sale.

Preventing Contingencies

When you offer your home for sale, act to prevent contingencies, if possible.

1. Give potential buyers copies of a disclosure statement and any inspections performed on the property.
2. Attempt to reach an agreement on each item that contains no contingencies. Giving a little in the negotiation now may save you time, worry, and money later.
3. Use a contingency only if you are not able to reach an agreement.
4. Use specific and definite wording in all contracts you prepare, so you and buyers have no misunderstandings.
5. Ask buyers to sign a statement that they will act in good faith to remove contingencies as soon as possible by obtaining whatever information, approval, or inspections are necessary.
6. Use a contingency release clause for the contingencies you specify in addition to the regular purchase contract.

Contingency Releases

Understand that a contingency release provides that

- You will continue to market your home until one of the following occurs:
  - You receive another offer that does not contain the contingencies you and the buyers agreed on.
  - Buyers remove the contingencies.
- If you receive another contract without the contingencies you specified, both of the following apply:
  - Buyers have the amount of time you agree on in hours or days to remove the contingencies.
  - If the buyers do not remove the contingencies, you may sell your home to the persons who offered you the contract without the contingencies.

Many variations of the contingency release form exist. Here we present the most up-to-date form available in California at the time of this writing. This Contingency

Release Clause Addendum is published by the California Association of Realtors. Check your state's version of this form against the descriptions of items in this section.

As the form notes, you have the right to continue to offer your property for sale.

Time Limit

If buyers fail to remove the contingencies within the time limit listed in the addendum,

1. The real estate purchase agreement as well as this contract shall end and have no effect.
2. You are to return buyers' deposit.

Receipt of Notice

The notice to buyers to remove contingencies is considered received by buyers when it meets the listed requirements. In this case, that is when either buyers or their agent receives delivery of this notice in person or by certified mail, *and* the notice is addressed as listed.

Step 3: Understand How to Handle Contingencies

You can take several steps to manage the contingencies that you negotiated into your contract. Use a copy of the Contingencies Worksheet—Working to keep track of the contingencies in the contract and how they are handled.

1. Use your copy of the purchase contract as a reference.
2. Mark an X in the box marked Working.
3. Mark an X for the contingencies that apply in the Used column.
4. Enter information regarding the checked contingencies.
5. As each contingency is met, insert an X in the Met column.
6. Be sure that you act in good faith to remove contingencies as soon as possible by obtaining whatever information, approval, or inspections are necessary.
7. Have buyers sign a contingency removal form for each contingency as soon as that contingency is met.
8. Realize that if a contingency in a contract is not met for any reason the contract is canceled *unless* you and buyers choose to negotiate a modification of the contingency.

After you have acted to prevent contingencies or, if necessary, removed contingencies and obtained statements from the buyers that they have been removed, you are ready to understand other possible offers you may receive on your property. These offers include leases, options, or lease options. They may be used alone or in combination with each other. They may also be used with purchase agreements.

CONTINGENCY RELEASE CLAUSE ADDENDUM
THIS IS INTENDED TO BE A LEGALLY BINDING CONTRACT. READ IT CAREFULLY.
CALIFORNIA ASSOCIATION OF REALTORS® (CAR) STANDARD FORM

This addendum is a part of the Real Estate Purchase Contract and Receipt for Deposit dated_____

Between _____ (Buyer)

and_____ (Seller)

regarding the real property described as_____

_____

Seller shall have the right to continue to offer subject property for sale.

Should a subsequent written offer be accepted by Seller, conditioned upon above named Buyer's Rights, Buyer

shall have _____ hours_____ days

following receipt of notice to remove and waive in writing the following condition(s) _____

_____

_____

_____

In the event Buyer(s) shall fail to remove the condition(s) within the above time limit, the Real Estate Purchase Contract and Receipt for Deposit and this agreement shall terminate and become null and void and Buyer's deposit shall be returned to Buyer.

Notice to Buyer to remove condition(s) shall be deemed to have been received by Buyer when Buyer, or his

agent, has received notice by delivery in person or by certified mail and addressed to _____

_____

If notice is given by mail Buyer shall have until 6:00 PM of the third day following the date of mailing, unless the notice provides otherwise, to deliver to Seller or Seller's agent Buyer's written agreement to remove and waive the contingencies.

The undersigned acknowledges receipt of a copy hereof.

RECEIPT IF DELIVERED IN PERSON
Receipt of this notice is acknowledged:

Dated _____   Buyer_____

Buyer_____

Dated _____   Seller_____

Seller_____

CONTINGENCIES WORKSHEET

[ ] <u>WORKING</u>   [ ] <u>COUNTER OFFER</u>

Property address:_____

Seller:_____ Buyer:_____

Date prepared:_____ Closing date:_____

Use this form for worksheet purposes only. For complete wording of each section, see your copy of your purchase contract.

<u>Used</u> <u>Met</u> <u>Contingency</u>

Additional Financing Terms (see Loans, Additional Terms)

Additional Terms and Conditions (see the specific term or condition)

Balance of Down Payment (see Down Payment, Balance)

[ ]   [ ]   **Buyer Approval**
[ ]   [ ]   Written notification of disapproval
[ ]   [ ]   Within ___ days
[ ]   [ ]   Balances adjusted in [ ] cash, [ ] other _____
[ ]   [ ]   _____

Closing (see Escrow)

[ ]   [ ]   **Condition of Property**
[ ]   [ ]   _____
[ ]   [ ]   _____
[ ]   [ ]   _____

[ ]   [ ]   **Condominium/PUD**
[ ]   [ ]   Buyers allowed _____ days from receipt to review the documents
[ ]   [ ]   Buyers approve
[ ]   [ ]   Buyers fail to notify you in writing (considered approval)
[ ]   [ ]   _____

Deposit (see Down Payment, Deposit)

[ ]   [ ]   **Diligence and Good Faith to Obtain Financing**
[ ]   [ ]   _____
[ ]   [ ]   _____

CONTINGENCIES WORKSHEET

<u>Used</u> <u>Met</u> <u>Contingency</u>

[ ] [ ] **Down Payment, Deposit**
[ ] [ ] Deposited into_____
[ ] [ ] $ _____
[ ] [ ] _____

[ ] [ ] **Down Payment, Increased Deposit**
[ ] [ ] Within ____ number of days
[ ] [ ] Deposited into_____
[ ] [ ] $ _____
[ ] [ ] _____

[ ] [ ] **Down Payment, Balance**
[ ] [ ] Deposited into_____
[ ] [ ] On or before _____
[ ] [ ] $ _____
[ ] [ ] _____

[ ] [ ] **Energy Conservation Retrofit**
[ ] [ ] [ ] buyers [ ] seller comply with
[ ] [ ] [ ] buyers [ ] seller pay for

[ ] [ ] **Escrow**
[ ] [ ] Signed instructions to _____
[ ] [ ] Within ____ days from seller's acceptance
[ ] [ ] Closing within ____ days from seller's acceptance
[ ] [ ] _____

Existing First Loan (see Loan, First Existing)

Existing Second Loan (see Loan, Second Existing)

[ ] [ ] **Geological inspection**
[ ] [ ] Buyers select professional within ____ days after seller's acceptance
[ ] [ ] Buyers deliver to seller within ____ days after seller's acceptance written claims of defects and written reports
[ ] [ ] Buyers approved
[ ] [ ] Buyers fail to give you written notice of disapproval (approval)
[ ] [ ] _____

Home Protection Plan (see Home Warranty)

[ ] [ ] **Home Warranty**
[ ] [ ] To be issued by_____

CONTINGENCIES WORKSHEET

Used Met Contingency

Home Warranty (continued)

[ ]   [ ]   Cost not to exceed $ _____

[ ]   [ ]   _____

Increased Deposit (see Down Payment, Increased Deposit)

[ ]   [ ]   **Loan, First Existing**
[ ]   [ ]   Buyers to [ ] assume, [ ] take title subject to
[ ]   [ ]   Approximate balance of $ _____
[ ]   [ ]   In favor of_____
[ ]   [ ]   Payable monthly at $ _____
[ ]   [ ]   Interest at _____ %
[ ]   [ ]   Loan [ ] fixed rate, [ ] other_____
[ ]   [ ]   Fees not to exceed $ _____
[ ]   [ ]   _____

[ ]   [ ]   **Loan, First New**
[ ]   [ ]   Amount of $ _____
[ ]   [ ]   Payable [ ] biweekly, [ ] monthly
[ ]   [ ]   At approximately $ _____
[ ]   [ ]   Interest at origination not to exceed _____%
[ ]   [ ]   Loan [ ] fixed rate, [ ] other_____
[ ]   [ ]   All due _____ years
[ ]   [ ]   Loan fee not to exceed $ _____
[ ]   [ ]   Maximum of _____ FHA/VA discount points
[ ]   [ ]   _____

[ ]   [ ]   **Loan, Second Existing**
[ ]   [ ]   Assume
[ ]   [ ]   Take title subject to
[ ]   [ ]   Balance of $ _____
[ ]   [ ]   In favor of _____
[ ]   [ ]   Payable monthly at $ _____
[ ]   [ ]   Interest at _____ %
[ ]   [ ]   Loan [ ] fixed rate, [ ] other_____
[ ]   [ ]   Buyers' fees not to exceed $ _____
[ ]   [ ]   _____

[ ]   [ ]   **Loan, Second New**
[ ]   [ ]   Amount of $ _____
[ ]   [ ]   Payable [ ] biweekly, [ ] monthly
[ ]   [ ]   At approximately $ _____
[ ]   [ ]   Interest at origination _____ %
[ ]   [ ]   Loan [ ] fixed rate, [ ] other_____

CONTINGENCIES WORKSHEET

<u>Used</u> <u>Met</u> <u>Contingency</u>

Loan, Second New (continued)
[ ]   [ ]   All due _____ years
[ ]   [ ]   Buyers' loan fee not to exceed $ _____
[ ]   [ ]   _____

[ ]   [ ]   **Loan Secured by Deed of Trust in Favor of Seller**
[ ]   [ ]   Deed of trust [ ] 1st, [ ] 2nd, [ ] 3rd
[ ]   [ ]   Amount of $ _____
[ ]   [ ]   Payable monthly at $ _____
[ ]   [ ]   Interest at _____%
[ ]   [ ]   All due [ ] ___ years, [ ] upon sale, [ ] upon transfer
[ ]   [ ]   Late charge of $ _____
[ ]   [ ]   Within _____ days of due date
[ ]   [ ]   _____
[ ]   [ ]   _____
[ ]   [ ]   _____
[ ]   [ ]   _____

[ ]   [ ]   **Loans, Additional Terms**
[ ]   [ ]   _____
[ ]   [ ]   _____
[ ]   [ ]   _____
[ ]   [ ]   _____
[ ]   [ ]   _____
[ ]   [ ]   _____

Note Secured by Deed of Trust in Favor of Seller (see Loan Secured by Deed of Trust in Favor of Seller)

[ ]   [ ]   **Other Terms and Conditions**
[ ]   [ ]   _____
[ ]   [ ]   _____
[ ]   [ ]   _____
[ ]   [ ]   _____
[ ]   [ ]   _____
[ ]   [ ]   _____
[ ]   [ ]   _____
[ ]   [ ]   _____
[ ]   [ ]   _____
[ ]   [ ]   _____
[ ]   [ ]   _____
[ ]   [ ]   _____
[ ]   [ ]   _____
[ ]   [ ]   _____

CONTINGENCIES WORKSHEET

Used Met Contingency

[ ]   [ ]   **Pest Control**
[ ]   [ ]   Within _____ days of seller's acceptance
[ ]   [ ]   Written inspection report by_____
[ ]   [ ]   Inspection of inaccessible areas
[ ]   [ ]   Work to repair damage
[ ]   [ ]   Work to correct conditions that cause infestation
[ ]   [ ]   Work to correct conditions likely to cause infestation
[ ]   [ ]   Other_____
[ ]   [ ]   _____
[ ]   [ ]   _____

[ ]   [ ]   **Physical Inspection**
[ ]   [ ]   Buyer to select inspector within _____ days
[ ]   [ ]   Written claims of defects delivered to seller within _____ days
[ ]   [ ]   _____

Planned Unit Development (see Condominium/PUD)

[ ]   [ ]   **Possession**
[ ]   [ ]   Possession delivered to buyers on close of escrow (COE)
[ ]   [ ]   Possession delivered to buyers not later than ___ days after COE
[ ]   [ ]   Or_____
[ ]   [ ]   _____
[ ]   [ ]   _____

[ ]   [ ]   **Price, Total Purchase $_____**

[ ]   [ ]   **Smoke Detector**
[ ]   [ ]   State requirements met
[ ]   [ ]   Local requirements met
[ ]   [ ]   Written statement of compliance _____
[ ]   [ ]   _____

[ ]   [ ]   **Special Studies Zone Disclosure**
[ ]   [ ]   Within _____ days from date of seller's acceptance
[ ]   [ ]   Buyers approved
[ ]   [ ]   Buyers failed to notify seller in writing of disapproval (considered approval)
[ ]   [ ]   _____

[ ]   [ ]   **Supplements**
[ ]   [ ]   Interim Occupancy Agreement
[ ]   [ ]   Residential Lease Agreement After Sale

CONTINGENCIES WORKSHEET

<u>Used</u> <u>Met</u> <u>Contingency</u>

Supplements (continued)

[ ]   [ ]   VA and FHA Amendments

[ ]   [ ]   _____

[ ]   [ ]   _____

[ ]   [ ]   _____

[ ]   [ ]   _____

[ ]   [ ]   _____

[ ]   [ ]   _____

[ ]   [ ]   **Tax Withholding**

[ ]   [ ]   You provide buyers an affidavit

[ ]   [ ]   You provide buyers a qualifying statement

[ ]   [ ]   _____

[ ]   [ ]   **Title**

[ ]   [ ]   Not disapproved by the buyers in writing

[ ]   [ ]   Within ___ days of receipt of current preliminary report

[ ]   [ ]   You furnish buyers a standard title insurance policy

[ ]   [ ]   You furnish buyers an extended title insurance policy

[ ]   [ ]   Issued by _____ Company

[ ]   [ ]   You are willing and able to eliminate buyers' disapprovals

[ ]   [ ]   _____

[ ]   [ ]   _____

[ ]   [ ]   _____

Total Purchase Price (see Price, Total Purchase)

[ ]   [ ]   **Transfer Disclosure**

[ ]   [ ]   Buyer has received and read

[ ]   [ ]   You provide buyers with transfer disclosure within ____ days

[ ]   [ ]   _____

CHAPTER 12

Understand Other Possible Offers

Buyers and sellers often use agreements in addition to, in combination with, or instead of the purchase offer. For example, you may lease your property to buyers before closing, buyers may lease the property to you after closing, buyers may lease your property with an option to buy, or you may give buyers an option to purchase only.

Step 1: Learn About Basic Contracts

Leases and options are the basic real estate contracts you may encounter in addition to purchase contracts.

Lease

A lease is a contract by which one party (lessor) transfers possession and use of property for a limited, designated term at a specified price and under the stipulated conditions to another party (lessee).

You can buy blank lease forms at your local stationery store or in some states from your Board of Realtors. Books available at your local library or bookstore contain sample leases. Consult with your attorney or real estate professional if you have questions concerning leasing. Also consider consulting your accountant or tax preparer to calculate your estimated tax consequences during the period you plan to lease the property.

ADVANTAGES
- Enables you to obtain income from a property that otherwise might be costing you money.
- You may feel free to move into another home if you know the home you are selling can be rented.

DISADVANTAGES
- Lessees may cause considerable damage before you can remove them.
- Lessees at times can be difficult to remove if there is a problem.

Option

An option is a contract that gives potential buyers (optionees) the *right* to purchase a property before the specified future date for the amount and under the conditions listed in the contract. Also, buyers agree to pay an added amount—an option fee—if they do not use the option.

ADVANTAGES
- If buyers do not use the option, they pay you an option fee.

DISADVANTAGES
- You may worry about whether the persons to whom you gave the option will purchase your home.
- Buyers can decide to purchase your property at any time within the lease period.
- You do not receive money for the sale until the property is sold, usually near or at the end of the lease period.
- Unless you negotiate otherwise, you cannot legally raise the property's price during the term of the contract.

If you use an option, consider
1. Using an attorney or a real estate professional to draw up the agreements, due to their somewhat complex nature.
2. Having buyers make a deposit toward a down payment.
3. Making the return of the deposit to the optionees contingent on your later successful sale of the property to other buyers.
4. Negotiating that the price of the property when the buyers exercise the option be a value to be determined by some mutually acceptable method.

Step 2: Learn About Other Contracts

In selling your home, you may also encounter combination contracts, including lease purchase and sale leaseback agreements, as well as lease and purchase options.

Lease Purchase Agreements

If you lease your property *to* buyers during the period *before* escrow closes, use a lease in combination with the purchase contract or a consolidated form, such as an Interim Occupancy Agreement.

ADVANTAGES
- You may feel free to move into another home if you know the home you are selling can be rented.
- You receive income from your property, which otherwise might be a drain on your cash flow.

DISADVANTAGES
- Buyers may see things about your home that they do not like and refuse to complete the sale.
- You may have difficulty getting buyers to vacate the property if they refuse to go through with the sale.
- Buyers who refuse to complete the sale might cause considerable damage before you can remove them.

Sale Leaseback Agreements

If you rent or lease your former home *from* buyers *after* escrow closes, use a lease in combination with a purchase contract or a specific sale leaseback form, such as an Interim Occupancy Agreement.

ADVANTAGES
- You may not have to bother moving more than once.
- After closing the sale, you will be in a better financial position to buy another home.

DISADVANTAGES
- You must move out of the home by the date you negotiate. If the escrow on your new home does not close on time, you may have no place to live.

Lease Option

If you agree to lease your property with an option to buy, use a lease option or a combination of a lease, an option, and a purchase contract.

ADVANTAGES
- Enables you to obtain income from a property, which otherwise might be costing you money.
- If buyers do not use the option, they pay you an option fee.

DISADVANTAGES
- You may worry about whether the persons to whom you gave the option will purchase your home.
- Buyers can decide to purchase your property at any time within the lease period.
- You do not receive money for the sale until the property is sold, usually near or at the end of the lease period.
- Unless you negotiate otherwise, you cannot legally increase the property price during the contract.
- After buyers live in the property, they may discover certain inconveniences that they did not expect and may try to avoid purchasing the property.

If you decide to use a lease option, consider
1. Requesting approval for the lease option from the lender.
2. Including a provision for buyers to forfeit the deposit if buyers decide not to purchase the property on a lease option.
3. Adding a clause that buyers make monthly lease payments to equal or exceed payments on the existing loan.
4. Inserting a provision that you credit buyers with a portion of the monthly lease payment toward the purchase price.
5. Calculating your estimated tax consequences during the period that you plan to lease the property.

Purchase Option

The purchase option contract states that potential buyers have the *right* to purchase the property before the specified future date for the amount listed and under the conditions specified in the contract. Also, they agree to pay an option fee that is applied to the purchase price if they use the option or forfeited if they do not. If you agree to grant a purchase option, use a purchase option form or a combination option and purchase contract.

ADVANTAGES
- You may have sold your home and not have to worry about marketing it any longer.
- You will receive some cash, the option fee, even if the sale is not completed.

DISADVANTAGES

- You may worry about whether the persons to whom you gave the option will purchase your home.
- Buyers can decide to purchase your property at any time within the option period.
- You do not receive money until the property is sold, usually near or at the end of the option period.
- You cannot increase the price for your property during the term of the contract. A price increase is illegal even if all other properties in the area increase substantially in value.

Step 3: Learn About Backup Offers

Backup offers are offers that you accept in a subordinate position to the offer you accepted previously. You may want to accept backup offers because of the possibility that a contract may become void in some way. Voiding can occur because contingencies in the primary purchase agreement are not satisfied or some other complication occurs (see Chapter 15). When the first offer fails, the next offer in line automatically becomes the primary offer. If you decide you want to accept backup offers, consider

- Telling the buyers from whom you accept the primary offer that you plan to accept backup offers.
- Negotiating backup offers in the same way you negotiated the primary purchase offer.
- Including a clause noting that it is a backup offer and as such is subject to the nonperformance of any previous offers.
- Including a statement allowing buyers to withdraw a backup offer in writing at any time before you notify them that their offer is in first position.
- Numbering each backup offer as you accept it to avoid priority disputes.
- Telling all the other offerors, including the buyers, when you accept another backup offer.

Step 4: Contract Basics

Remembering some basic information can help you use contracts effectively.

Familiarity with Contracts

An important aspect of achieving your goals is your familiarity with the contracts you will be using. Your understanding of the contracts and ability to fill them in to accurately reflect your decisions are essential in saving you money and anxiety in selling your home.

The advantages of preprinted contracts are that they

- Cover important areas you might not think to include if you were writing the agreement yourself.
- Are written in commonly accepted legal terminology.
- Are intended to be legally binding agreements.

Wording Priorities

The following priorities exist in the event of discrepancies or inconsistencies in the contracts, in the order shown:

1. Written words usually take priority over printed and typed wording.
2. Typed words generally take priority over printed wording but not over written wording.
3. Specific provisions in a contract usually supersede the general provisions.

After you study the types of other offers you may encounter, you are now ready to learn about and perhaps make a counter offer.

CHAPTER 13
Handle Counter Offers

You will probably receive offers for your property that do not satisfy your expectations in such areas as price, financing, inspections, and/or occupancy. Making an offer of your own (counter offering) indicates to buyers that you

- Are not willing to accept the offer as written.
- Are motivated to sell your home.
- Are willing to negotiate.
- Desire different terms in the places you have made changes.

Step 1: Prepare for Counter Offers

Few sellers receive exactly the terms they ask for on the first offer. If you understand at the beginning that you are likely to write a counter offer, you will probably find the counter offer process easier.

Understand the Purchase Contract
In order to fully understand the purchase offer, consider
1. Reading the completed real estate purchase contract that the buyers submitted.
2. Listing each item you want to change under its appropriate section number and heading on a pad of paper.
3. Leaving room after each item to write the response you want.
4. Reading the list and entering the response you desire.
Example: Section 1, Selling Price, buyers offered $195,000 and I want $205,000.

Estimate of Proceeds Worksheet—Counter Offer
Estimate the amount you will receive from the sale of your home as modified by the counter offer.
1. Make a copy of the Estimate of Proceeds Worksheet—Preliminary from Chapter 9.
2. Check the box preceding Counter Offer at the top of the worksheet.
3. Gather documents necessary to prepare the Estimate of Proceeds Worksheet—Counter Offer, including the
   a. Counter offer you are preparing.
   b. Latest purchase offer buyers presented to you.
   c. Estimate of Proceeds Worksheet—Working that you previously prepared.
   If you have not prepared the Estimate of Proceeds Worksheet—Working, prepare

the Estimate of Proceeds Worksheet—Counter Offer, using the instructions provided in Chapter 9, as well as those provided in this chapter.
4. Insert an **X** in front of the words *Counter Offer* on a copy of the Estimate of
Proceeds Worksheet and fill in the requested information.
5. List on the worksheet the amount of each charge for the items that you intend
to pay. Use the amount from the most current available document listed in
steps 1a to 1d. Use an amount from an earlier document only if that is the most
current information available.
6. If the item is not listed on any of the documents, check the source of information
shown in Chapter 9 for the approximate cost of this item.
7. Understand that for any charges you do not itemize, escrow will generally assign
a payor of these charges in agreement with local customs.

Contingencies Worksheet—Counter Offer

Prepare the Counter Offer Contingencies Worksheet included in Chapter 12 so that
you understand exactly what contingencies apply.
1. Make a copy of the Contingencies Worksheet.
2. Mark an **X** in front of the words *Counter Offer* on the Contingencies Worksheet,
then fill in the requested information.
3. Use the following references for preparing the worksheet.
   a. Your counter offer.
   b. Your Working Contingencies Worksheet.
   c. The purchase offer.
4. Check the contingencies that apply.
   a. Check the most current contingencies that apply from the documents in the
   order listed before consulting the next document.
   b. Check only those contingencies that remain unchanged from the Working
   Contingencies Worksheet and the purchase offer.
5. Enter the appropriate information about each contingency using the appropriate
source of information.

Step 2: Understand Counter Offers

If your changes are relatively simple and few in number, use a form similar to the
counter offer form. Many variations of this form exist. Here we present the most up-
to-date form published in California at the time of this writing. The Counter Offer is
published by the California Association of Realtors.

Changes or Amendments

Consider entering the changes or amendments by
1. Listing sections and changes in the order in which they appear in your real
estate purchase contract. In this way the counter offer may be most easily understood. Legally, changes and amendments may be made in any order.
2. Writing the section number and/or letter designation as well as the section
caption. Designations and captions
   • Are most easily understood if listed in the same order as those in the real
   estate purchase contract you want to change.
   • Make sections of the agreement easier to locate.

CALIFORNIA
ASSOCIATION
OF REALTORS

COUNTER OFFER
THIS IS INTENDED TO BE A LEGALLY BINDING AGREEMENT – READ IT CAREFULLY.
CALIFORNIA ASSOCIATION OF REALTORS® (CAR) STANDARD FORM

This is a counter offer to the: ☐ Real Estate Purchase Contract and Receipt for Deposit, ☐ Mobile Home Purchase Contract and Receipt for Deposit, ☐ Business Purchase Contract and Receipt for Deposit, ☐ Other _____
dated _____ , 19 ____ , on property known as: _____
in which _____ is referred to as Buyer
and _____ is referred to as Seller.

Seller accepts all of the terms and conditions in the above designated agreement with the following changes or amendments:
_____
_____
_____
_____
_____
_____
_____
_____
_____
_____
_____
_____
_____
_____
_____
_____
_____
_____
_____

The Seller reserves the right to continue to offer the herein described property for sale and accept any offer acceptable to Seller at any time prior to personal receipt by Seller or _____ , Seller's authorized agent, of a copy of this counter offer, duly accepted and signed by Buyer. "Accept," as used herein, includes delivery in person, by mail, or by facsimile.

Unless this counter offer is accepted on or before _____ , 19 ____ at _____ AM/PM, it shall be deemed revoked and deposit shall be returned to the Buyer. Seller's acceptance of another offer shall revoke this counter offer. This counter offer and any supplement, addendum, or modification relating hereto, including any photocopy or facsimile thereof, may be executed in two or more counterparts, all of which shall constitute one and the same writing.

Receipt of a copy is acknowledged.

Date _____ 19_____   Seller _____

Time _____   Seller _____

☐ The undersigned Buyer accepts the above counter offer, **OR**
☐ The undersigned Buyer accepts the above counter offer with the following changes or amendments:

Unless the following changes or amendments are accepted and a copy duly accepted and signed by Seller is personally delivered to Buyer or _____ , the agent obtaining the offer on or before _____ ,
19____ at _____ AM/PM, it shall be deemed revoked and deposit shall be returned to Buyer. Receipt of a copy is acknowledged.
_____
_____
_____
_____

Date _____ 19_____   Buyer _____

Time _____   Buyer _____

Receipt of signed copy on _____ , 19____ at _____ AM/PM, by Seller _____
or Seller's authorized Agent _____ is acknowledged.
                              (Initials)

THE FOLLOWING IS REQUIRED ONLY IF BUYER HAS MADE CHANGES OR AMENDMENTS ABOVE:
Seller accepts Buyer's changes or amendments to Seller's counter offer and agrees to sell on the above terms and conditions. Seller acknowledges receipt of a copy and authorizes Broker(s) to deliver a signed copy to Buyer.

Date _____ 19_____   Seller _____

Time _____   Seller _____

┌─ OFFICE USE ONLY ─┐
Reviewed by Broker or Designee _____
Date _____

Copyright © 1986, 1987, CALIFORNIA ASSOCIATION OF REALTORS®
525 South Virgil Avenue, Los Angeles, California 90020
REVISED 4/89

CO-14

EQUAL HOUSING
OPPORTUNITY

- Are not intended to be part of the contract.
3. Write the changes and amendments you want to make for the section you listed. Be definite and specific.

Until you receive a copy of this counter offer accepted and signed by buyers, you have the right to
1. Continue to market the property described in this contract for sale.
2. Accept any offer that is acceptable to you.

Seller

All persons holding title must sign this contract, unless one person has power of attorney for another.

Step 3: Understand Counter Offer Logistics

Understanding logistics of counter offers can aid you in handling them most effectively.

Writing a Counter Offer

When you make a counter offer, be aware of several points:
1. The counter offer must be in writing. Like offers, counter offers are not valid unless written.
2. The length of time buyers have to accept your counter offer should be stated clearly. Sellers usually offer an acceptance time ranging from several hours to several days.

Revoking a Counter Offer

You may revoke your counter offer any time before buyers accept your counter offer *and* communicate their acceptance of your counter offer in writing.

Accepting Another Purchase Offer

You may accept another offer as long as buyers to whom you made a counter offer have not accepted the counter offer.

Buyers Accepting Your Counter Offer

Understand that to establish a binding legal contract, buyers must accept and communicate their acceptance
- In writing.
- Within the time limits allowed by your counter offer.
- Before you revoke the counter offer.

Timing

You and buyers may continue to make as many counter offers as you wish, until you agree on the terms or decide to discontinue the process. When you and buyers continue to make offers and counter offers, consider
1. Making or accepting from buyers only *written* offers or counter offers.
2. Stating clearly the length of time buyers have to accept your counter offer.
3. Choosing the form to use depending upon the changes involved:
   - Use a counter offer form to make counter offers for which the changes are relatively few and simple.

- Write a counter offer using a real estate purchase contract for changes that are numerous and/or complex.

4. That you may revoke your counter offer any time (within time limits specified in contract) before buyers accept your counter offer *and* communicate their acceptance.

5. That buyers may also revoke their offer any time (within the time limits specified in the contract) before you accept their offer *and* communicate your acceptance.

After completing the negotiation process—including possible counter offers and signing a written real estate purchase contract to sell your home—you are ready to learn about and prepare for closing.

CHAPTER 14
Understand Closing Basics

Closing or settlement is the process in which funds and property title are transferred between you and the buyers. Although closing could be accomplished by you and buyers simply getting together and exchanging money and documents, most property transactions today use an escrow type of closing.

Step 1: Understand Escrow

Escrow is a type of closing by which you and buyers deposit money and/or documents with a neutral third party. You and buyers give the third party instructions to hold and disburse documents and funds after certain conditions are met. Whoever handles the closing acts as an agent for both you and buyers. This person is often referred to as the *escrow holder.*

ADVANTAGES

Consider having an escrow because of the complexity of the closing process. The advantages of escrow are that a neutral third party is responsible for
- Keeping documents and funds safe.
- Making computations.
- Receiving and distributing funds.
- Drawing up, acquiring, and recording documents.
- Carrying out any other terms of the contract.
- Determining that all conditions have been satisfied.
- Ensuring that buyers receive the appropriate documents.
- Ensuring that you receive the appropriate funds.
- Providing an accounting for the transfer process.
- Complying with federal, state, and local tax regulations.

DISADVANTAGES

The disadvantage of having an escrow is the slight cost involved.

Functions of Escrow

Following is a short list of the functions that escrow holders often perform while they act as impartial stake holders and communicate with everyone involved about the transaction. Escrow holders
- Prepare escrow instructions.

- Prepare and assemble relevant documents.
- Obtain signatures.
- Proceed with title search by
  1. Requesting the title search.
  2. Receiving and reviewing preliminary title report to determine what actions to take to conform to the condition of title required in the escrow instructions.
  3. Requesting demands (demand for payoff) from lenders, if you desire to pay off existing loans.
  4. Requesting an explanation of liens against the property as listed on the preliminary title report.
  5. Analyzing taxes on the report to be sure terms are correct and conform to the escrow instructions.
  6. Receiving demands from lenders.
  7. Entering demands from lenders into the file.
- Proceed processing a new loan, if any, concurrently with the title search by
  1. Requesting or preparing a new loan application.
  2. Obtaining a loan approval in the form of a loan commitment letter from the lender.
  3. Examining approved loans to be sure that terms are correct and conform to escrow instructions.
  4. Requesting loan documents.
- Proceed with a loan takeover (assumption), if any, concurrently with the title search and the processing of a new loan (if applicable) by
  1. Requesting from lenders beneficiary statements giving transfer terms and payment status for each loan.
  2. Receiving and reviewing each beneficiary statement.
  3. Entering each beneficiary statement into the file.
  4. Reviewing each loan's transfer terms and payment status to determine if approval is necessary to record.
- Review the file to determine that
  1. All conditions have been met.
  2. All documents are drawn (prepared).
  3. All documentation is correct.
  4. All documents are available for signatures.
- If the file is complete, proceed by
  1. Calculating costs.
  2. Requesting signatures on all unsigned documents.
- Complete the closing by
  1. Sending documents to the title company.
  2. Requesting and obtaining funds from the buyer.
  3. Returning loan documents (usually the note, signed disclosure statements, and instructions) to lender.
- Fund the loan (request and obtain loan funds from lender).
- Request recording (official entry of transactions, liens, satisfaction of mortgages, and reconveyances into the permanent record of a county).
- Close the file.
- Prepare buyers' and seller's closing statements.
- Disburse (distribute) funds.
- Complete closing.
- Send final documents to all interested parties (seller, buyer, and lender).

- Prepare federal, state and local tax documents (1099s, FIRPTAs, deed tax stamps, and so on).

Lenders usually require escrow as a condition of making a loan. Some states require escrow for the sale of houses only or in cases such as court sales—including public administration and probate sales. Check with lenders or escrow companies to determine whether escrow on your home is required by law.

Because of the complexity of the process involved, having an escrow holder can do much to protect you when you sell your home.

Actions Prohibited for Escrow Holders

Escrow holders are usually prohibited from
- Offering advice.
- Negotiating with you and buyers.
- Revealing information about the escrow to persons who are not a party to the transaction.
- Preparing or revising escrow instructions without the authorization of you *and* the buyers.

Requirements of a Valid Escrow

A valid escrow arrangement is a legal and binding written contract between a buyer and seller. Requirements for a legal and binding contract include factors described here.

Competency of Buyers and Seller

To be competent, you and buyers must meet certain requirements set by your state. You and buyers often must
- Be natural persons (not corporations) who meet all the following criteria:
  - Adult (at least a minimum age set by your state laws) or emancipated minors (state laws vary but often include being lawfully married or divorced, on duty in the armed forces, or emancipated by court order).
  - Mentally competent.
  - Not a felon deprived of civil rights.
- Be artificial persons such as corporations, partnerships, or a joint venture. Individuals from such entities who sign documents must have the authority to act as a representative of the entity.
- Have a legal right (such as power of attorney) to enter into contracts involving the property.

Consideration

Consideration is anything of value that influences a person to enter into a contract, such as money, a deed, a service, an item of personal property, an act (including the payment of money), or a promise (including the promise to pay on a loan).

If consideration is an act or service, that act or service must be performed *after* you and buyers enter into the contract.

Lawful Object

To be legally enforceable, the promises and the consideration must be legal.

Mutual Agreement

There must be agreement between you and buyers about the wording and conditions.

Selection of an Escrow Holder

Depending on the area, the party that acts as escrow holder can include independent escrow companies, title companies, escrow departments of lending institutions (banks, savings and loans, and so on), attorneys, and real estate brokers.

Consider choosing an escrow holder who is willing to take the time to explain to you what is happening and what you need to do and is located within a convenient distance from your current residence so you can deliver and sign documents easily.

Timing of Selection

Select an escrow holder during this period of preparation for closing if you have not already done so.

Step 2: Establish an Escrow

To set up an escrow account, you must open the escrow and provide the escrow holder with information for the escrow instructions.

Opening an Escrow

After you select an escrow holder, open the escrow by following these steps:

1. Contact the escrow holder by telephone or in person.
2. Give the escrow holder all of the relevant information regarding the sale.
3. Deposit the buyers' earnest money with the escrow holder, preferably in person *or* if necessary by certified mail.

Providing Take Sheet Information

The escrow officer collects information necessary to prepare escrow instructions on a form called a "take sheet." Data the escrow holder may need to prepare escrow instructions includes the following.

Property Description

From your deed or title insurance policy, the property description includes
- Property address
- Legal description
- Type of property

Parties to the Transaction

From the purchase contract, the list of parties includes
- Your name, address, and telephone number.
- Buyers' name, address, and telephone number.

Escrow Information

From the purchase contract, the escrow information includes
- Time period.
- Proposed closing date.

Sales Price

From the purchase contract, the sales price lists
- Amount.
- Terms.

Loans Currently on the Property

From your payment statement or lender, loan information includes data about mortgages, trust deeds, and/or home equity lines of credit, specifically

- Loan number, amount, and rate of interest.
- Amount of monthly principal and interest payments.
- Lender's name, address, and telephone number.

Loans Buyers Want to Put on the Property

From the purchase contract, buyers' loan information includes data regarding

- Loan amount and rate of interest.
- Amount of monthly principal and interest payments.
- Lender's name, address, and telephone number.
- Proposed beginning and due dates of the loan.
- Existence or absence of an acceleration clause in the loan.
- Whether buyers requested notice of delinquency of payment.
- Amount of the loan fee.

Vesting of the Title

How the title is to be vested when the property is transferred can be obtained from the purchase contract.

Conditions of the Title

Title conditions are specified in the purchase contract and include conditions, covenants, and restrictions.

Buyers' and Seller's Costs

Information regarding who pays which costs can be obtained from the purchase contract. Unless you have specified otherwise in the documents you submit to escrow, the escrow holder usually writes escrow instructions designating costs based on area custom. You and buyers may agree on any division that does not conflict with legal requirements in your state and area. Be sure you and buyers

1. Reach an agreement about each possible cost.
2. Communicate your agreement to the escrow officer.

Rental Information

If the property is being rented or leased, provide current information regarding names of tenants along with their rental amounts, payment dates, and security deposits.

Escrow Instructions

Escrow instructions are the written agreement between you and buyers that translates the contract into a form used by the escrow holder to conduct and close the escrow.

Understand Escrow Instructions

The escrow holder attempts to prepare escrow instructions, using the take sheet as a guideline, so that the intent and conditions are identical to those of the purchase agreement. The escrow holder then asks you and buyers to read and sign the escrow instructions. Consider

1. Reading the escrow instructions carefully.
2. Being sure that the intent and conditions of escrow instructions are identical to those in the purchase contract.
3. Asking questions about items you do not understand or ones that do not appear to match those in the purchase contract.

4. Signing escrow instructions *only* when you are satisfied that all items reflect *exactly* the terms of the purchase contract.

Amending Escrow Instructions

You and buyers can make amendments (changes) only when you both agree to the amendments. To amend any escrow instruction,

1. Discuss the change with buyers.
2. Obtain the buyers' agreement to the change.
3. Request the escrow holder prepare documents for the change.
4. Request that documents containing the change be sent to both you and the buyers.
5. Both you and the buyers sign documents authorizing the change.
6. Both you and the buyers return the documents to escrow.

Step 3: Handle Escrow Responsibilities

Both you and the buyers have responsibilities for completing some items in the escrow process. The steps you will be asked to take and the order in which you are asked to take them vary depending on the details of your sale, requirements of your state, usual procedure in your area, and process the escrow company uses. Ask your escrow holder to inform you and the buyers what each one of you should do and when you should do it.

After you have established the escrow and understand the basics of the escrow process, you are ready to address any complications that may arise as a result of that escrow.

CHAPTER 15
Handle Closing Complications

You, the buyers, or circumstances beyond the control of either may create complications you must resolve in order to close the sale of your property. Such complications might include
- Your acceptance of another offer on your home when you have used a kick-out provision in your real estate purchase contract.
- Your and buyers' agreement to changes in the contract.
- Breach of contract.
- Destruction of your property.
- Disputes with buyers.
- Proclaiming your contract invalid, if all else fails.

Step 1: Remove Contingencies

Contingencies, as you saw earlier, are conditions on which a valid agreement depends. These conditions must be met within the time period stated in the contract. If even *one* contingency is not met within that period for any reason, the contract is voidable. This means that you and/or buyers may cancel the contract. You and buyers may also negotiate a contract modification.

To prevent contingencies from becoming major difficulties,
1. Make a good faith attempt to meet the requirements of the contingencies for which you are responsible as soon as possible. Obtain required information, approvals, and/or inspections as well as making required repairs. Buyers may be prone to take legal action if you do not make a good faith attempt.
2. Cooperate with people hired by the buyers. These people include persons who need information and those who must gain access to your property.
3. Request buyers sign a separate copy of a notice that a contingency was removed for each contingency listed in the purchase contract, as each separate contingency is met.

Step 2: Handle Unmet Contingencies

If a contingency for which you or buyers are responsible is not met for any reason, the contract is over. Why it was not met may be important in influencing your action.

Consider the likelihood that you and the buyers will be able to meet the terms of the conditions within a time period acceptable to you both before you choose what action to take.

Renegotiate

Renegotiation could be the least expensive option, especially if you extend only the time limits for meeting contingencies that have a high likelihood of being met. Consider renegotiating your present contract if

- Buyers made what you consider a good faith attempt but were unable to meet the terms of the contingencies within the time limits on which you agreed.
- Buyers still want to purchase your property.
- You feel buyers *will* be able to meet the terms of the contingencies within a time period acceptable to you both.

If you decide to renegotiate, choose the type of form for the written contract, depending on the number and nature of the changes. Use a new purchase contract for numerous and/or major changes.

Contract Supplement

Make uncomplicated and/or minor additions or deletions to the purchase contract using a contract supplement form similar to this addendum.

Many variations of the contract supplement exist. Here we present the form current in California at the time of this writing. The Contract Supplement/Addendum is published by the California Association of Realtors. The spaces to be filled in on this form are largely self-explanatory.

Consider listing the section number and designation for each addendum before you list the terms or conditions. Section numbers and designations make the items easier to locate in the contract.

Distribute copies of forms containing any modifications to buyers, escrow holder, your attorneys, and yourself.

Remarket

Remarketing may take a substantial amount of time and expense, depending on how long it takes you to find buyers and the length of closing involved. Remarketing may cost significantly less than dealing with buyers who try to win concessions from you. Consider remarketing your property and selling it to other buyers if you feel current buyers

- Will not be able to meet contingencies in a manner acceptable to you for any reason.
- Have not made what you consider a good faith effort to meet contingencies but are still interested in buying your home.
- Seem to have slowed the closing process, especially if they are aware that you have certain time or money limitations.

Step 3: Accept an Offer Without Contingencies

Whether you can legally accept another offer without the contingencies from different buyers depends on whether you have used a contingency release form or a similar agreement when you signed the purchase contract.

CONTRACT SUPPLEMENT/ADDENDUM
THIS IS INTENDED TO BE A LEGALLY BINDING CONTRACT - READ IT CAREFULLY.
CALIFORNIA ASSOCIATION OF REALTORS® (CAR) STANDARD FORM

The following terms and conditions are hereby incorporated in and made part of the: ☐ Real Estate Purchase Contract and Receipt for Deposit, ☐ Mobilehome Purchase Contract and Receipt for Deposit, ☐ Business Purchase Contract and Receipt for Deposit, ☐ other_____

dated_____ , 19_____ , on property known as: _____

in which _____ is referred to as Buyer

and _____ is referred to as Seller.

_____
_____
_____
_____
_____
_____
_____
_____
_____
_____
_____
_____
_____
_____
_____
_____
_____
_____
_____
_____
_____

The undersigned acknowledge receipt of a copy of this page, which constitutes Page_____ of_____ Pages

Date_____   Date _____

Buyer_____   Seller _____

Buyer_____   Seller _____

┌─ OFFICE USE ONLY ─┐
Reviewed by Broker or Designee _____
Date _____

EQUAL HOUSING
OPPORTUNITY
SF-A7-SF

DS-14

Contingency Releases

Contingency releases supply wipe-out or kick-out provisions to your purchase contract for those contingencies you specify to be the buyer's responsibility. They provide that you will continue to market your home until one of the following occurs:

- Buyers remove those contingencies you have indicated.
- You receive another offer to purchase your home that does not contain the contingencies you specified. Buyers then have the amount of time you agreed on to remove the contingencies. If the buyers fail to remove the contingencies, you may sell your home to the persons who offered you the contract without the contingencies.

Consider basing your actions on whether you signed a contingency release when you signed the purchase contract.

- If you have *not* used a contingency release type form or a similar contract, do *not* accept another offer. Accepting another offer opens you to possible legal action.
- If you used a contingency release type form or a similar contract to supply a wipe-out or kick-out provision, you may continue to market your property.
  1. You may continue to market until you accept another offer to buy your home that does not contain any of the contingencies you specified.
  2. Inform the first buyers that
     a. You accepted another offer.
     b. They have the time agreed on in the contingency release in which to remove and waive the specified contingencies.

Contingency Removal Requests

Consider using a contingency removal request type form to notify buyers to remove and waive the contingencies agreed on in a contingency release type form. This form serves as official notice to buyers that you have accepted another written offer. Many variations of this form exist. Here we present the current form in California at the time of this writing. The Notice to Buyer to Remove and Waive Contingencies is published by the California Association of Realtors.

The first buyers have the amount of time you both agreed to in the purchase contract to sign a firm agreement without the specified contingencies. One way to sign a firm contract without the specified contingencies is to have buyers sign a notice of contingency removal notice type form.

If buyers fail to remove the contingencies within the time limit given, by signing a contingency removal notice or similar form.

1. The real estate purchase contract, plus all the rights and duties under that contract, end and become invalid.
2. You will return the buyers' deposit.

Contingency Removal Notice

Using a contingency removal notice, buyers can remove and waive conditions agreed on in a contingency release form. On any form of this type expect the buyers to have

- Entered the conditions to which they voluntarily give up claim.
- Agreed to buy the property in accord with all other terms and conditions.

If the first buyers *remove* those contingencies you have specified, you *must* sell your home to the first buyers.

NOTICE TO BUYER TO REMOVE AND WAIVE CONTINGENCIES

CALIFORNIA ASSOCIATION OF REALTORS® (CAR) STANDARD FORM

TO: _____

_____

_____

In accordance with the Contingency Release Clause Addendum to Real Estate Purchase Contract

and Deposit Receipt dated _____

between _____ (Buyer)

and _____ (Seller)

regarding real property described as _____

_____

You are hereby notified that Seller has accepted a written offer conditioned upon your rights to remove the contingencies outlined in the Contingency Clause Addendum.

Under the terms of the Addendum, you have until _____
at 6:00 P.M. to remove said contingencies. In the event of your failure to remove the contingencies with the time limit specified, the Real Estate Purchase Contract and Deposit Receipt and all of the rights and obligations thereunder shall terminate and become null and void and your deposit shall be returned.

Dated _____   SELLER _____

                                SELLER _____

RECEIPT IF DELIVERED IN PERSON

Receipt of this notice is acknowledged:

Dated _____   BUYER _____

                                BUYER _____

FORM CRCN-11

OFFICE USE ONLY
Reviewed by Broker or Designee _____
Date _____

EQUAL HOUSING OPPORTUNITY
SF-Oct-88

If the first buyers *fail to remove* those contingencies you specified, your contract with these buyers is void. After your contract with the first buyers is void, you may then open an escrow to sell your property to the buyers who offered you a contract without those contingencies.

Step 4: Handle Other Complications

A number of other complications might occur while your property is in escrow.

Revocation
Revocation is contract cancellation after a time limit expires. The cancellation is by whomever performed according to the contract when the other party did not perform according to the contract. Handle revocation in the way that helps you achieve your desired results.

- Have the escrow holder return whatever you put into escrow if you do not want to continue the sale of your house to those buyers. Both you and the buyers are entitled to the return of the documents and funds that you deposited in escrow.
- Renegotiate the contract and open another escrow if you want to continue to sell your home to those buyers. You cannot continue with the initial escrow once it is canceled.

Breach of Contract
Breach of contract means failure to perform as promised without a legal excuse (a good reason). If you file a suit for breach of contract, in most states escrow holders must retain funds and documents until cases have been decided by the courts or by arbitration. What legally might be considered a breach of contract depends on the circumstances. For answers to questions regarding breach of contract, consult your attorney. Actions that are often considered breaches of contract by courts include

- Your refusing *without* a legitimate reason to sell your home to buyers after you have signed a valid contract. Valid reasons for your refusal might include buyers failing to apply for a loan that they need to purchase the home or not having sufficient funds to cover a check.
- Buyers refusing without a sound reason to buy your home after they have signed a valid contract with you. Valid reasons for buyers' refusal might include unsatisfactory home or pest control inspection reports, their failure to sell property on which your sale is contingent, and their failure to obtain suitable financing.

Death or Incapacity
If you or the buyers die or become incapacitated, the timing of these events determines the effect on the sale. Generally, if

- You die or become incompetent *before* you deliver the deed to escrow, buyers
  - ○ Cannot receive the title through that escrow.
  - ○ May sue representatives of your estate for specific performance (a court order requiring a party to perform according to the terms of the contract).
  - ○ May negotiate a new contract with your heirs and set up a new escrow.
- You die or become incompetent *after* depositing the deed in escrow, the escrow is not revoked. Buyers may still deposit the purchase price into escrow and receive the deed if all the other terms of the escrow are met.

- The buyer dies before you deliver the deed to escrow, the deed is void.
- The buyer becomes mentally incapacitated before you deliver the deed to escrow, the deed is still valid.
- The buyer dies or becomes mentally incapacitated after you deliver the deed to escrow, the escrow is not necessarily revoked.

Property Destruction

Usually, the person with whom responsibility for costs of property destruction rests depends on the circumstances:
- Buyers are responsible if they have either assumed legal title or physical possession.
- You are responsible if buyers have neither assumed legal title nor assumed physical possession.

To protect yourself if fire, flood, earthquake, or other devastating incident should destroy the property, consider keeping your hazard insurance policy in effect until the close of escrow. If the home is destroyed, you thus do not lose a tremendous amount of money.

Assignment by Seller

Assignment is the transferring to another of an entire property including all rights to the property. How you assign your interest or proceeds determines whether you must obtain the consent of the assignee. The assignee is the person to whom the interest or proceeds transfer. If you assign your interest or any portion of your interest
- *Contingent on* the close of escrow, the consent of the assignee is generally not required.
- *On* the close of escrow, escrow may require the assignee's consent.

Mutual Consent and Cancellation

If you and buyers both agree to cancel an escrow, you may do so. Under these circumstances, both you and buyers are entitled to the return of documents and funds you deposited.

Implications

If a real estate professional represents you in a sale in which you and the buyers mutually consent and cancel, the broker
- Must return the deposit to the buyers.
- Is considered to have earned the commission by providing ready, willing, and able buyers who entered into the contract.
- May sue you to obtain a commission if he or she has a contract with you.

Consider protecting yourself by
1. Seeing your attorney before you cancel a purchase contract.
2. Using a contract release form when both you and the buyers want to declare your purchase contract invalid.

Contract Release

A contract release should contain wording indicating that you and buyers jointly release each other from any and all of the following, which each may have against the other up to the date of the release agreement.
- Claims—demands for money or property, and/or rights to payments.
- Actions—suits brought in courts.

- Demands—legal rights or obligations asserted in courts.

A release should also contain instructions to the broker or escrow holder regarding the distribution of the deposit, including amounts and to whom to disburse the funds.

Disputes

The escrow holder is a neutral stakeholder and therefore is not the proper person to make decisions in controversies between you and buyers. If you and buyers have a dispute,

- The escrow holder usually does nothing until you and buyers resolve the situation.
- In prolonged disputes, the escrow holder sometimes initiates a court interpleader action requesting that a court take custody of deposited funds and make a judgment as to their disbursement.
- Consider consulting an attorney if you feel you and buyers have a binding contract and you have a dispute about anything other than a simple default (failure of a person to fulfill an obligation or perform a duty). An attorney may aid you in resolving the dispute without court action.
- If you and the buyers have agreed to arbitration,
  - Your controversy is to be heard by a disinterested person who will give you both a chance to speak and then make a decision on the case.
  - You must take and abide by the judgment of that person if you have agreed to binding arbitration.

Now that you have handled all the complications that have occurred prior to closing, you are ready for closing the sale of your house, which is the subject of Chapter 16.

CHAPTER 16
Close!

Closing is the successful completion of a real estate transaction in which funds are disbursed and title is transferred from seller to buyers. To close most effectively, we suggest that you have the buyers perform a walk-through inspection, understand how escrow closes, and reconcile the closing statement.

Step 1: Perform Walk-through Inspection

A walk-through inspection is proof that you have left the property in the condition in which you agreed to leave it. Although this step is not generally legally necessary, like disclosures it provides proof that you have complied with the terms of your contract.

Understand Walk-through Inspection
A walk-through inspection, usually done by you and buyers within a few days before escrow closes, is an inspection verifying that
- All systems and appliances are in good working order except as noted in your contract.
- You made all repairs you agreed to make.
- You replaced all items you agreed to replace.
- You have removed all your personal items from the house.
- You have left the house in the condition you agreed on with the buyers or at least swept, vacuumed, and dusted.

Prepare Walk-through Inspection Worksheet
Consider using the Walk-through Inspection Worksheet to conduct your walk-through inspection.
1. Fill in the heading of the worksheet.
2. If item is acceptable on inspection, have buyers write their initials in the Okay column.
3. If an item needs to be fixed, have buyers write a **X** in the Fix column and write how the item needs to be fixed.
4. Write in additional items in the spaces provided.
5. Have the buyers sign a copy of the completed worksheet.
6. Obtain a copy of the completed worksheet for your records.

WALK-THROUGH INSPECTION WORKSHEET

Sellers: _____ Buyers:_____

Address:_____

Move in date: _____ Current date:_____

Initial under Okay for items that appear in satisfactory condition. Check Fix
if item needs to be handled and write what needs to be done under Notes.

Okay Item   Fix Notes

Outside
_____ Plantings   [ ] _____
_____ Sprinkler system   [ ] _____
_____ Walls/fences/gates   [ ] _____
_____ Patio/deck   [ ] _____
_____ Pool/spa   [ ] _____
_____ Outdoor/electrical   [ ] _____
_____ Well/pump   [ ] _____

Utilities
_____ Heating system   [ ] _____
_____ Cooling system   [ ] _____
_____ Indoor electrical   [ ] _____
_____ Bathroom plumbing   [ ] _____
_____ Kitchen plumbing   [ ] _____

Appliances
_____ Water heater   [ ] _____
_____ Range/hood   [ ] _____
_____ Oven   [ ] _____
_____ Microwave   [ ] _____
_____ Dishwasher   [ ] _____
_____ Disposal   [ ] _____
_____ Smoke detectors   [ ] _____
_____ Security devices   [ ] _____

Other
_____ Doors/windows   [ ] _____
_____ Window coverings   [ ] _____
_____ Floor coverings   [ ] _____
_____ Mirrors   [ ] _____
_____ Sinks/showers/tubs   [ ] _____

Buyer: _____   **Buyer:**_____

Step 2: Understand Closing Escrow

Understanding how the escrow transaction closes can make you comfortable with a process many buyers and sellers find very confusing.

Closing Escrow

An escrow is complete when all conditions listed in the escrow instructions are met and all acts performed. When an escrow is complete, the escrow holder disburses the funds and documents to close the escrow.

Closing Costs

Closing costs are expenses that must be paid before the escrow can close. Closing costs are generally from 1.5 percent to 3 percent of the sales price of your home. The party that pays each cost generally depends on the arrangements you negotiated with buyers. Closing costs should be quite close to those you estimated on the last Estimate of Proceeds Worksheet you completed. Discrepancies are often due to forgetting to re-calculate costs after you change dates on which some of these costs depend.

Step 3: Reconcile Closing Statement

Reconciling your closing statement is much like checking an invoice for goods and services. Make sure you were charged only for items for which you agreed to pay and for the amount you agreed to pay.

Understand Closing Statements

A *closing statement* is a written accounting that specifies the distribution of all funds involved in the sale. This document is also called an *escrow* or *settlement statement*. A closing agent or escrow holder issues separate closing statements to you and the buyers. On each statement, the debits must equal the credits.

Many variations of closing statements exist. Here we present a copy of the HUD-1 Settlement Statement published by the U.S. Department of Housing and Urban Development. This statement is available and in general use throughout the country.

Regarding the settlement statement, note that

- Although all possible charges are not specifically listed on this form, the form provides ample space for the enumeration of each charge.
- The large darkened areas on your form (on the left in the sample shown) represent the areas where the buyers' charges were listed. The closing agent or escrow holder calculates the transaction as a whole on his or her copy. Because the buyers' side of the sale does not directly concern you, the area where that data occurs is darkened on your statement. The buyers' statement has similar darkened areas in the spaces where the details of your transaction are listed.

Reconcile the Closing Statement

To reconcile your closing statement,

1. Compare your closing statement to the appropriate Estimate of Proceeds Worksheet, that is, the last one you used to calculate your estimated proceeds.
2. If there is a significant difference between your estimate and what you were

HUD-1 Rev 5/78

FORM APPROVED OMB NO 63R1501

A.		B. TYPE OF LOAN						
		1.	FHA	2.	FMHA	3.		CONV. UNINS
U.S. DEPARTMENT OF HOUSING AND URBAN DEVELOPMENT		4.	VA	5.	CONV. INS.			
		6. FILE NUMBER				7. LOAN NUMBER		
SETTLEMENT STATEMENT		8. MORTGAGE INSURANCE CASE NUMBER						

C. NOTE: *This form is furnished to give you a statement of actual settlement costs. Amounts paid to and by the settlement agent are shown. Items marked "(p.o.c.)" were paid outside the closing; they are shown here for informational purposes and are not included in the totals.*

D. NAME OF BORROWER:	E. NAME OF SELLER:
F. NAME OF LENDER:	G. PROPERTY LOCATION:

H. SETTLEMENT AGENT	PLACE OF SETTLEMENT	I. SETTLEMENT DATE

K. SUMMARY OF SELLER'S TRANSACTION	
400. GROSS AMOUNT DUE TO SELLER:	
401. Contract sales price	
402. Personal property	
403.	
404.	
405.	
Adjustments for items paid by seller in advance	
406. City/town taxes to	
407. County taxes to	
408. Assessments to	
409.	
410.	
411.	
412.	
420. GROSS AMOUNT DUE TO SELLER	
500. REDUCTIONS IN AMOUNT DUE TO SELLER:	
501. Excess deposit (see instructions)	
502. Settlement charges to seller (Line 1400)	
503. Existing loans taken subject to	
504. Payoff of first mortgage loan	
505. Payoff of second mortgage loan	
506.	
507.	
508.	
509.	
Adjustments for items unpaid by seller	
510. City/town taxes to	
511. County taxes to	
512. Assessments to	
513.	
514.	
515.	
516.	
517.	
518.	
519.	
520. TOTAL REDUCTION AMOUNT DUE SELLER	
600. CASH AT SETTLEMENT TO/FROM SELLER	
601. Gross amount due to seller (Line 420)	
602. Less reductions in amount due seller (Line 520)	
603. CASH (TO) (FROM) SELLER	

L. SETTLEMENT CHARGES

	PAID FROM SELLER'S FUNDS AT SETTLEMENT
700. TOTAL SALES/BROKER'S COMMISSION based on price $ @ % =	
Division of Commission (line 700) as follows:	
701. $ to	
702. $ to	
703. Commission paid at settlement	
704.	
800. ITEMS PAYABLE IN CONNECTION WITH LOAN	
801. Loan Origination Fee %	
802. Loan Discount %	
803. Appraisal Fee to	
804. Credit Report to	
805.	
806.	
807.	
808.	
809.	
810.	
811.	
900. ITEMS REQUIRED BY LENDER TO BE PAID IN ADVANCE	
901. Interest from to @ $ /day	
902. Mortgage Insurance Premium for months to	
903. Hazard Insurance Premium for years to	
904. years to	
905.	
1000. RESERVES DEPOSITED WITH LENDER	
1001. Hazard insurance months @ $ per month	
1002. Mortgage insurance months @ $ per month	
1003. City property taxes months @ $ per month	
1004. County property taxes months @ $ per month	
1005. Annual assessments months @ $ per month	
1006. months @ $ per month	
1007. months @ $ per month	
1008. months @ $ per month	
1100. TITLE CHARGES	
1101. Settlement or closing fee to	
1102.	
1103.	
1104.	
1105. Document preparation to	
1106. Notary fees to	
1107.	
1108. Title insurance to	
(Includes above items numbers	
1109. Lender's coverage $	
1110. Owner's coverage $	
1111.	
1112.	
1113.	
1200. GOVERNMENT RECORDING AND TRANSFER CHARGE	
1201. Recording fees: Deed $; Mortgages $; Release $	
1202. City/County tax/stamps: Deed $; Mortgage $	
1203. State tax/stamps: Deed $	
1204.	
1205.	
1300. ADDITIONAL SETTLEMENT CHARGES	
1301.	
1302. Pest inspection to	
1303.	
1304.	
1305.	
1400. TOTAL SETTLEMENT CHARGES *(enter on Lines 103, Section J and 502, Section K)*	

charged, check with your closing agent or escrow holder for an explanation of the discrepancy.

Closing agents and escrow holders may distribute your proceeds check to you even though they have not completed the closing statement in its finished form. For safety's sake and for your permanent records,

- Make a copy of your proceeds check before you cash it.
- Keep the copy of your proceeds check in your property records file with the other documents about the transaction.

Congratulations for selling your home without a broker. Remember, after you close the escrow on your home, sooner or later you must handle the tax consequences of your sale. Handling your taxes is the subject of Chapter 17.

CHAPTER 17
Handle Taxes

Selling a home has important tax consequences. Because tax laws recently underwent—and are continuing to undergo—significant changes, consider contacting your accountant or tax preparer for more current and detailed information.

Step 1: Calculate Tax Costs

Tax laws may directly affect you when you sell your home.

24-month Rule

When you sell your *principal residence*, you must defer gain and thus any tax consequences if you buy or construct another principal residence within 24 months before or after your sale of the first property. The *gain* is adjusted sales price minus adjusted basis. To qualify, the transaction must meet certain criteria.

- Your principal residence must be the home in which you live the majority of the time.
- Your principal residence may be a house, condominium, mobile home, or even a houseboat, yacht, or cooperative apartment.
- You must plan to live in your new residence.

Complete Deferral of Gain

If the adjusted sales price of your new residence is *equal to or greater than* the adjusted sales price of your old residence, you completely defer the gain until a later date. The deferred gain lowers your basis in the new residence dollar for dollar.

1. For adjusted sales price of your old residence, subtract closing costs on old residence from sales price of old residence, for example:

Sales price of old residence	$ 174,000
Closing costs of old residence	− 4,000
Adjusted sales price of old residence	$ 170,000

2. *Basis* is the cost of your residence when you purchased it including down payment, loans used, and closing costs. If you deferred gain from selling a former residence, your basis should be listed on Form 2119 of your federal tax return for the year you sold your former residence.
3. For *adjusted basis* of your old residence add costs of capital improvements on

old residence to basis of old residence. Capital improvements are additions to your property that are permanent, increase property value, and have a useful life of at least one year. Use total cost of the improvements from the last page of the Capital Improvement Worksheet in Chapter 2, for example:

Basis of old residence	$ 75,000
Capital improvements on old residence	+ 15,000
Adjusted basis of old residence	$ 90,000

4. For the gain on your old residence, subtract adjusted basis of the old residence from adjusted sales price of old residence. You defer paying taxes on this gain, for example:

Adjusted sales price of old residence	$ 170,000
Adjusted basis of old residence	− 90,000
Gain deferred on old residence	$ 80,000

5. For adjusted sales price of your new residence, add the sales price of new residence to closing costs on new residence, for example:

Sales price of new residence	$ 180,000
Closing costs of new residence	+ 5,000
Adjusted sales price of new residence	$ 185,000

6. For your basis in the new residence, subtract the gain deferred on the old residence from adjusted sales price of the new residence, for example:

Adjusted sales price of new residence	$ 185,000
Gain deferred on old residence	− 80,000
Basis in new residence	$ 105,000

Partial Deferral of Gain

If the adjusted sales price of the new residence is less than the adjusted sales price of the old residence, you partially defer gain until a later date.

The amount on which you must pay capital gains tax at once is the difference between the adjusted sales price of old residence and the adjusted sales price of new residence. Any remaining gains *must* be deferred. The deferred amount reduces your basis in your new residence dollar for dollar.

1. For adjusted sales price of your old residence, subtract the closing costs on old residence from the sales price of old residence, for example:

Sales price of old residence	$ 205,000
Closing costs on old residence	− 5,000
Adjusted sales price of old residence	$ 200,000

2. *Basis* is the cost of your home when you purchased it, including down payment, loans, and closing costs. If you deferred gain from the sale of a former home your basis should be listed on Form 2119 of your federal tax return for the year in which you sold your former home.

3. For the adjusted basis of your old residence, add costs of capital improvements

on old residence to basis of old residence. See Complete Deferral of Gain earlier in this chapter for more information regarding capital improvements. The following is an example of calculation of adjusted basis on an old residence:

Basis of old residence		$ 75,000
Capital improvements on old residence	+	25,000
Adjusted basis of old residence		$ 100,000

4. For your gain on your old residence subtract the adjusted basis on the old residence from adjusted sales price of your old residence. You defer paying taxes on this gain on the old residence, for example:

Adjusted sales price of old residence		$ 200,000
Adjusted basis of old residence	−	100,000
Gain deferred on old residence		$ 100,000

5. For the adjusted sales price of your new residence, add the sales price of new residence to closing costs on new residence, for example:

Sales price of new residence		$ 180,000
Closing costs on new residence	+	5,000
Adjusted sales price of new residence		$ 185,000

6. For gain that is immediately recognized (on which you pay taxes) on your old residence, subtract the adjusted sales price of new residence from the adjusted sales price of the old residence, for example:

Adjusted sales price of old residence		$ 200,000
Adjusted sales price of new residence	−	185,000
Gain recognized on old residence		$ 15,000

7. For gain deferred on your old residence, subtract the gain recognized on your old residence from gain on the old residence, for example:

Gain on old residence		$ 100,000
Gain recognized on old residence	−	15,000
Gain deferred on old residence		$ 85,000

8. For your basis in the new residence, subtract the gain deferred on your old residence from adjusted sales price of the new residence, for example:

Adjusted sales price of new residence		$ 185,000
Gain deferred on old residence	−	85,000
Basis in new residence		$ 100,000

If you feel that you will owe capital gains tax on the sale of your home, consider
- Filling in the Capital Improvements Worksheet.
- Preparing the Final Tax Implications Worksheet or consulting your accountant or tax preparer.

You cannot take a capital loss on the sale of your principal residence. See the section on converting a principal residence into a rental property.

You can usually defer gain on the sale of your residence only once every 24 months; however, exemptions exist. Consult your accountant or tax preparer for current regulations if you

- Plan to sell because of work-related reasons.
- Are in the armed forces.
- Plan to buy two or more residences within 24 months.
- Plan to buy a replacement home that is not in the United States.

Over-55 One-time Exclusion

A taxpayer (or spouse) who is 55 or older before the date he or she sells the home can be granted a one-time exclusion of up to $125,000 of gain, provided that both of the following occur:

- Neither taxpayer nor spouse used this exclusion of gain on the sale of a residence after July 20, 1981.
- The home sold was owned and used as a principal residence for three of the last five years (calculated on a day-by-day basis) before the sale.

Contact your accountant or tax preparer for current rules if any of the following occurs:

- Your spouse died at age 55 or older and you are not yet 55.
- You want to revoke a previously used exclusion to shield a larger amount of gain now.
- You want to combine the 24-month rule and the over-55 one-time exemption to defer any gain above the $125,000 exclusion.

Tax-deductible Expenses

If you itemize deductions, some of the costs of the sale of your home may be tax deductible. Check with your accountant or tax preparer for the current status of tax deductibility of marketing costs, closing costs, and moving expenses.

Marketing Costs

The costs of marketing efforts, including fix-up expenses (improvements, repairs, and attractiveness items) as well as advertising may be deductible from your adjusted sales price if they are both

- Performed during the 90-day period before you place your property on the market.
- Paid for within 30 days after the closing date.

Closing Costs

Closing costs such as prepaid interest, prepaid taxes, points, escrow fees, title fees, and recording fees are deductible.

Moving Costs

Moving expenses are deductible as an itemized expense on Schedule A of your federal income tax forms.

Installment Sale Imputed Interest

You may sell your home and help buyers finance the purchase price by extending them credit using a seller carry back loan. If you receive your sales price over more than one year, in effect, you have made an installment sale. You spread your gain and thus any tax consequences over more than one tax year.

The IRS requires that you charge a minimum interest rate on seller carry back financing. If you do not charge the minimum rate, the IRS will assign (impute) a rate the service says you should have charged. The IRS will tax you as if you had received interest at the higher rate, plus the service will penalize you for not having paid this tax earlier, for example:

- You carry back a $15,000 second loan at 6 percent interest.
- IRS minimum interest rate is 9 percent.
- Therefore, the IRS imputes a 9 percent rate on the loan you made to buyers.
- The IRS taxes you as if you had received interest at 9 percent and also charges you a penalty.

Conversion of a Principal Residence

You can convert your principal residence into rental property and vice versa. With rental property, you

- May take repairs and maintenance expenses as deductions.
- Must take depreciation. Currently, depreciation for residential property is calculated on a 27.5-year or 40-year straight line method. Subtract depreciation from your basis.
- May take a loss on the sale.

If you convert rental property into your principal residence and then sell, you

- May not deduct repairs and maintenance.
- Must subtract accrued depreciation from the basis in calculating your gain.
- May not take a loss on the sale.

Consult your accountant or tax preparer if either of these situations applies.

Foreign Investment in Real Property Tax Act (FIRPTA)

You may be asked to sign an affidavit stating that you are not a nonresident alien for the purposes of U.S. income taxation in order to comply with FIRPTA regulations. The Foreign Investment in Real Property Tax Act (FIRPTA) is a federal law designed to make sure that foreign nationals selling property in the United States pay capital gains tax on their profit.

Buyers may be liable to the IRS for up to 10 percent of the sales price, plus penalties and interest, if

- Buyers are nonresident aliens for U.S. income taxation.
- No exemptions apply.
- Buyers do not deduct and withhold the required tax.

FIRPTA requires that buyers deduct and withhold 10 percent of the sales price to pay the tax unless certain exemptions apply. Exemptions are as follows:

- Buyers purchase your home to use as their personal residence and the price they paid was not over $300,000.
- You as seller signed an affidavit that you are not a nonresident alien for the purposes of U.S. income taxation.
- The buyers established an exemption under IRS code.

IRS Form 1099S

Since January 1, 1987, the closing agent is required to provide you and the IRS with a completed Form 1099S entitled "Statement for Recipients of Proceeds from Real

Estate Transactions," for the IRS. This form contains information regarding your name, address of the property sold, sales price, and closing date.

The IRS checks Form 1099S with your tax return—specifically, Form 2119—to see if the numbers match.

IRS Form 2119

For the return of the year you sell your home, the Internal Revenue Service requires you to file Form 2119, entitled "Sale or Exchange of Principal Residence." This form's sections include

1. Facts about you and the home you sold.
2. Calculation of your gain.
3. Computation of your one-time exclusion if you or your spouse is age 55 or older.
4. Calculation of your gain to be postponed, as well as adjusted basis of your new residence.

Be careful to comply with regulations regarding this form, which at the time of this writing include

- Filing Form 2119 with your tax return for the year of the sale in order to begin the statute of limitations.
- Filing Form 2119 whether or not you bought another residence.
- Sending an amended Form 2119 to the IRS when you do complete the replacement purchase within the 24-month period.
- Filing Form 1040X to apply for an income tax refund if you report and pay tax on your gain but later buy or build a residence within a two-year period.

Step 2: Prepare Final Tax Implications Worksheet

Use the parts of the Final Tax Implications Worksheet to
1. Calculate your gain on the sale of your residence.
2. Determine whether you want to completely or partially defer the gain.

Complete the worksheets to get an idea of what your tax ramifications may be. Consider checking with your accountant or tax preparer to verify your calculations and obtain more current and detailed information. Laws in this area have recently been undergoing significant changes.

Step 3: Report and Pay Taxes

After you read this chapter, understand what you need to report, and calculate the results, we recommend that you
1. Report the results of your sale as required, even when no taxes are due.
2. Pay taxes on the sale when due.

Moving is not technically considered part of selling your home, although you generally move close to the time you sell. By understanding moving and handling it effectively you can save time and money. Moving is the subject of Chapter 18.

FINAL TAX IMPLICATIONS WORKSHEET

Name: _____ Date:_____

Address:_____

GAIN ON SALE OF OLD RESIDENCE

1. Adjusted sales price of old residence

    Sales price of old residence   _____
    Closing costs of old residence   − _____
    Adjusted sales price of old residence   = _____

2. Adjusted basis of old residence

    A.   Basis of old residence from IRS Form 2119   _____
    B.   Capital improvements on old residence from   + _____
          Capital Improvements Worksheet
    Adjusted basis of old residence   = _____

3. Gain on old residence

    Adjusted sales price of old residence   _____
    Adjusted basis of old residence   − _____
    Gain on old residence   = _____

        Gain on sale = Taxable gain (for persons not using
        the Over-55 One-time Exclusion).

4. Taxable gain if using Over-55 One-time Exclusion

    Gain on old residence   _____
    Over-55 One-time Exclusion   − $ 125,000
    Taxable gain   = _____

FINAL TAX IMPLICATIONS WORKSHEET

COMPLETE DEFERRAL OF GAIN

5. Adjusted sales price of old residence (from #1) _____

6. Sales price of new residence _____
Closing costs of new residence + _____
Adjusted sales price of new residence = _____

7. Adjusted sales price of new residence _____
Adjusted sales price of old residence − _____
Adjusted sales price difference = _____
   A. IF adjusted sales price difference is a <u>positive</u> number or <u>0</u>, proceed with step #8.

   B. IF adjusted sales price difference is a <u>negative</u> number, proceed with the section entitled Partial Deferral of Gain located at the bottom of this sheet.

8. Adjusted sales price of new residence _____
Gain deferred on old residence − _____
Basis in new property = _____

PARTIAL DEFERRAL OF GAIN

Gain on old residence _____
Gain recognized on old residence − _____
Gain deferred on old residence = _____

Adjusted sales price of new residence _____
Gain deferred on old residence − _____
Basis in new residence = _____

CHAPTER 18
Move!

Selling your home usually requires a move. Understanding and applying certain techniques can keep money in your pocket when you move.

Step 1: Prepare for Moving

You can save money and aggravation by preparing for your move ahead of time.

Decide What to Move
Decide what you don't want to move beforehand and then handle the preparations so that you have less to move.
1. Consume or give away excess food and beverages.
2. Sell items you do not need or use but that are worth selling.
3. Give away items you don't need or use that are not worth selling but are still usable. Get a receipt for your donation if it is tax deductible.
4. Discard items that are unusable.
5. Sell, donate, or discard heavy but relatively inexpensive items that are not cost effective to move, including lumber, firewood, old appliances, and plants. Unless plants are rare or expensive, buying new plants after you move is cheaper and easier. Soil and pots are often heavy. Loading plants is up to the moving van driver's discretion because of potential pests. Some states have strict rules about plant materials. Check with states in which you plan to travel.
6. Dispose of potentially hazardous substances that are always dangerous and often illegal to ship, such as
   - Flammables, combustibles, and explosives, including propane from propane tanks.
   - Pressurized containers of all types.
   - Pesticides, herbicides, and other poisons.

Obtain Written Relocation Policies
Obtain written relocation policies if your employer is going to pay for part or all of the move.

Check Homeowner's Insurance
Check your homeowner's insurance to see
   - Whether your policy covers moving, including liability; cargo protection, both loss and theft; equipment damage; and medical expenses.

- Whether it contains a floater for valuable items, in addition to life insurance.
- The limits of each coverage on your policy.

Step 2: Plan Your Move

You can have a moving company move your goods, move them yourself, or use a combination of methods. Before you decide what method to use, understand what is involved with each method.

Moving Companies

By understanding what is involved with a move by professional movers, you can usually save yourself money.

Cost Factors

Moving companies base the costs of moving your goods on several factors.

Weight. Movers weigh the truck before and after your goods are loaded to determine the weight of your shipment.

Distance. Movers use charts that give the basic cost per 100 pounds. These costs are calculated for a range of weights and a range of distances.

Insurance. Movers include protection against damage and loss based on a required minimum amount per pound, *if* you request coverage. The actual value of items is usually much greater than the minimum per pound coverage. Actual value is depreciated value of item at the present time, not full cost of replacing item.

Consider

1. Buying higher coverage than the minimum provided. Buy coverage for at least actual value, if not the replacement value.
2. Inquiring about options for liability coverage available through the moving company.
3. Obtaining temporary coverage for the move if your homeowner's policy does not contain moving coverage.

Storage. Storage charges are based primarily on weight but may vary widely from area to area. Other charges might include a

- Handling fee for unloading truck.
- Delivery charge for delivering goods to a new location.
- Flat access fee plus an hourly access rate for access to your goods during storage.

Delivery. Delivery is included in the price of the move during normal working hours. For weekend, holiday, or after-hours delivery at

- Your request, movers usually add an additional charge.
- Driver's request, movers should not charge you extra.

Moving Special Items. Professional movers usually charge extra for moving certain large heavy items, including but not limited to

- Pianos, organs, and grandfather clocks.
- Hot tubs, Jacuzzis, spas, and whirlpool baths.
- Play houses and tool sheds.
- Automobiles, motorcycles, golf carts, and snowmobiles.
- Trailers of all types.
- Boats, unmounted campers, campers, and mini-motor homes.
- Riding mowers, farm equipment, and tractors.

Other Common Charges. Other charges by professional movers may include but are not limited to

- Providing moving containers such as cartons.
- Packing and/or unpacking.
- Disassembly and/or assembly of items.
- Carrying items up or down flights of stairs.
- Carrying items an excessive distance.
- Pick up and/or delivery at locations other than your home.
- Extra time over estimate.

Tips. Although definitely not required, giving the movers a small tip after loading and again after unloading your belongings is a nice gesture.

Usual Moving Company Procedure

Many moving companies perform a regular estimate using these steps:

1. Estimator makes a price estimate of your move based upon cost factors listed earlier.
2. Movers determine the weight of your shipment by weighing the truck before and after loading, and finding the difference.
3. You pay the total charge based on shipment weight in cash or certified check *before* the driver will unload your belongings.
4. If the total amount you owe is greater than estimated total amount plus 10 percent, you pay only the estimated amount before the driver will unload the truck.
5. You pay the balance within the period the company indicates, often 30 days.

Money-saving Ideas

You may save money when using a professional mover by

1. Finding out which moving companies have the best reputations in your area and dealing with only these companies.
2. Calling the three top companies.
   a. Ask each company whether it takes your shipment to its destination or transfers it to another company. Transfer often means extra handling for your goods and potential extra problems for you.
   b. If the company transports your goods to its destination, ask the company to provide an estimate.
3. Letting each estimator know that you are getting several other estimates and comparing price and quality.
4. Asking the estimator to list what services are provided as well as to itemize the price for each service.
5. Asking whether there is a time of the year, month, and/or week (an off period) when you can get a lower price.
6. Asking whether the company will repay you for expenses you must pay if delivery is delayed through no fault of yours, and if so
   a. What items are included.
   b. What you must do to be repaid.
7. Asking estimator to provide additional estimates
   a. Guaranteed estimate—A binding estimate guaranteeing that you pay only the price quoted and no more. Ask for how long price is guaranteed.
   b. Not over estimate—An estimate guaranteed not to be over a specified amount in spite of the actual shipment weight. If weight on which estimate is based is *greater* than the estimate, you pay only estimated amount. If weight is

less than the estimate, you pay an amount based on the actual shipment weight.

    c. Discounted estimate—An estimate for which some or all services are discounted from rates stated in published tariff books. If published rates increase between your estimate and your move, your cost often increases, even if you receive the same discount. Consider

        1. Requesting to see the rates stated in the tariff book.

        2. Asking how much the rates you were quoted are discounted.

        3. Inquiring for how long this discount applies.

        4. Asking when the estimator expects the next rate increase.

8. If your estimate is the guaranteed or not over type, ask when you move whether you qualify to have extra items added without paying any additional fees. (Due to the manner in which tariff books are set up combined with the estimated weight of your goods, your shipment may or may not qualify.)

9. Make sure that each estimate is complete and accurate. Estimates are good *only* for items listed in estimate.

10. Tell each estimator that you will not be making a decision at this time because you want to compare estimates.

11. Compare estimates and choose the company that you want to move your goods.

12. Call the company you have chosen and ask the customer service person to prepare an order for service. Consider being sure that the order is

    • A complete and accurate list of items you want to move.

       ◦ You can add or delete items after you sign the service order and before you move by signing an addendum stating what you are adding or deleting.

       ◦ Companies usually charge extra for added items.

       ◦ Drivers may refuse to load unlisted items.

    • Cancelable by you at any time without a charge because the service order is *not* a contract.

13. Driver will ask you to sign a bill of lading, which is the contract between you and the moving company. Sign the bill of lading only when you are sure that it

    a. Is correct.

    b. Corresponds in all details to the estimate, the service order, *and* the addenda.

    c. States the company's responsibilities and liability.

    d. States your responsibilities.

    e. States the services to be rendered and their prices.

14. When the van arrives to load or unload your shipment,

    a. Accompany the person who is doing the inventory.

    b. Be sure all items are listed and their condition is accurately described on your and their inventory sheets.

    c. If you do not agree with the person's description of condition, note your description and initial the note on both sheets.

    d. Sign sheets *only* when you feel everything is listed and accurately described.

15. File a claim after the move for lost items, damaged items, and/or extra expenses incurred if delivery was delayed through no fault of yours.

ADVANTAGES

    • Everything can be moved at one time.

    • Movers are trained to move your goods quickly and effectively.

- This method is less tiring and involves less chance of injury for you.
- Movers must estimate costs correctly within certain limits.

DISADVANTAGES
- This method is expensive.
- You must pay when you are moved because most moving companies do not accept credit cards.

Move-It-Yourself

Moving your goods yourself is based on size and type of vehicle, accessories, type of move, and insurance.

Cost Factors

The cost of moving is based on several factors.

Size of Vehicle. To determine the size of vehicle you need for the move, consider
1. Getting estimates from professional movers for
   a. The full move.
   b. Moving selected items. Get a breakdown of costs so if you decide to do various aspects yourself you can judge how much you might save.
   c. The number of cubic feet of area the load will occupy. Remember, chances are that you are not as adept at loading and may use more space than a professional.
2. Obtain information from vehicle rental companies and follow their instructions for estimating. They may
   a. Suggest you do an inventory and add the estimated cubic feet that each item you move occupies.
   b. Recommend a vehicle to use by the size of your home.

Type of Vehicle. The vehicle you rent may depend on the type of move you make.
- Local moves give you more options, you may
  ○ Rent a large vehicle and move everything at once.
  ○ Rent a smaller vehicle and move over a longer period of time. This enables you to use some items such as pads, straps, and perhaps even some cartons several times. It also permits you to rest between loads and not drive yourself to exhaustion.
- Long distance moves are generally most effectively handled using the largest vehicle that accommodates your belongings and that you can handle comfortably and safely.

Moving Accessories. In addition to the truck consider renting the following:
- Hand truck or dolly—A heavy-duty hand truck with straps is made for moving large, heavy items like appliances but is useful even for stacks of boxes.
- Furniture blankets/pads and straps—Strap blankets or pads on furniture for protection.
- Extension mirrors—For safety, consider using extension mirrors on *both* sides, whether you are renting a vehicle that lacks extension mirrors or are using your own vehicle to tow a trailer.

Insurance. Movers usually include coverage against damage and loss based on required minimum amount per pound *if* you request coverage. The actual value of items is usually much greater than the minimum per pound coverage. The actual value is the depreciated value of the item at the present time, not the full cost of replacing the item. Consider

- Obtaining higher coverage than the minimum provided at least to the actual value if not to the replacement value.
- Inquiring about what options for liability coverage are available through the moving company and their costs.
- Obtaining temporary coverage for the move if your homeowner's policy does not contain moving coverage.

Type of Move. The move you make also determines the amount the rental company charges.

- For round trips, you rent the vehicle and return it to the same dealer. For trailers, you generally pay a daily charge; for trucks, you usually pay a daily rate plus mileage.
  - Be sure you have a binding reservation for a round-trip rental; otherwise, you may not find a vehicle available even though you have reserved one.
  - Dealers prefer to rent to one-way movers because income is greater for the amount of work involved.
- For one-way trips, you rent a vehicle from one dealer and return it to another dealer.
  - Ask a renting dealer to look for a drop-off point that is handy to your destination and has the lowest charges.
  - Reserve your vehicle well in advance, particularly if you desire automatic transmission, air conditioning, and/or a loading ramp or a hydraulic lift gate.

Travel Expenses. You will have some travel expenses no matter how you travel to your new home. If you move your own goods, some of these expenses will be greater than usual.

- Gas consumption approximations can be obtained from the dealer from whom you rent the vehicle.
- Road taxes, charged by some states that require trip permits, and tolls are often higher with a truck or trailer. An automobile club may have information about these costs.
- Lodging and food costs increase if you travel more slowly.

Deposits. Deposits are up-front costs on the equipment you rent, which the rental company refunds after you return the equipment. The company may deduct charges from the deposit, including

- Extra mileage or time.
- Loss of or damage to equipment.
- Gas (if you return the vehicle filled with less gas than when you received it).

ADVANTAGES
- This method is less expensive than using professionals.
- Agencies usually accept credit cards; you can pay later.
- You can move at a convenient time.

DISADVANTAGES
- You may break or mar some of the items you move.
- You may become physically and emotionally exhausted.
- You may hurt yourself packing and lifting heavy objects.
- You may be liable if someone is hurt while helping you.

- You may be more apt to have a traffic accident while using equipment to which you are not accustomed.
- You may estimate expenses incorrectly.

Other Savings

Save money when you move by
1. Sending out items for cleaning or repair *before* moving, then having items delivered or picking them up after you move (for local moves).
2. Obtaining cartons that fit your needs.
   a. Obtain cartons at local stores. Ask employees of liquor stores, supermarkets, office supplies, and computer stores to save sturdy cartons with tops for you. Also try moving companies with supplies of boxes from unpacking other peoples moves.
   b. Buy cartons from moving companies, both commercial and do-it-yourself, that
      - Sell book, dish, and wardrobe cartons, in addition to utility cartons in several sizes. Being uniform, these cartons are more easily loaded than an assortment from various sources.
      - Have cartons constructed to meet the needs of the loads they are designed to carry.
      - Offer recommendations about what to pack in which size cartons and how to pack.
   c. Packing some items yourself, at least clothes and unbreakables.
   d. Shipping heavy items you will not need immediately by slower, less-expensive methods.
      - Consider shipping items such as books, magazines, some appliances, piano or organ, pool table, sports equipment, and vehicles.
      - Contact carriers for rates, including cartage, express, freight forwarding companies; parcel-shipping services including the post office, bus companies, and railroads.
3. Using a combination of methods,
   a. Have movers pack and move heavy items that you need right away or find hard to handle.
   b. Pack and ship heavy items you do not need immediately by slower, less expensive methods.
   c. Pack and move lightweight items yourself.
   d. Keep valuables with you.

Step 3: Inventory Your Home

An inventory can take the form of a written list, photos, videos, and/or receipts. In case of items lost or damaged during your move, burglary, or disasters (such as fire or flood), you will have information for insurance purposes. For the most complete inventory, use a combination of these methods of recording your home's contents.

Written List

List items by name, how many you have, the year they were purchased, and their present value. This method is inexpensive but time-consuming to use. Combined with photographs or videos, it provides good coverage.

Receipts

Keep the original receipt or a copy for each major item you have on your inventory. Store the receipts in a lockbox or other safe place outside your home in case of fire or other disaster. This method is easy and provides the best documentation. It provides the best protection when combined with photographs or videos.

Photographs or Videos

Take photographs or videos of the items as they are placed in your home. Take closeups of especially valuable items. This method may be relatively expensive, especially if you must rent equipment as well as buy the film or tapes. It provides proof of the condition of the items.

Step 4: Handle Address Changes and Records Transfers

Use the Address Change/Transfer Records Worksheet to aid you in notifying your correspondents of your address change and transferring your records.

Prepare Address Change/Records Transfer Worksheet

Address Changes

To handle your change of address, record the names and addresses of the professionals and companies on the form, noting especially those from which you need to transfer records.

1. Make an X in the Address column and write data requested about parties to whom you want to send address change notices under each applicable heading.
2. Prepare address change notices.
   a. Get post card address change forms at your local post office or use your own post cards or letters.
   b. Include the date that the address change takes effect.
3. Make an X in the Did column as you prepare each notice.
4. Mail the notices.

Records Transfer

1. On one line of each category, make an X in the Record column and write information about the party *from* whom you wish records to be transferred.
2. On the next line write **To** in Record column and write data about party *to* whom you wish records transferred.
3. Contact the parties from whom you wish the records to be transferred. Inform them
   A. You want records transferred.
   B. The name and address to whom you wish the records to be sent.
4. When you have sent a letter or contacted the party by telephone make an X in the Did column.

Step 5: Stop (and Possibly Start) Services

To stop services at your old home and start them at your new home, complete and use the Stop and Start Services Worksheet.

ADDRESS CHANGE/RECORDS TRANSFER WORKSHEET

Name: _____ Date effective: _____
Old address:_____
New address: _____

For records insert *F* for From or *T* for To within the brackets [ ].

Ad-dress	Rec-ord	Did	Name	Address	Telephone

Accountant

[ ]	[ ]	[ ]	_____	_____	_____
[ ]	[ ]	[ ]	_____	_____	_____
[ ]	[ ]	[ ]	_____	_____	_____

Attorneys

[ ]	[ ]	[ ]	_____	_____	_____
[ ]	[ ]	[ ]	_____	_____	_____
[ ]	[ ]	[ ]	_____	_____	_____

Banks, Savings and Loans, and so on

[ ]	[ ]	[ ]	_____	_____	_____
[ ]	[ ]	[ ]	_____	_____	_____
[ ]	[ ]	[ ]	_____	_____	_____
[ ]	[ ]	[ ]	_____	_____	_____

Book Clubs

| [ ] | [ ] | [ ] | _____ | _____ | _____ |
| [ ] | [ ] | [ ] | _____ | _____ | _____ |

Catalog Companies

[ ]	[ ]	[ ]	_____	_____	_____
[ ]	[ ]	[ ]	_____	_____	_____
[ ]	[ ]	[ ]	_____	_____	_____
[ ]	[ ]	[ ]	_____	_____	_____
[ ]	[ ]	[ ]	_____	_____	_____

Charge Cards

[ ]	[ ]	[ ]	_____	_____	_____
[ ]	[ ]	[ ]	_____	_____	_____
[ ]	[ ]	[ ]	_____	_____	_____

ADDRESS CHANGE/RECORDS TRANSFER WORKSHEET

Ad- dress	Rec- ord	Did	Name	Address	Telephone

Charge Cards (continued)

[ ] [ ] [ ] _____ _____ _____
[ ] [ ] [ ] _____ _____ _____
[ ] [ ] [ ] _____ _____ _____
[ ] [ ] [ ] _____ _____ _____
[ ] [ ] [ ] _____ _____ _____

Chiropractor

[ ] [ ] [ ] _____ _____ _____
[ ] [ ] [ ] _____ _____ _____
[ ] [ ] [ ] _____ _____ _____
[ ] [ ] [ ] _____ _____ _____

Clubs

[ ] [ ] [ ] _____ _____ _____
[ ] [ ] [ ] _____ _____ _____
[ ] [ ] [ ] _____ _____ _____
[ ] [ ] [ ] _____ _____ _____
[ ] [ ] [ ] _____ _____ _____
[ ] [ ] [ ] _____ _____ _____
[ ] [ ] [ ] _____ _____ _____

Credit Bureau

[ ] [ ] [ ] _____ _____ _____

Department Stores

[ ] [ ] [ ] _____ _____ _____
[ ] [ ] [ ] _____ _____ _____
[ ] [ ] [ ] _____ _____ _____
[ ] [ ] [ ] _____ _____ _____
[ ] [ ] [ ] _____ _____ _____

Dentist/Orthodontist

[ ] [ ] [ ] _____ _____ _____
[ ] [ ] [ ] _____ _____ _____

ADDRESS CHANGE/RECORDS TRANSFER WORKSHEET

Ad- Rec-
dress ord Did Name   Address   Telephone

Dentist/Orthodontist (continued)

[ ]   [ ] [ ] _____ _____ _____

Doctors

[ ]   [ ] [ ] _____ _____ _____
[ ]   [ ] [ ] _____ _____ _____
[ ]   [ ] [ ] _____ _____ _____
[ ]   [ ] [ ] _____ _____ _____
[ ]   [ ] [ ] _____ _____ _____

Draft Board

[ ]   [ ] [ ] _____ _____ _____

Friends

[ ]   [ ] [ ] _____ _____ _____
[ ]   [ ] [ ] _____ _____ _____
[ ]   [ ] [ ] _____ _____ _____
[ ]   [ ] [ ] _____ _____ _____
[ ]   [ ] [ ] _____ _____ _____
[ ]   [ ] [ ] _____ _____ _____
[ ]   [ ] [ ] _____ _____ _____
[ ]   [ ] [ ] _____ _____ _____
[ ]   [ ] [ ] _____ _____ _____
[ ]   [ ] [ ] _____ _____ _____
[ ]   [ ] [ ] _____ _____ _____
[ ]   [ ] [ ] _____ _____ _____
[ ]   [ ] [ ] _____ _____ _____
[ ]   [ ] [ ] _____ _____ _____

Insurance Companies

[ ]   [ ] [ ] _____ _____ _____
[ ]   [ ] [ ] _____ _____ _____
[ ]   [ ] [ ] _____ _____ _____
[ ]   [ ] [ ] _____ _____ _____
[ ]   [ ] [ ] _____ _____ _____
[ ]   [ ] [ ] _____ _____ _____

Internal Revenue Service

[ ]   [ ] [ ] _____ _____ _____

ADDRESS CHANGE/RECORDS TRANSFER WORKSHEET

Ad- Rec-
dress ord Did Name   Address   Telephone

Investments

[ ] [ ] [ ] _____   _____   _____
[ ] [ ] [ ] _____   _____   _____
[ ] [ ] [ ] _____   _____   _____
[ ] [ ] [ ] _____   _____   _____
[ ] [ ] [ ] _____   _____   _____
[ ] [ ] [ ] _____   _____   _____

Lenders

[ ] [ ] [ ] _____   _____   _____
[ ] [ ] [ ] _____   _____   _____
[ ] [ ] [ ] _____   _____   _____
[ ] [ ] [ ] _____   _____   _____

Magazines

[ ] [ ] [ ] _____   _____   _____
[ ] [ ] [ ] _____   _____   _____
[ ] [ ] [ ] _____   _____   _____
[ ] [ ] [ ] _____   _____   _____
[ ] [ ] [ ] _____   _____   _____
[ ] [ ] [ ] _____   _____   _____
[ ] [ ] [ ] _____   _____   _____
[ ] [ ] [ ] _____   _____   _____
[ ] [ ] [ ] _____   _____   _____

Motor Vehicle Registration

[ ] [ ] [ ] _____   _____   _____

Newspapers

[ ] [ ] [ ] _____   _____   _____
[ ] [ ] [ ] _____   _____   _____
[ ] [ ] [ ] _____   _____   _____
[ ] [ ] [ ] _____   _____   _____

Ophthalmologist, Optometrist, Oculist

[ ] [ ] [ ] _____   _____   _____
[ ] [ ] [ ] _____   _____   _____

ADDRESS CHANGE/RECORDS TRANSFER WORKSHEET

Ad- Rec-
dress ord Did Name   Address   Telephone

Pharmacy

[ ] [ ][ ] _____   _____   _____
[ ] [ ][ ] _____   _____   _____

Post Office

[ ] [ ][ ] _____   _____   _____

Record Clubs

[ ] [ ][ ] _____   _____   _____
[ ] [ ][ ] _____   _____   _____

Relatives

[ ] [ ][ ] _____   _____   _____
[ ] [ ][ ] _____   _____   _____
[ ] [ ][ ] _____   _____   _____
[ ] [ ][ ] _____   _____   _____
[ ] [ ][ ] _____   _____   _____
[ ] [ ][ ] _____   _____   _____
[ ] [ ][ ] _____   _____   _____
[ ] [ ][ ] _____   _____   _____
[ ] [ ][ ] _____   _____   _____
[ ] [ ][ ] _____   _____   _____
[ ] [ ][ ] _____   _____   _____
[ ] [ ][ ] _____   _____   _____
[ ] [ ][ ] _____   _____   _____

Religious Organizations

[ ] [ ][ ] _____   _____   _____
[ ] [ ][ ] _____   _____   _____

Schools

[ ] [ ][ ] _____   _____   _____
[ ] [ ][ ] _____   _____   _____
[ ] [ ][ ] _____   _____   _____
[ ] [ ][ ] _____   _____   _____
[ ] [ ][ ] _____   _____   _____

Social Security Administration

[ ] [ ][ ] _____   _____   _____

ADDRESS CHANGE/RECORDS TRANSFER WORKSHEET

Ad- dress	Rec- ord	Did	Name	Address	Telephone

Stockbroker

[ ] [ ] [ ] _____ _____ _____
[ ] [ ] [ ] _____ _____ _____

Tax Preparer

[ ] [ ] [ ] _____ _____ _____
[ ] [ ] [ ] _____ _____ _____

Tenants

[ ] [ ] [ ] _____ _____ _____
[ ] [ ] [ ] _____ _____ _____
[ ] [ ] [ ] _____ _____ _____
[ ] [ ] [ ] _____ _____ _____
[ ] [ ] [ ] _____ _____ _____

Unions

[ ] [ ] [ ] _____ _____ _____
[ ] [ ] [ ] _____ _____ _____

Veterans Administration

[ ] [ ] [ ] _____ _____ _____

Veterinarian

[ ] [ ] [ ] _____ _____ _____
[ ] [ ] [ ] _____ _____ _____

Voter Registration

[ ] [ ] [ ] _____ _____ _____

1. Make an **X** in To Call column for each service you wish to stop or start.
2. Write the name of party providing service in the Name column.
3. Write the telephone number of party providing service in Telephone column.
4. Call the party providing service and request that service be stopped or started, as appropriate.
5. Make an **X** in Notified column after you complete the call.

Thank you for using this book to successfully sell your home yourself and move. After you are settled in your new location, we would like to hear from you, in care of the publisher, about your experience using *How to Sell Your Home Without a Broker.*

STOP AND START SERVICES WORK SHEET

Name: _____ Date effective: _____
Old address:_____
New address: _____

To Noti-
Call fied Service   Name   Telephone

STOP

[ ] [ ] Cleaner   _____ _____
[ ] [ ] Dairy Delivery   _____ _____
[ ] [ ] Diaper Service   _____ _____
[ ] [ ] Drinking Water   _____ _____
[ ] [ ] Fuel Oil   _____ _____
[ ] [ ] Garbage Collection   _____ _____
[ ] [ ] Gas   _____ _____
[ ] [ ] Landscaping Service   _____ _____
[ ] [ ] Laundry Service   _____ _____
[ ] [ ] Maid   _____ _____
[ ] [ ] Newspaper   _____ _____
[ ] [ ] Pest Control   _____ _____
[ ] [ ] Pool   _____ _____
[ ] [ ] Sewer   _____ _____
[ ] [ ] Telephone   _____ _____
[ ] [ ] Trash   _____ _____
[ ] [ ] Water   _____ _____
[ ] [ ] Water Softener   _____ _____
[ ] [ ] Other   _____ _____

START

[ ] [ ] Cleaner   _____ _____
[ ] [ ] Dairy Delivery   _____ _____
[ ] [ ] Diaper Service   _____ _____
[ ] [ ] Drinking Water   _____ _____
[ ] [ ] Fuel Oil   _____ _____
[ ] [ ] Garbage Collection   _____ _____
[ ] [ ] Gas   _____ _____
[ ] [ ] Landscaping Service   _____ _____
[ ] [ ] Laundry Service   _____ _____
[ ] [ ] Maid   _____ _____
[ ] [ ] Newspaper   _____ _____
[ ] [ ] Pest Control   _____ _____
[ ] [ ] Pool   _____ _____
[ ] [ ] Sewer   _____ _____
[ ] [ ] Telephone   _____ _____
[ ] [ ] Trash   _____ _____
[ ] [ ] Water   _____ _____
[ ] [ ] Water Softener   _____ _____
[ ] [ ] Other   _____ _____

Appendix

The sample forms in this appendix illustrate the types of calculations you make in selling your home without a broker.

The Asking Price Determination Worksheet helps you arrive at a reasonable asking price based on prices of comparable properties for sale or recently sold in your area.

The Ownership Costs Worksheet helps you total costs of utilities and services for the previous year for your property.

The Net Proceeds Worksheet is helpful when you calculate the money you will have remaining after you deduct charges against the asking price.

Use the Repairs Worksheet to determine what repairs are necessary as well as what person or company will make them, the deadlines for completion, and the approximate costs.

The Estimate of Proceeds Worksheet helps you calculate the estimated costs, encumbrances, and credits and debits from your sale.

ASKING PRICE DETERMINATION WORKSHEET

Address:_____

Property Information   Price

Property Address	Bedrm	Bath	Square feet	Remarks	For Sale	Sold

Source: My home

3334 Burgundy	3	2	1800	Pool, Spa, Air		

Source: Neighbors

3216 Muslo	3	2	1600	Tiny Yard	279,000	
3305 Fosca	4	2	1700	Pool, Spa		305,000

Source: Real estate professionals

3444 Venado	3	2	1600	Air	285,000	
3424 Muslo	3	2	1800	Pool, Spa, Air	315,000	
3321 Burgundy	4	2½	1900	Pool, Spa		315,000

Source: Appraiser

Source: Title companies

3106 Burgundy	3	2	1650	Spa, Air	295,000	

Most comparable
   For sale _____3424 Muslo_____   315,000
   Sold _____3305 Fosca_____   305,000

ASKING PRICE $ 310,000

OWNERSHIP COSTS WORKSHEET

Name: _Steve and Barbara Balaban_

Address: _3334 Burgundy_

Year	Month	Electric	Gas/Oil	Water	Sewer	Trash
90	January	$ 100–	$ 115–	$ 60–	$ 35–	$ 50–
90	February	95–	105–	55–	35–	
90	March	105–	110–	65–	35–	50–
90	April	75–	95–	60–	35–	
90	May	75–	85–	65–	35–	50–
90	June	75–	65–	70–	35–	
89	July	115–	40–	75–	35–	50–
89	August	125–	30–	75–	35–	
89	September	110–	40–	70–	35–	50–
89	October	105–	55–	65–	35–	
89	November	100–	65–	60–	35–	50–
89	December	120–	95–	60–	35–	
	Total	$ 1200–	$ 900–	$ 780–	$ 420–	$ 300–
	+ Number of months	12	12	12	12	12
	=Average/month	$ 100–	$ 75–	$ 65–	$ 35–	$ 25–

Year	Month	Taxes	Insurance	Home-owner's Fees	Bond	
90	January		$ 90–		$ 100–	
90	February				100–	
90	March				100–	
90	April	$ 1200–	90–		100–	
90	May				100–	
90	June				100–	
89	July		90–		120–	
89	August				120–	
89	September				120–	
89	October		90–		120–	
89	November	1200–			120–	
89	December				120–	
	Total	$ 2400–	$ 360–		$ 1320–	
	+ Number of months	12	12		12	
	= Average/month	$ 200–	$ 30–		$ 110–	

NET PROCEEDS WORKSHEET

Name:____Steve and Barbara Balaban____Date:__4/11/90____

Address:____3334 Burgundy____

Asking price $ 310,000

Charges against asking price

Mortgage costs

1st Mortgage/Trust deed (TD)   + $ 65,000
1st Mortgage/TD prepayment penalty   + $ 0
2nd Mortgage/Trust deed (TD)   + $ 95,000
2nd Mortgage/TD prepayment penalty   + $ 0

Marketing costs

Improvement costs   + $ 0
Repair costs   + $ 1,700
Attractiveness costs   + $ 400
Advertising costs   + $ 1,200

Closing costs   + $ 6,300
(Use 1.5% to 3.0% of asking price)

Total of charges against asking price   − $ 169,600

Net Proceeds   = $ 140,400

REPAIRS WORKSHEET

Name: _Steve and Barbara Balaban_

Address: _3334 Burgundy_

		To Be Done			**Call to repair/**	**Estimate**
Do	**Did**	**By**	**Date**	**Job**	**telephone number or material needed**	

Lawn

Do	Did	By	Date	Job	Call to repair	Estimate
[ ]	[ ]			Bare spots replanted		
[✓]	[✓]	SB	6/15	Lawn fertilized	2 bags fertilizer	$45
[ ]	[ ]			Other		

Plantings

Do	Did	By	Date	Job	Call to repair	Estimate
[✓]	[ ]	SB	6/21	Dead plants removed		
[✓]	[ ]	SB	6/21	Dead plants replaced	2 bushes	$60
[ ]	[ ]			Dead limbs removed		
[ ]	[ ]			Other		

Driveway and Walks

Do	Did	By	Date	Job	Call to repair	Estimate
[ ]	[ ]			Holes patched		
[ ]	[ ]			Concrete repaired		
[✓]	[ ]	BB	7/1	Asphalt sealed	Asphalt Inc 942-1616	$350
[ ]	[ ]			Gravel smoothed		
[ ]	[ ]			Other		

Walls and Fences

Do	Did	By	Date	Job	Call to repair	Estimate
[ ]	[ ]			Sections repaired		
[ ]	[ ]			Sections painted		
[✓]	[✓]	BB	6/18	Termite and rot free	No Pests 436-9193	$200
[ ]	[ ]			Other		

Patios and Decks

Do	Did	By	Date	Job	Call to repair	Estimate
[ ]	[ ]			Smooth surface		
[ ]	[ ]			Stained or painted		
[ ]	[ ]			Termite and rot free		
[ ]	[ ]			Railings sturdy		
[ ]	[ ]			Other		

Pools and Spas

Do	Did	By	Date	Job	Call to repair	Estimate
[✓]	[ ]	BB		Free of algae	Pool Clean 943-1923	$150
[ ]	[ ]			Motor works		
[ ]	[ ]			Filter works		
[ ]	[ ]			Pool cleaner works		
[ ]	[ ]			Cover in good repair		
[ ]	[ ]			Other		

Subtotal #1 $805

ESTIMATE OF PROCEEDS WORKSHEET

[✓] PRELIMINARY   [ ] WORKING   [ ] COUNTER OFFER

Seller _Steve Balaban_ Buyer_____
Property _3334 Burgundy_____
Selling price _$ 310,000_____ Type of financing _____New_____
Date prepared _4/16/90___ Proposed closing date _6/11/90_____

ESTIMATED COSTS

Pay	Cost		Amount	Notes
[ ]	Appraisal fee	$	_____	
[ ]	Assessments		_____	[ ] Prorate, $ from page 3
[ ]	Assumption fee		_____	
[✓]	Attorney fees		650	
[ ]	Beneficiary statement		_____	
[ ]	Credit report		_____	
[ ]	Delinquent payments		_____	
[✓]	Demand fees		75	
[✓]	Document preparation		75	
[✓]	Drawing deed		25	
[✓]	Escrow/closing fees		750	
[ ]	Homeowner's insurance		_____	
[ ]	Homeowner's assn. fee		_____	[ ] Prorate, $ from page 3
[✓]	Home warranty		300	
[ ]	Impounds		_____	[ ] Prorate, $ from page 3
[✓]	Interest		1800	[ ] Prorate, $ from page 3
[ ]	Loan origination fee		_____	
[✓]	Loan tie-in fee		75	
[ ]	Notary fee		_____	
[✓]	Pest control inspection		50	
[✓]	Pest control repair		325	
[ ]	Physical inspection fee		_____	
[ ]	Points		_____	
[ ]	Prepayment penalty		_____	
[✓]	Property taxes		400	[ ] Prorate, $ from page 3
[✓]	Reconveyance fee		75	
[ ]	Recording fee		_____	
[ ]	Satisfaction of mort.		_____	
[✓]	Subescrow fee		50	
[ ]	Survey fee		_____	
[✓]	Title insurance		1100	
[ ]	Title search fee		_____	
[✓]	Transfer tax		400	
[ ]	Other _____		_____	

TOTAL EST. COSTS $ 6,150

ESTIMATE OF PROCEEDS WORKSHEET

Type of worksheet [✓] PRELIMINARY [ ] WORKING [ ] COUNTER OFFER

ESTIMATED ENCUMBRANCES

Pay Encumbrance	Amount	Notes
[✓] 1st loan	$ 65,000	
[✓] 2nd loan	95,000	Due 6/11/2000
[ ] 3rd loan		
[ ] Improvement bonds		
[ ] Liens		
[ ] Other		
TOTAL ENCUMBRANCES	$ 160,000	

ESTIMATED CREDITS

Pay Credits	Amount	Notes
[ ] Assessments	$	
[ ] Bonds		
[ ] Homeowner's assoc. dues		
[ ] Impounds		
[ ] Insurance		
[ ] Interest		
[ ] Property taxes		
[ ] Rental payments		
TOTAL EST. CREDITS	$ Ø	

ESTIMATED DEBITS

	Amount	Notes
Total estimated costs	$ 6,150	From page 1
Total estimated encumbrances	160,000	From page 2
TOTAL EST. DEBITS	$ 166,150	

CALCULATIONS

Proposed selling price	$	315,000
Total estimated debits	−	166,150
Subtotal	=	148,850
Total estimated credit	+	Ø
SELLER'S EST. PROCEEDS	=	148,850
Note financed by you (seller)	−	Ø
Seller's estimate of cash	=	
from sale	$	148,850

ESTIMATE OF PROCEEDS WORKSHEET

Type of worksheet ☑ PRELIMINARY [ ] WORKING [ ] COUNTER OFFER

Item prorated_____

PRORATIONS
1. Assume a 30 day month and 360 day year for estimate purposes.
   a. To borrow days from Month column, subtract 1 month from Month column and add 30 days to Day column.
   b. To borrow months from Year column, subtract 1 year from Year column and add 12 months to Month column.
2. Seller does not pay costs for the day of the closing.
3. For items for which you have not paid, such as interest and property taxes, enter value on the proper line under the heading Estimated Costs.
4. For items for which you prepaid, such as insurance, taxes, and rents, enter value on the proper line under the heading Estimated Costs.

Total days for which the payment applies

	Year	Month	Day					
Ending	___	6	30	Year ___	× 360 =	___ days
-Starting	___	5	1	+ Month 1	× 30 =	30 days
	___	1	30	+ Day 30	× 1 =	30 days
				Total days (a)		60

Actual days for which the seller must pay

	Year	Month	Day			
Ending	___	6	11	Year ___	× 360 =	___ days
-Starting	___	5	1	+ Month 1	× 30 =	30 days
	___	1	10	+ Day 10	× 1 =	10 days
				Actual days (b)		40

Payment per day
Total payment required (c)		$ 2700⁻
Total days (a)	+	60
Payment per day (d)	= $	45⁻

Seller's payment required
Payment per day (d)		$ 45⁻
Actual days (b)	×	40
Seller's payment (e)	= $	1800⁻

Seller's credit for item that has been paid in advance
Total payment required (c)	$ _____
Seller's payment (e)	− $ _____
Seller's credit for item	= $ _____

Index

In this index, page numbers of blank forms are shown in **boldface** type.